POSTCARD HISTORY SERIES

Osterville

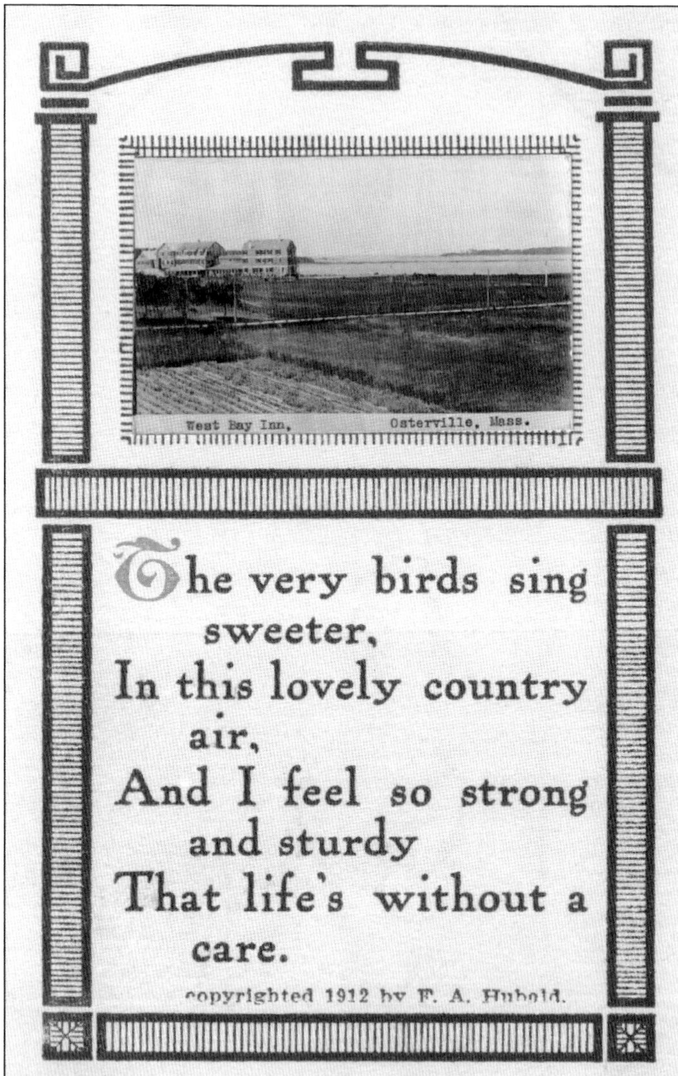

The sentiments of this postcard reflect how thousands felt as they returned to Osterville every summer to swim at the beaches, sail in the bays, or enjoy village life filled with churches, shops, a theater, library, and more. A charming image of the West Bay Inn, one of the most popular of the grand hotels by the sea, completes this postcard mailed in 1913. (Courtesy of the Osterville Historical Museum.)

ON THE FRONT COVER: Sailors prepare for one of many Crosby-built catboat and Wianno Senior races on the pier of the Wianno Yacht Club overlooking Nantucket Sound in 1914. This scene embodies the love of the sea and what drew thousands to return to Osterville summer after summer at the turn of the 20th century and still draws them today. (Courtesy of the Osterville Historical Museum.)

ON THE BACK COVER: A typical Osterville Village scene from the 1920s is shown in this image. The sign for the Star Theatre can be seen in the center with the Methodist Church on the right. On the left, two ladies stroll on the sidewalk past the library on the right. (Courtesy of the Osterville Historical Museum.)

POSTCARD HISTORY SERIES

Osterville

Jennifer Morgan Williams

ARCADIA PUBLISHING

ISBN 978-1-4671-2133-0

Published by Arcadia Publishing
Charleston, South Carolina

Printed in the United States of America

Library of Congress Control Number: 2013946825

For all general information contact Arcadia Publishing at:
Telephone 843-853-2070
Fax 843-853-0044
E-mail sales@arcadiapublishing.com
For customer service and orders:
Toll-Free 1-888-313-2665

Visit us on the Internet at www.arcadiapublishing.com

For John, Emily, Sarah, Abigail, and Jack.
Sans vous, il n'y a pas de moi.

Contents

Acknowledgments

I would like to thank all of the dedicated volunteers at the Osterville Historical Museum, led by our board president Kathy Capo. All of them contributed to the vast amount of research in documenting the story of Osterville. Osterville's own historian Paul Chesbro and his three groundbreaking books in A History of the Village series have been invaluable resources. Chesbro and Chester A. Crosby III's *Osterville: A Walk Through the Past*, Shirley Eastman's Images of America: *Osterville*, and *Osterville–Twice Remembered* by the Leonard family have likewise been most helpful. I would also like to thank the folks who helped to tell the story of our nautical heritage through the Crosby boats, and among them are the following: Malcolm Crosby, Jim Eastman, Dave Trimble, Ann W. Crosby, Rod Rowland, Will Price, Dick Whitman, and Al Lawson.

All images used in this book come from the collection of the Osterville Historical Museum. These postcards were donated from a number of private collections, including my own. A special thanks to the extensive postcard collections donated by Andrea Leonard, George Kilbourne, and Mari Poss, herself a former postcard dealer.

Thanks also goes to my husband, John, who helped me identify many Osterville scenes.

I have been collecting postcards for decades. They have always intrigued me as they present small vignettes of a moment in time. From the beautiful image on the front, the name of the sender and the address of the recipient, the message written, the stamp used, and the final mark of time with a cancellation, postcards capture a glimpse into the past. The collector is left to imagine the rest.

For all of those who have called Osterville home, this book is dedicated to you.

Introduction

You know how the time flies
Only yesterday was the time of our lives
We were born and raised in a summer haze
Bound by the surprise of our glory days.

The lyrics of "Someone Like You" by Adele are befitting the postcards contained within these pages. Osterville of the late 1800s to early 1930s represented the "glory days" to many. This small seaside village, once a summer home to the native Wampanoag tribe and one of the seven villages of Barnstable, drew many to its beautiful seaside. Majestic inns dotted the coastal landscape while Crosby boatbuilders were creating what was to become a world-renowned class of racing boats and a style of boat designed for these Cape Cod waters.

In 1798, brothers Daniel and Jesse Crosby Jr. paid $9 to lease land on North Bay. They came from the nearby village of Centerville and operated a lumber mill. North Bay was soon lined with four Crosby boatyards actively producing wooden boats.

In 1850, two Crosby brothers, C. Worthington and Horace S. Crosby, attended a séance held by their mother, Tirzah Lovell Crosby. It was a time when séances were commonplace, a time of mysticism. She told them that they were destined to build a boat that could tack in these shallow Cape Cod waters and be "quick as a cat." And the Crosby cats were born.

Its wide and deep design makes the catboat unique. It is wide to not turn over and deep to carry as much fish as possible. The mast is also at the bow of the boat, and the rudder is so big (for easy maneuvering) that it is often called a "barn door." The waters around Osterville were plentiful with oysters, clams, cod, and scores of other fish, and if you were not building boats, you were most likely fishing.

In a colonial tradition, the Crosbys carved half-hull models of these boats by eye before building them. Some of these half-hull models are extremely valuable. If they did not like the model they were carving, a builder would simply toss it into the wood stove to keep the boat shop warm.

Around the boatyards, you would find many oyster shanties, including one belonging to Joseph Crosby, and commercial boats transporting the prized oysters. Since the days of the native Wampanoag, oysters were valuable and highly prized. Sometimes called the "fruit of Cape Cod," oysters even played a role in the naming of the village. In 1648, Pilgrim captain Miles Standish purchased a large swath of land from the Wampanoags for two brass kettles, a hoe, and a promise to help build a fence. A portion of that land, today's Osterville, was named Oyster Island Village. It morphed to Oysterville, and then, it was officially changed in 1815 to Osterville.

In the late 1800s, Osterville was a destination. People would come to Osterville and stay not for a day or a long weekend, but for months at a time. A typical visitor would arrive by train at the West Barnstable train station where Capt. Daniel Bursley would pick them up in his stagecoach. The horse-drawn carriages would travel a loop throughout Osterville to places like East Bay Lodge, Wianno, and West Bay Inn. The horses would return to the stables behind the Henry Foster Lewis house on Main Street before repeating the journey.

Once ensconced at your summer inn or club, you were actively engaged in any number of activities of the day. Guests could enjoy reading by the fire, sewing in a rocker on one of many porches, practicing archery on the lawns, partaking in foxhunts or a stroll in the gardens, or perhaps a short sail to one of the bathing pavilions on the bays. Often, the same families would return to the same inns year after year, creating a community of regular "summer friends." There was also a great camaraderie amongst summer staff members who were housed on the campuses of the inns and clubs. They were charged with everything from tennis lessons to housekeeping and wait staff duties.

The wealthy summer families that flocked to Osterville were instrumental in the formation of the exclusive clubs that soon opened: the Wianno Club, Oyster Harbors, and Seapuit. All of them were known for their fine dining, golf, bathing beaches, sailing, and more. These influential families—some, like the DuPonts and Mellons, magnets of industry at the time—commissioned the Crosbys to build a new design class of racing boats—the Wianno Seniors.

Horace Manley Crosby designed the Wianno Senior for racing on Nantucket Sound. In the summer of 1914, a total of 14 boats entered the fleet. When President Kennedy sailed off Hyannisport in the 1950s and 1960s, he was in his wooden Crosby-built Wianno Senior, *The Victura*, hull No. 94. The boat resides now at the JFK Library in Boston but still returns to Osterville for upkeep.

While private homes have turned into retail shops on Main Street and Wianno Avenue, the heart of it all remains very similar to the late 1800s and early 1900s. The Osterville Baptist Church is a central focal point in the village, as is the Daniel Block of storefronts whose architecture can be easily recognized today. Just down the road, the Pattison Block also retains a similar facade. Long gone are the A&P Grocery Store, drugstore, and movie theater, but retail spaces, including an art gallery, now flourish. The diamond-shaped windows of the original Methodist Church on Main Street can still be seen at what is now Checkerberry House Interiors. Likewise, the Kalas' Fruit Store, located at the beginning of town near the hay scales, was known to many as "Charlie's" or the "penny candy store" until it closed in 2000. Now, Vintage Flowers occupies the same space.

With the advent of the automobile, Daniel Bursley's stables turned into the garage for Midway Gas Station in the 1920s. The automobile brought with it new destinations within easy traveling distance. No longer were the inns as full as they once were. As the financial crisis grew with the stock market collapse, some of the inns fell into disrepair or some fell victim to fire. The Seapuit Club with its golf course was subdivided into house lots in the 1950s, and East Bay Lodge was demolished in the late 1990s to make way for condominiums.

Still remaining are the grand clubs of Wianno and Oyster Harbors. The Wianno Yacht Club now resides on Bridge Street and looks into West Bay. The village library was rebuilt in 2012 on the corner of West Bay Road and Wianno Avenue. Dowses Beach and Armstrong-Kelley Park are well-loved attractions for all. The bays are also still filled with boats. On many summer days, you can still see the fleet of Wianno Seniors, both wooden and fiberglass, racing in the Max Crosby Regatta or the Scudder Cup. The Cape Cod Catboat Association also does a "sail around" each summer during their annual Townie Hornor rendezvous in Osterville.

What also remains are the families—the Crosbys, Leonards, Lovells, Crockers, Davises, Hansens, Fullers, and more—and the spirit of this seaside village called Osterville. And that "summer haze" that still beckons many to return year after year—or to never leave.

One

The Village

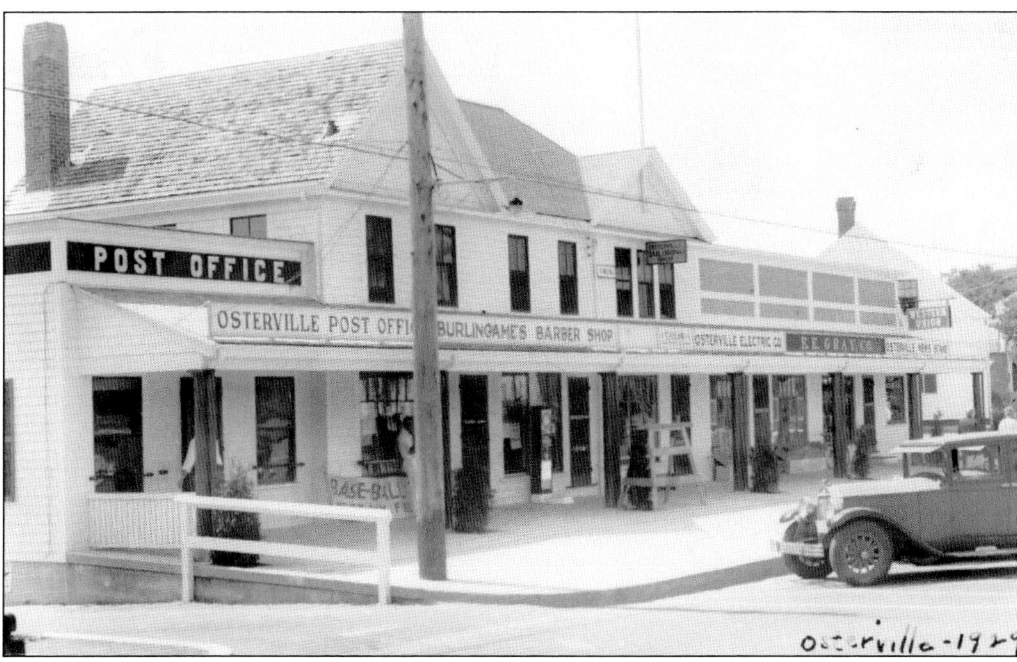

The Daniel Block, which is on the right as one turns onto Wianno Avenue from Main Street, was the center of activity in the village in 1929 with tenants including the post office, the Burlingame's Barbershop, and Western Union. The block was developed by builders Charles and Robert Daniel who came to Osterville in 1879. Although the stores have changed, the Daniel Block still looks essentially the same today.

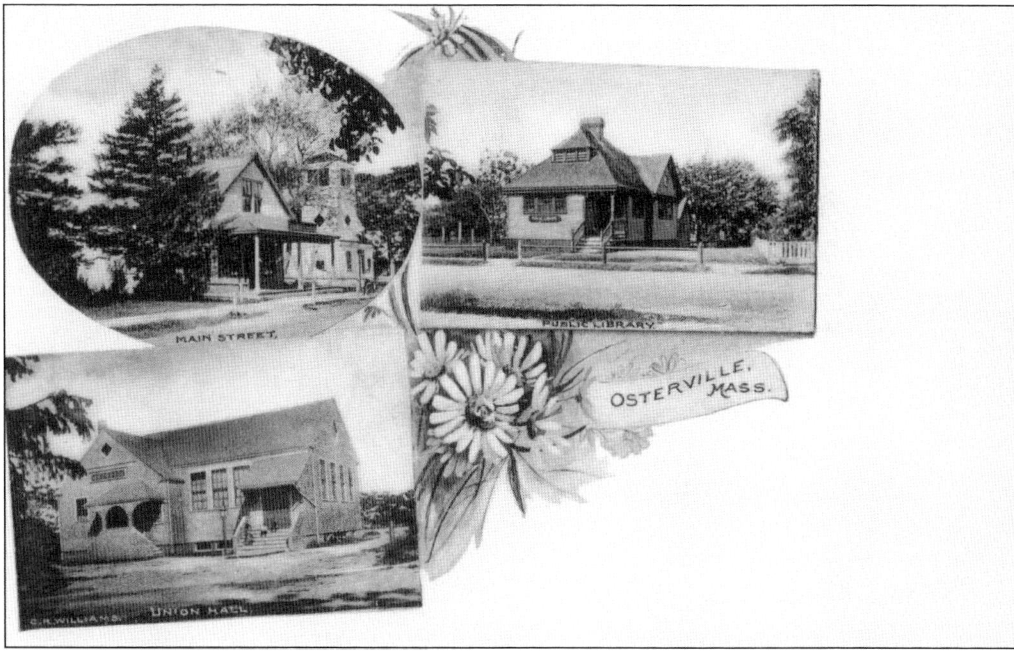

At top left is the view of Main Street with the Methodist Church on the right. Horace Scudder Parker's grocery store can be seen just to the left of the church. He opened the business in this location in 1895. At top right is the public library that was across the street from the Methodist Church. Pictured at bottom is the Union Hall, which later became Veterans Hall, on the corner of West Bay Road and Main Street. This is the view from across West Bay Road.

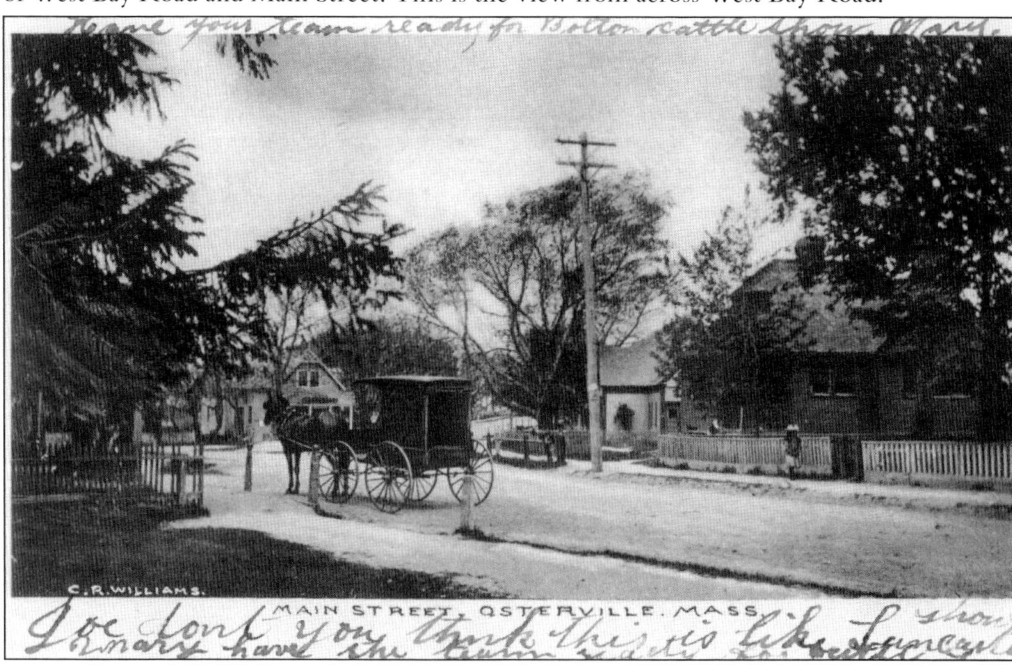

This is a view looking west on Main Street toward the intersection with Parker Road and Bay Street with the Kalas' Fruit Store, known to many as the "penny candy store" or simply "Charlie's" after owner Charlie Kalas, in the distance beyond the horse and the public library on the right.

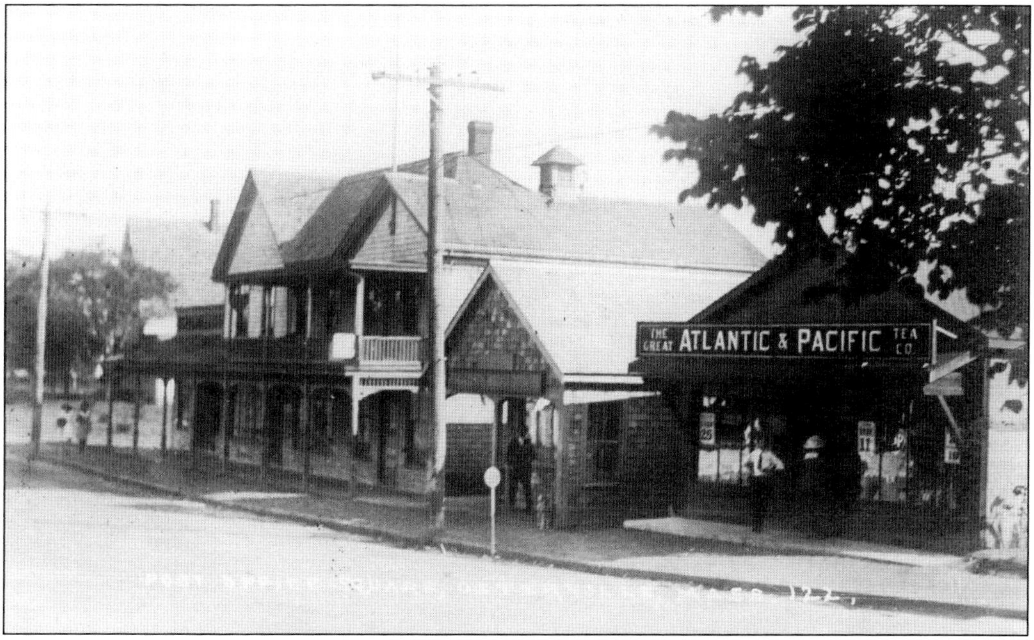

The start of Wianno Avenue began with the Great Atlantic and Pacific Tea Company (later known as the A&P Supermarkets), and the Daniel Block is beyond but harder to identify with the covered porch on the second floor and the dark trim paint. The space occupied by the building between the Daniel Block and the Great Atlantic and Pacific Tea Company would later be used to expand the Daniel Block west, closer to the beginning of Wianno Avenue.

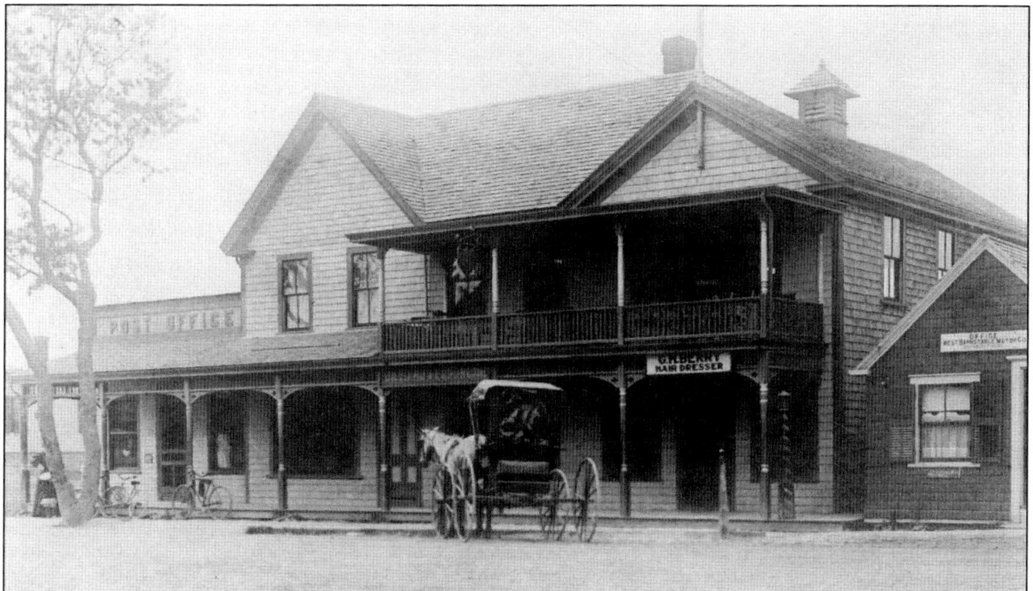

Here is another view of the Daniel Block on Wianno Avenue with the post office at the left end. Before becoming known as the Daniel Block, this section was called the Crocker Block in the 1890s and housed James H. Crocker's ice cream saloon. The office for the West Barnstable Motor Company is on the right.

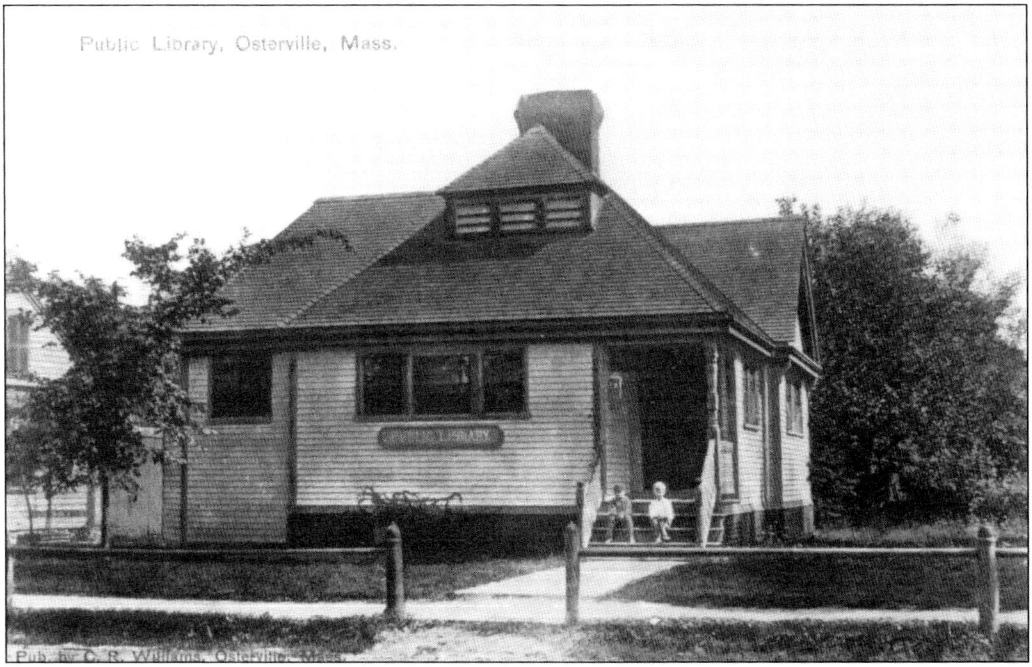

The Osterville Public Library was located on Main Street across from the Methodist Church. Walter Scudder is the little boy in white sitting on the stairs. The building later was expanded into what became the Osterville House and Garden Building.

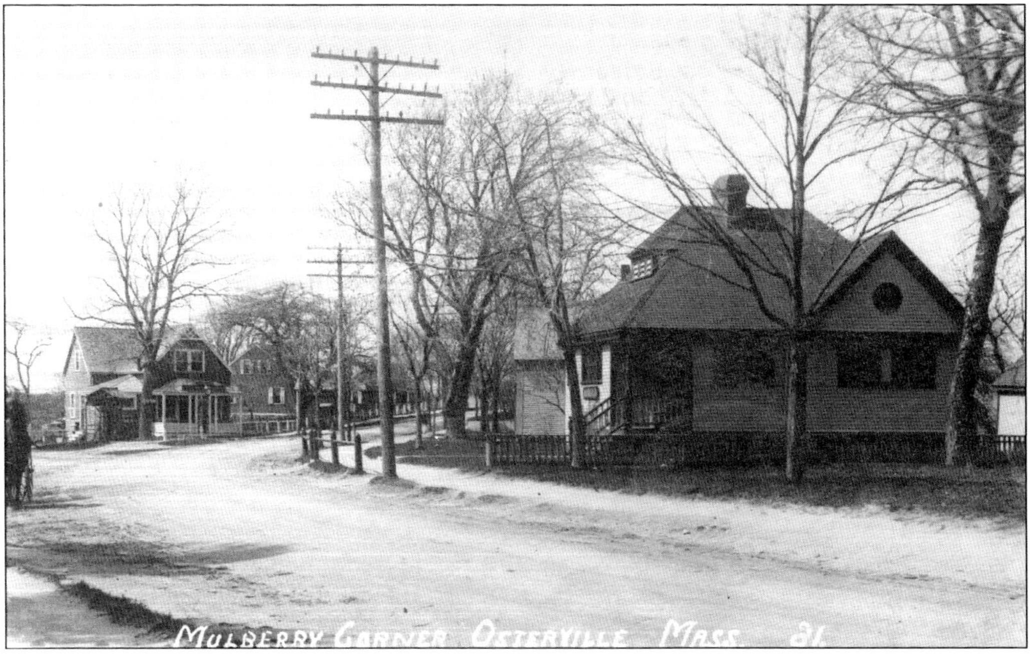

Looking west on Main Street toward the country store, one sees the public library on the right. This shows the original location of the Kalas' Fruit Store. In the 1920s, it would be moved back 40 feet from the road—thanks to a horse-and-pulley system—to make way for the expansion of Main Street and a paved road.

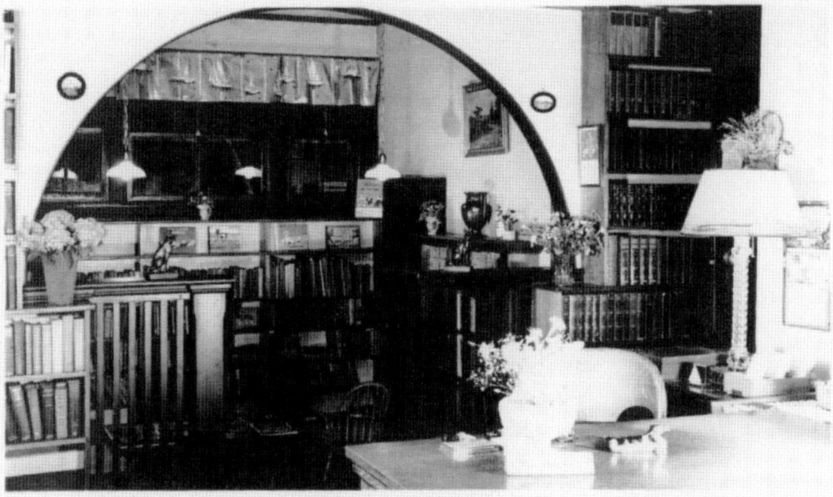

Pictured are two views inside the library at its Main Street location. The library originally cost $3,000 to build, and William Lloyd Garrison, an abolitionist from Boston who summered in Osterville, donated the money. Katherine Hinckley was the first librarian, and in the postcard above, one can see the archway leading into the children's room. This archway can still be seen today in the Oyster Island Emporium's retail shop.

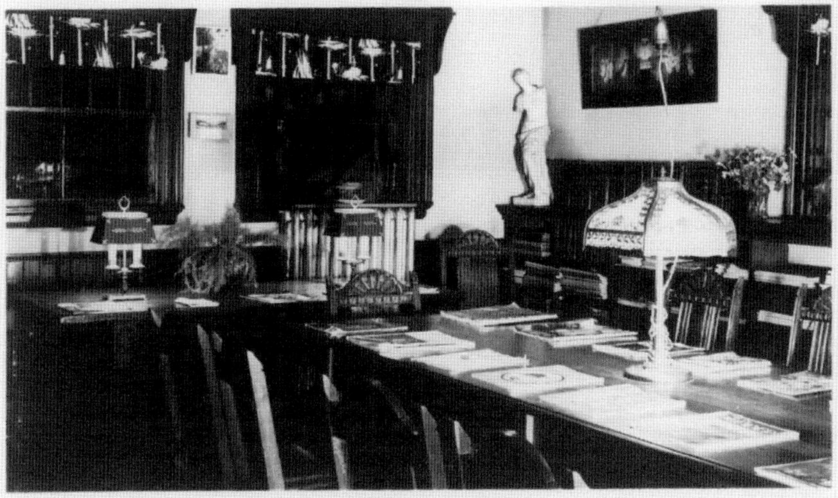

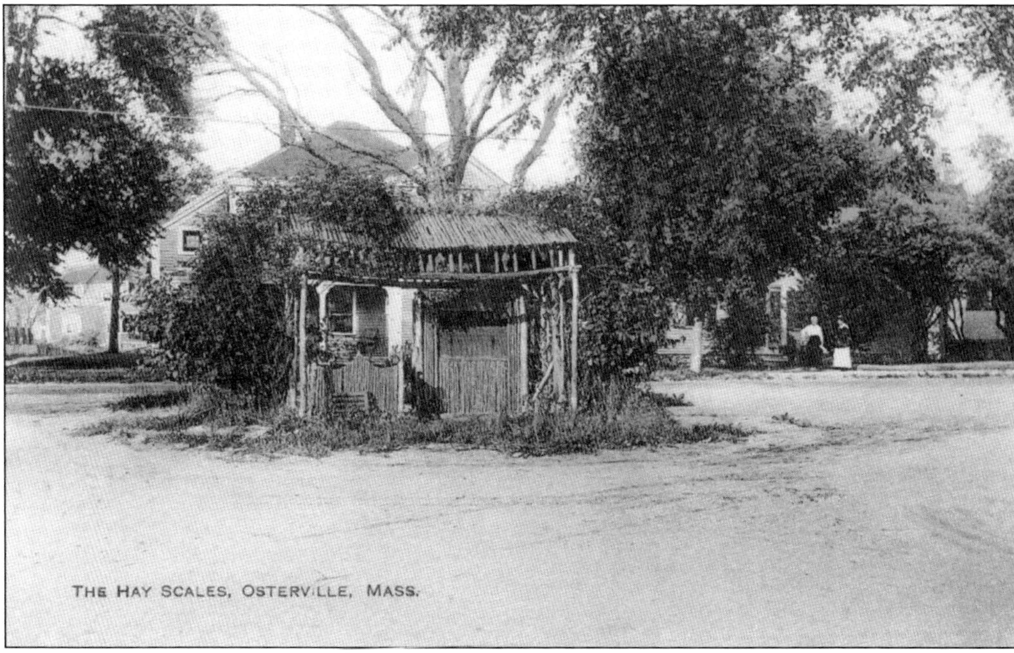

Here are the hay scales on the island at the intersection of Main Street, Bay Street, and Parker Road. This is the view looking north from Parker Road. The hay scales were used to measure everything from hay and coal to ice harvested from Neck Pond—one of the many glacial kettle ponds in the area.

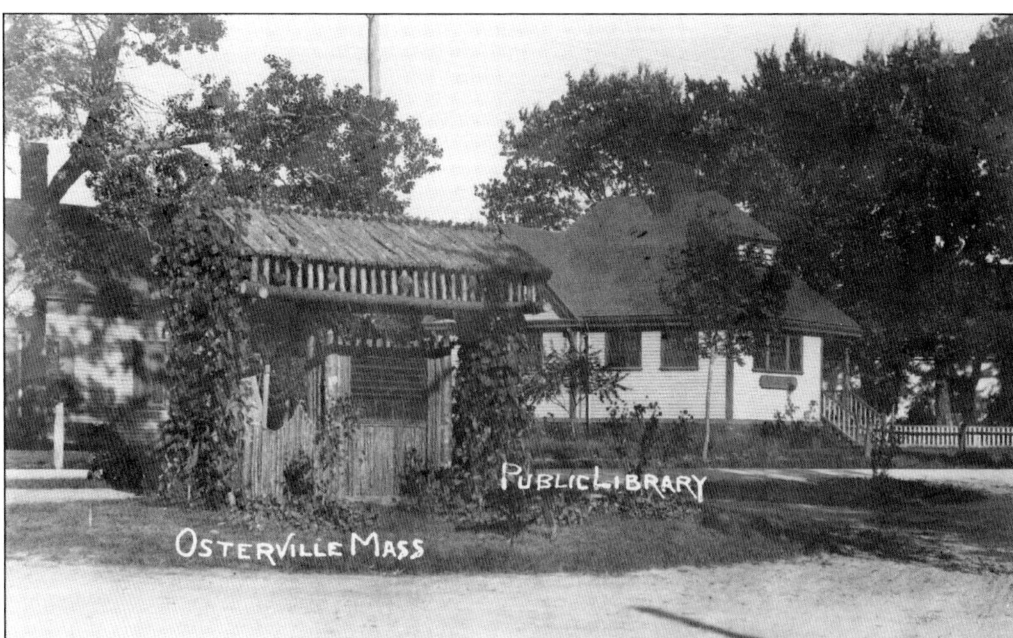

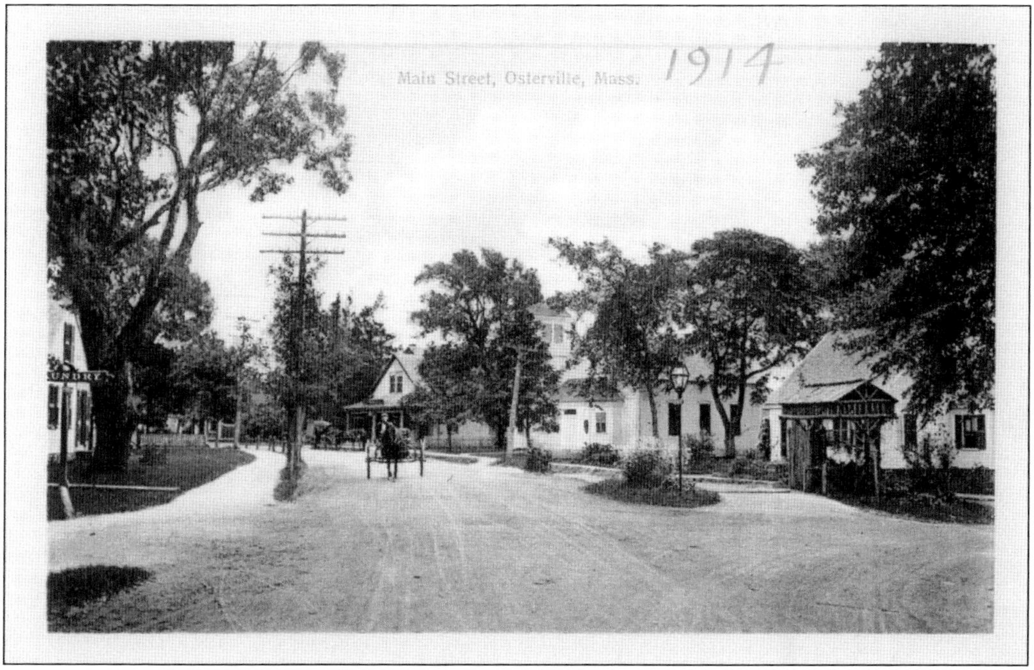

The above postcard is looking east on Main Street with the hay scales and Parker Road on the immediate right. Pictured below is the reverse of the postcard above; it is looking west on Main Street with the hay scales and the Kalas' Fruit Store on the left and the library on the right. An official "weigher" operated the hay scales. An iron scale was underneath wooden planks, and carts were either pushed or pulled on top for an accurate measurement.

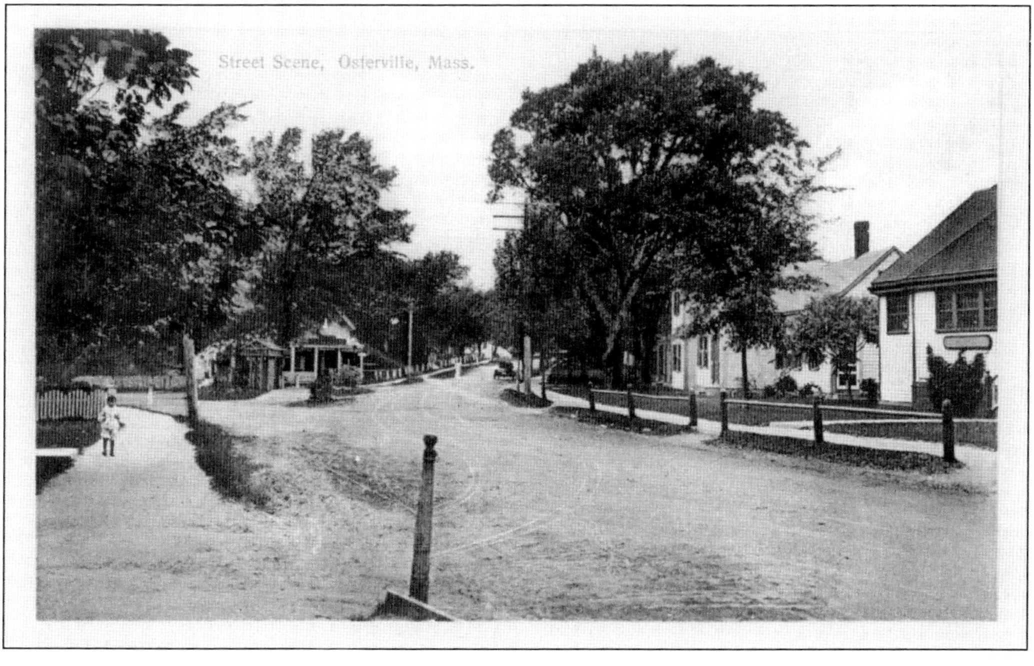

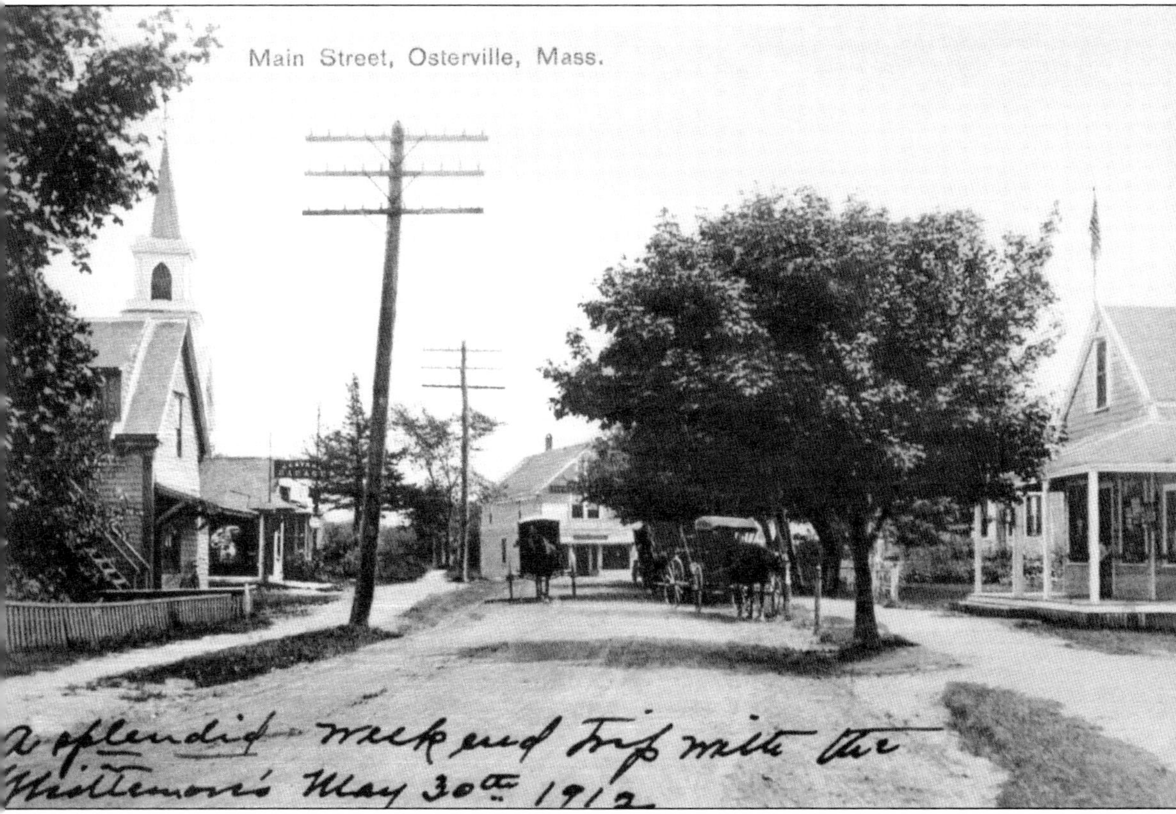

This view is looking east on Main Street in 1912. The steeple of the Baptist church can be seen on the left. The first building on the left is owned by Joseph Tallman Sr., and next is Carl Lagergren's central garage. Crocker's store is in the rear center of the image. To the right is Carrie Rich Williams's ice cream parlor with the porch. It is interesting how narrow the street was in comparison to modern day.

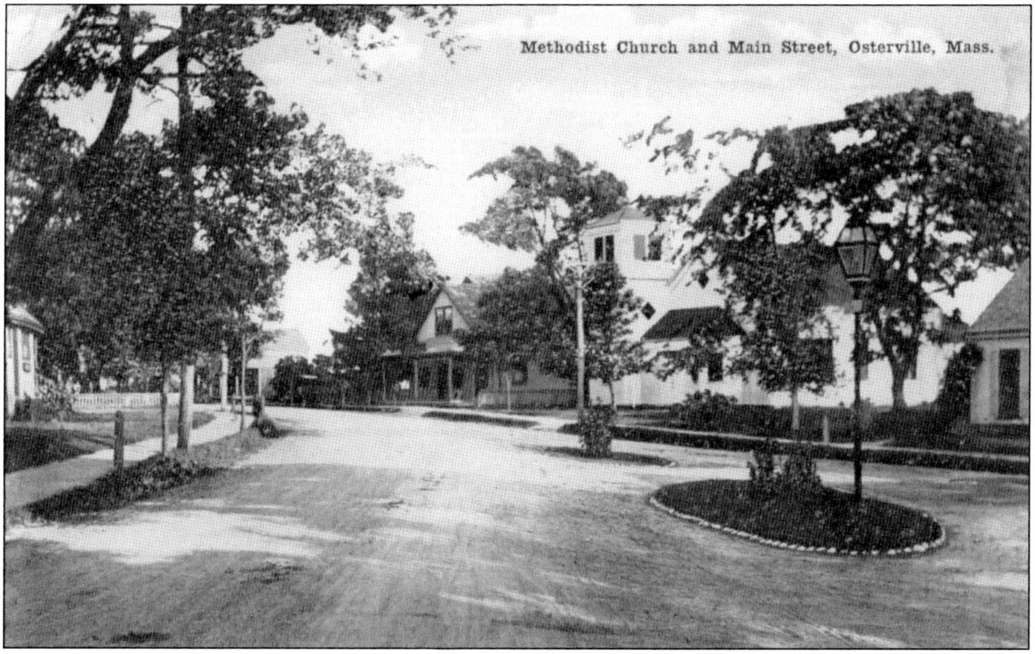

This pre-1921 postcard shows Main Street looking east with the Methodist Church on the right. Below, one can see Main Street looking west with the Kalas' Fruit Store on the left and the public library on the right. The fruit store building was erected in 1890 by Charles Crosby, and in 1915, James Kalas bought the property. Note that the hay scales have been replaced with plantings and a flagpole. The boulder at the base of the flagpole was added in 1929 to honor World War I war veterans.

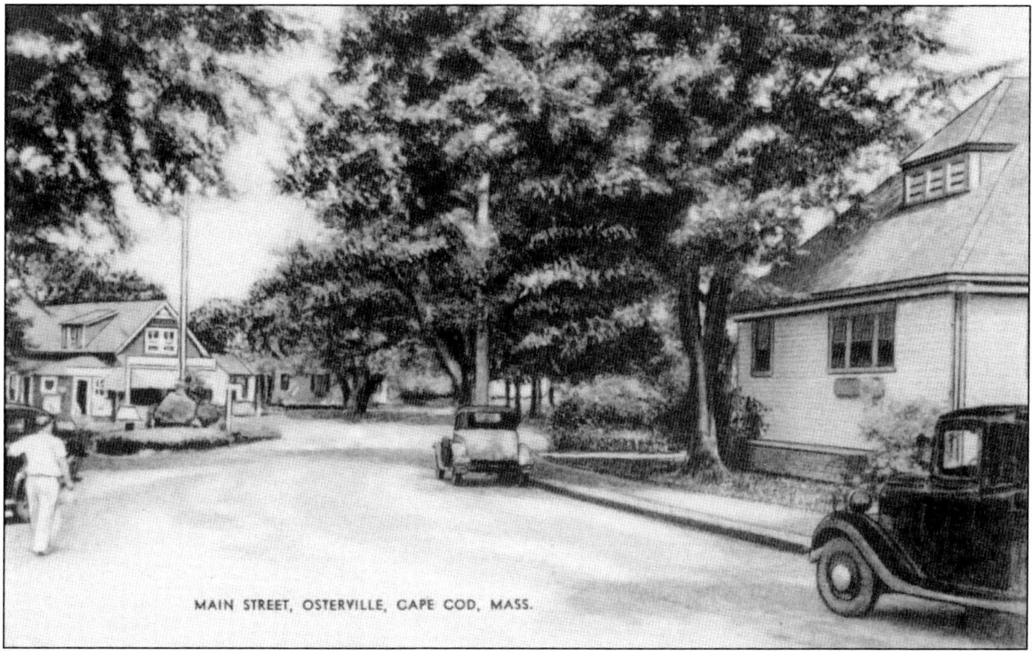

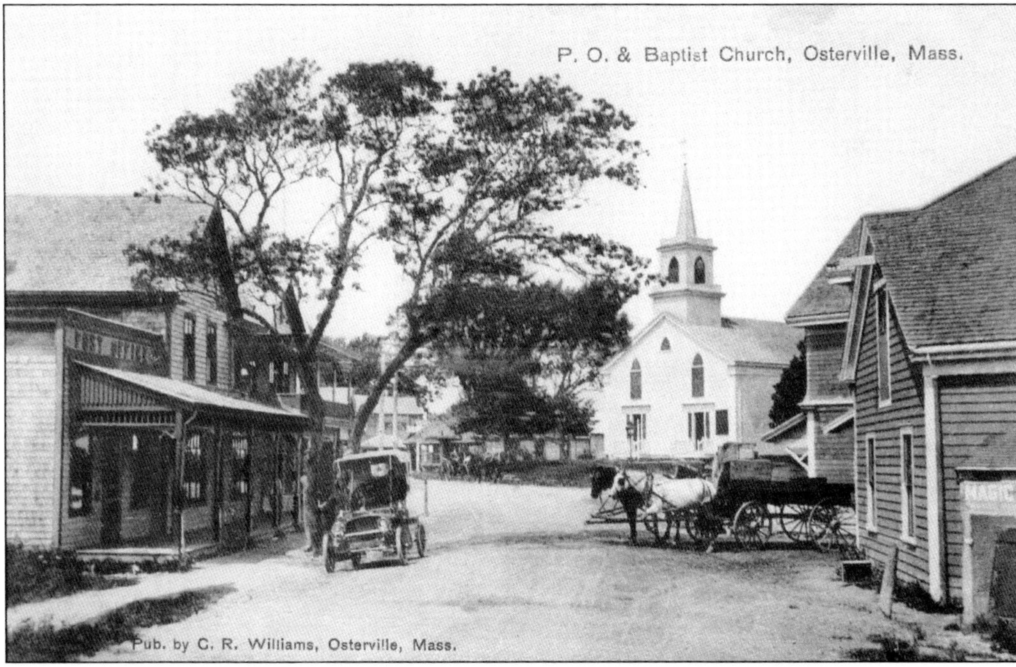

This is a view of Wianno Avenue looking west toward the intersection with Main Street. The Daniel Block with the post office is on the left, and Israel Crocker's General Store is on the right. Crocker's store opened in 1866 and carried everything from fancy meats and cheeses to flour and sundries. Crocker had one of the first telephones in Osterville, and he and his wife lived at the corner of West Bay Road and Wianno Avenue (the site of the current village library). The postcard below shows a 1939 reverse of the previous postcard looking southeast across Main Street down Wianno Avenue with the Daniel Block on the right and Crocker's store on the left.

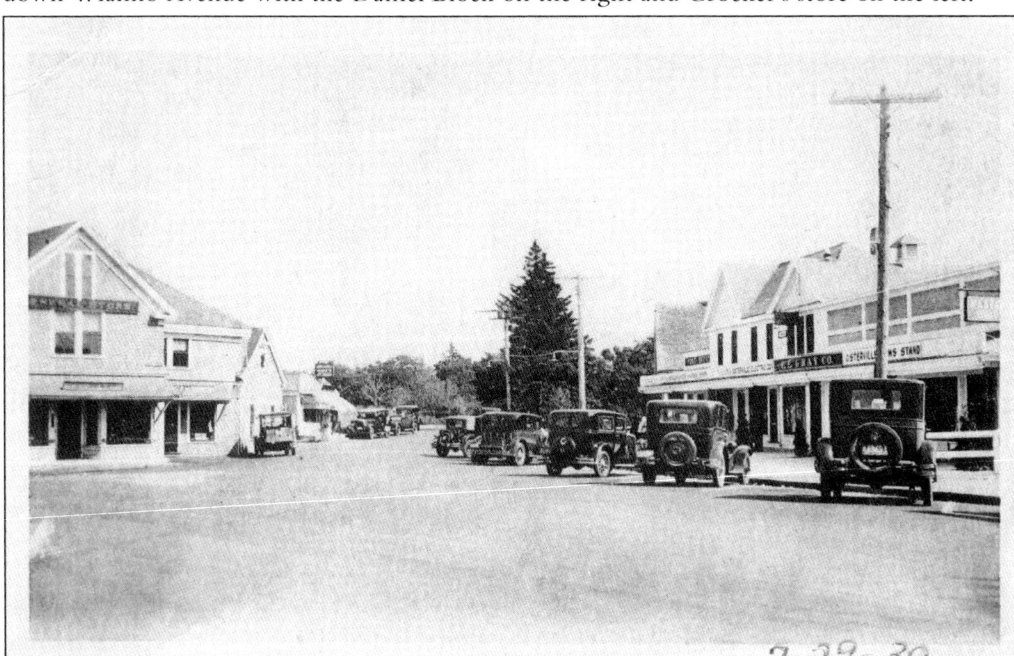

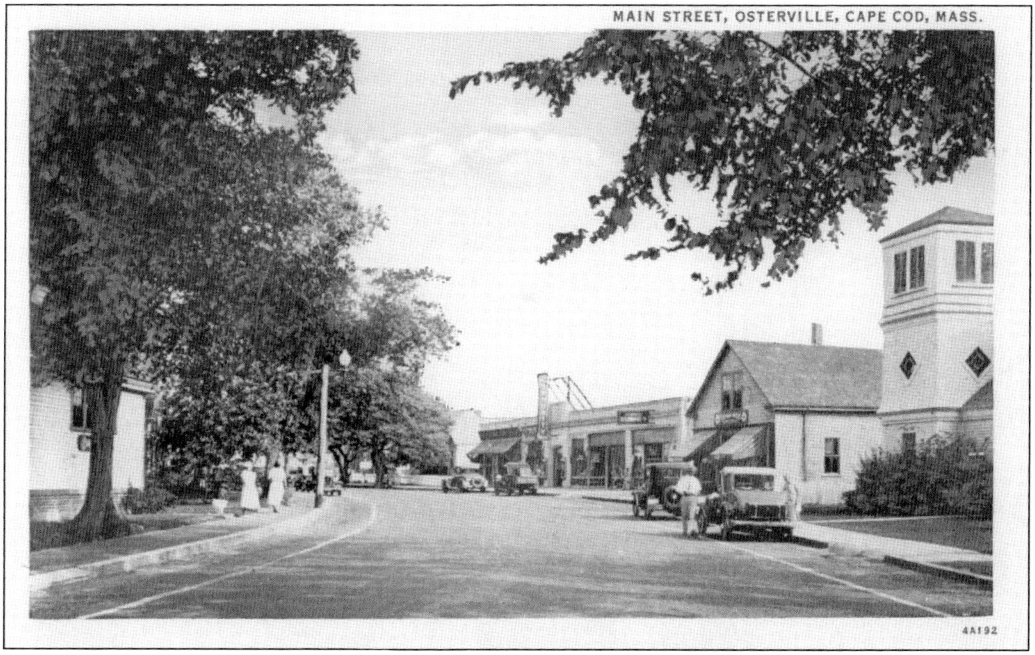

The view is looking east on Main Street toward the building housing the Star Theatre movie house and the Great Atlantic and Pacific Tea Company. The Star Theatre was built and owned built by Frank Williams, a carpenter. The interior featured cherry woodwork and had raised seats for 300. It was only the third building in Osterville to be electrified. The Methodist Church is on the right in both images.

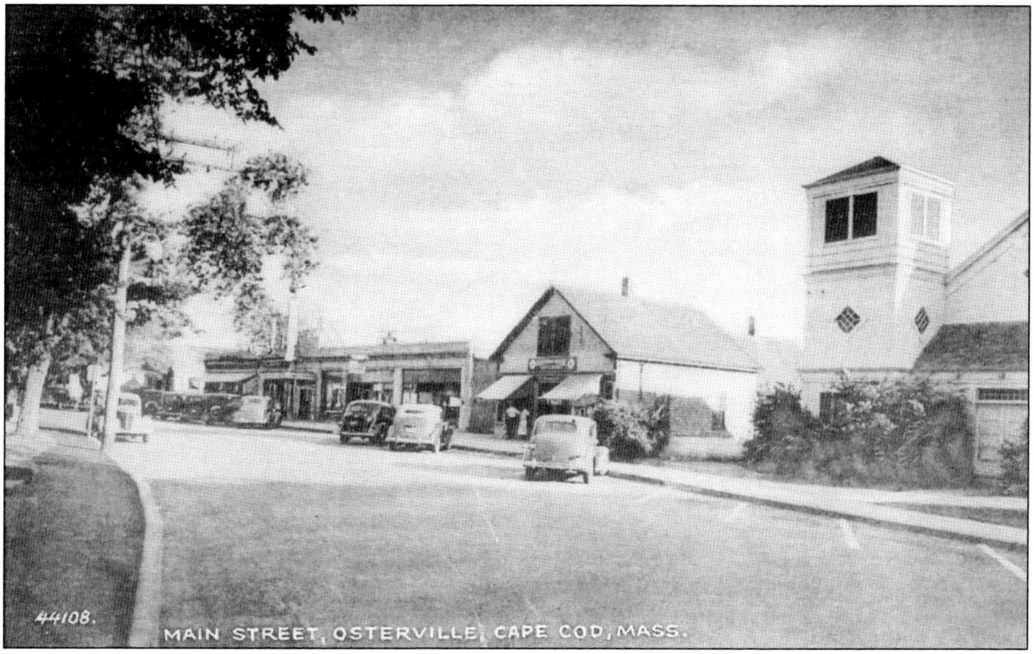

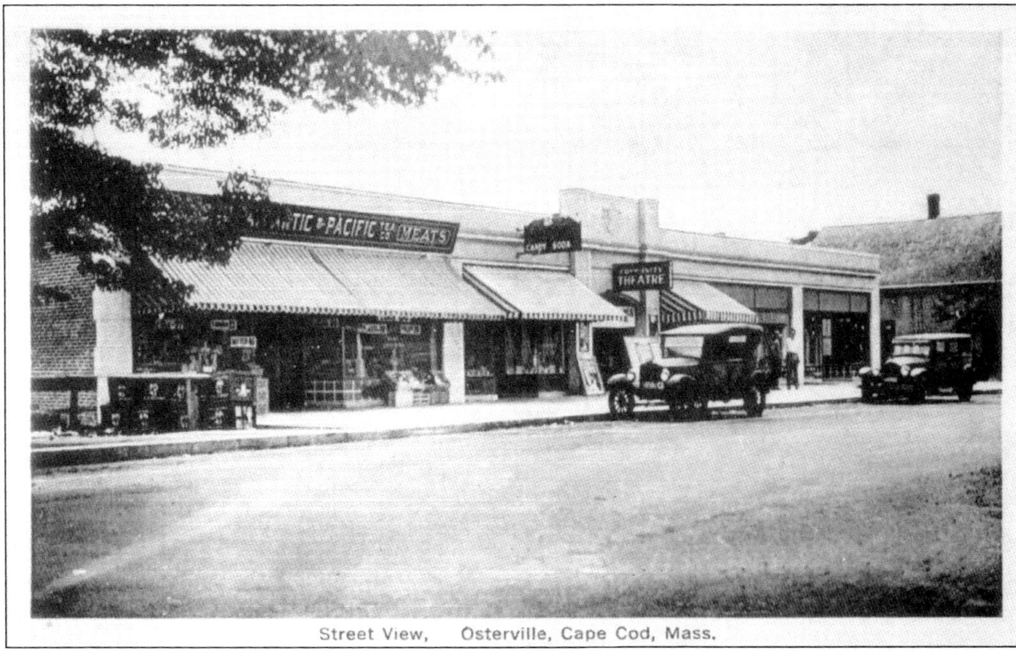

This is the view south across Main Street, just west of the intersection with Wianno Avenue. The Great Atlantic and Pacific Tea Company has moved a couple of buildings west and now anchors the left end of the building. When the Pattison Block was completed in 1928, a wooden ramp was added to the Star Theatre (open since 1913) to give it more frontage on the street. It formed a tunnel of sorts to the seating in the rear.

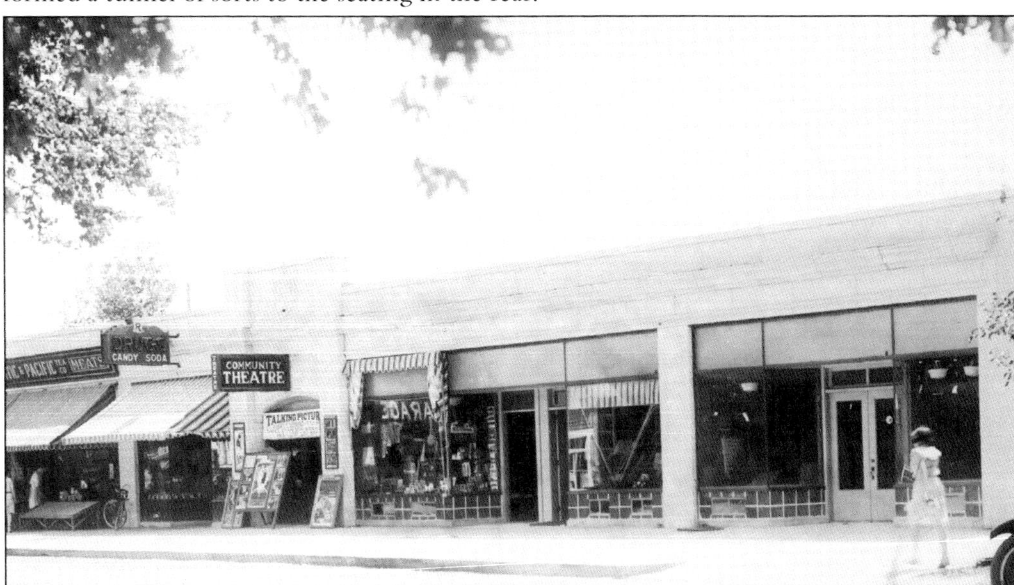

This postcard is looking east on Main Street at the Star Theatre. The Star Theatre ran "two-reeler" shows on Tuesday, Thursday, and Saturday evenings. Admission was 10¢, and the theater was packed on most nights. It provided evening entertainment for year-round residents as well as summer visitors. Often during the changing of the reels, local entertainment was provided by folks singing or playing a musical instrument.

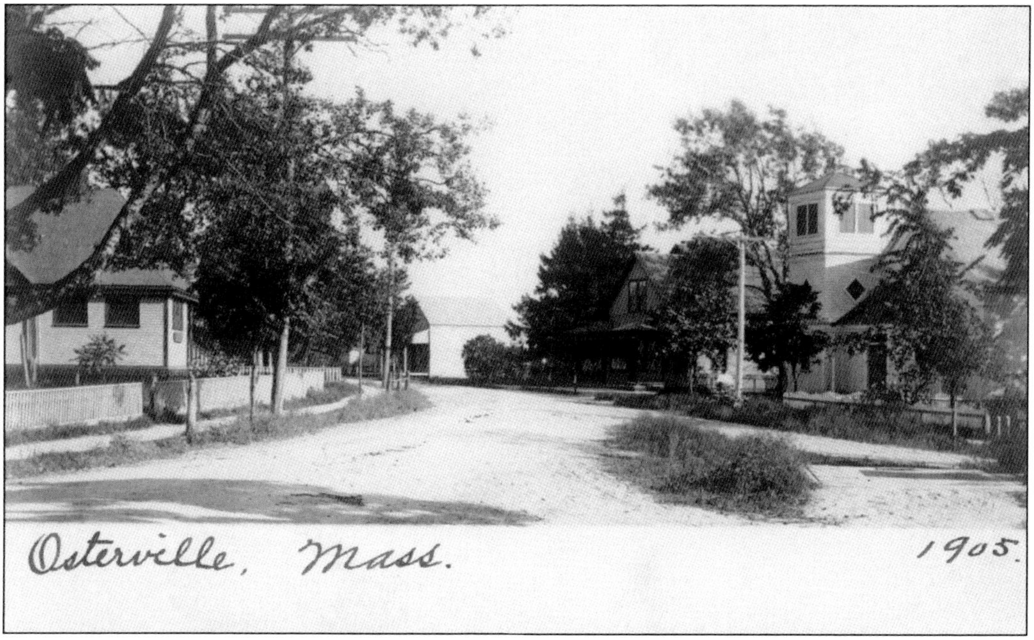

This view is looking east on Main Street in 1905 with hay scales to the immediate right. The Methodist Church is on the right, and the library is on the left. Katherine Hinckley served as the Osterville librarian for 37 years, from 1917 to 1954. During her time at the library, books used to be brought to beachgoers at Dowse's Beach to encourage reading.

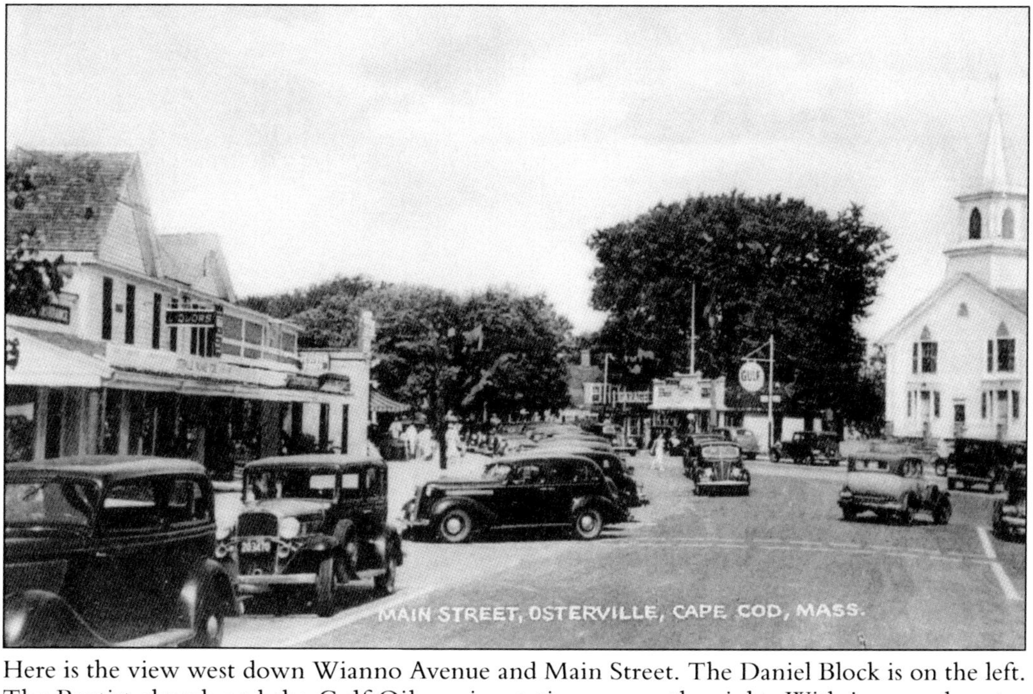

Here is the view west down Wianno Avenue and Main Street. The Daniel Block is on the left. The Baptist church and the Gulf Oil service station are on the right. With increased motor traffic, a total of seven gas stations could be found in Osterville at one point.

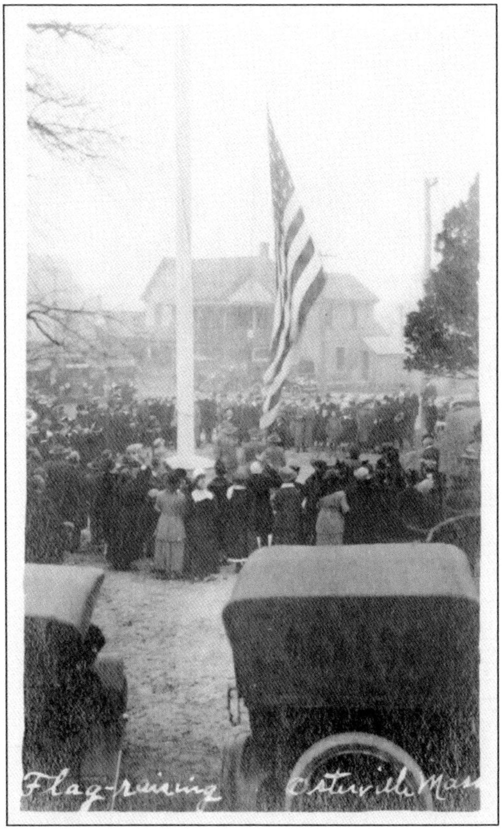

This postcard captures the historic flag raising on Main Street at the intersection with Wianno Avenue to celebrate Armistice Day on November 17, 1918, following World War I. The pole itself is a salvaged mast from a vessel that ran aground off Wianno Beach.

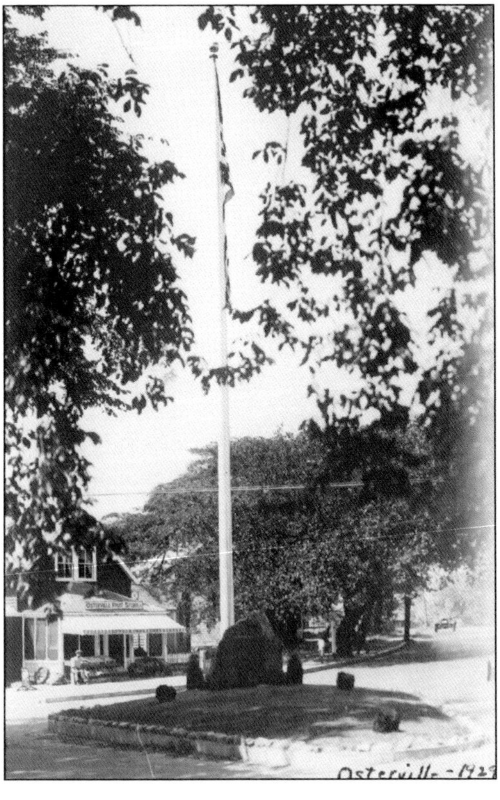

This 1929 scene is looking west on Main Street toward the Kalas' Fruit Store. Prior to the Kalas family purchasing the building in 1919, the space was the location of Edith Crosby's Dry Goods Store. The flag has been an important part of village life. As a young girl, Pansy Kalas, who lived and worked with her family in their fruit store, raised and lowered the flag faithfully during World War II.

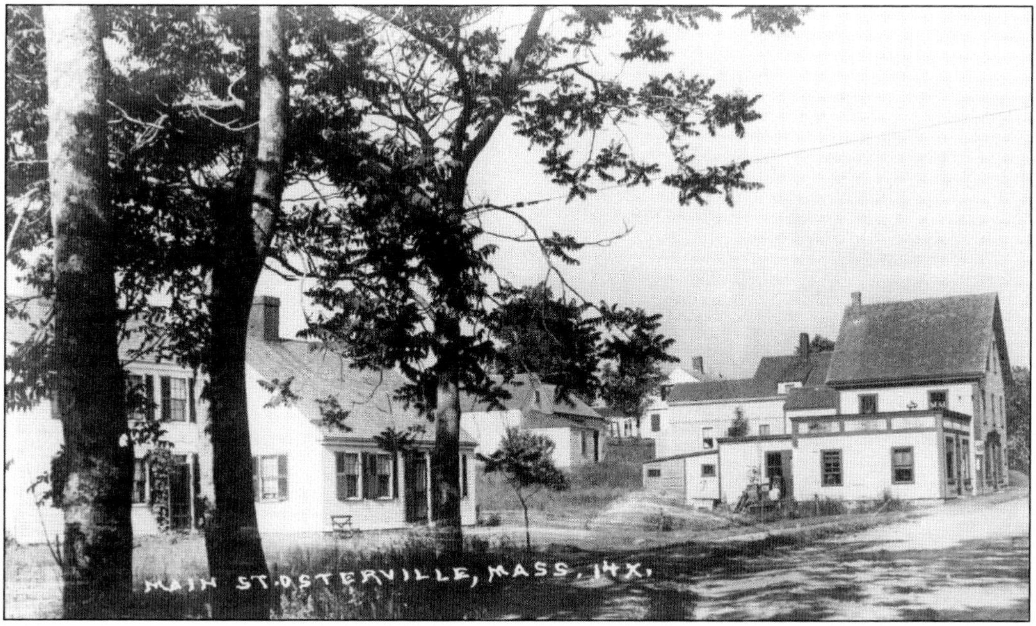

The card above shows Nehemiah Lovell's house on the left; it later became David Fuller Sr.'s home. Today's Fancy's Market (previously Fuller's Market and E.C.C. Swift's) can be seen on the right. The postcard below shows the house of Dr. William Kinney at the corner of West Bay Road (on the left) and Main Street. Across West Bay Road is the location of the Union Hall that later became the Veterans Hall. The card was mailed on July 28, 1922, and was addressed to a Miss Mildred Lewis in Belmont, Massachusetts. The note reads, "Sorry to have missed you before you left for camp, but hope you will write to me while you are gone and you will have a lovely time." Young Mildred Lewis had her tonsils removed by Dr. Kinney in the barn of her family home, shown on the next page.

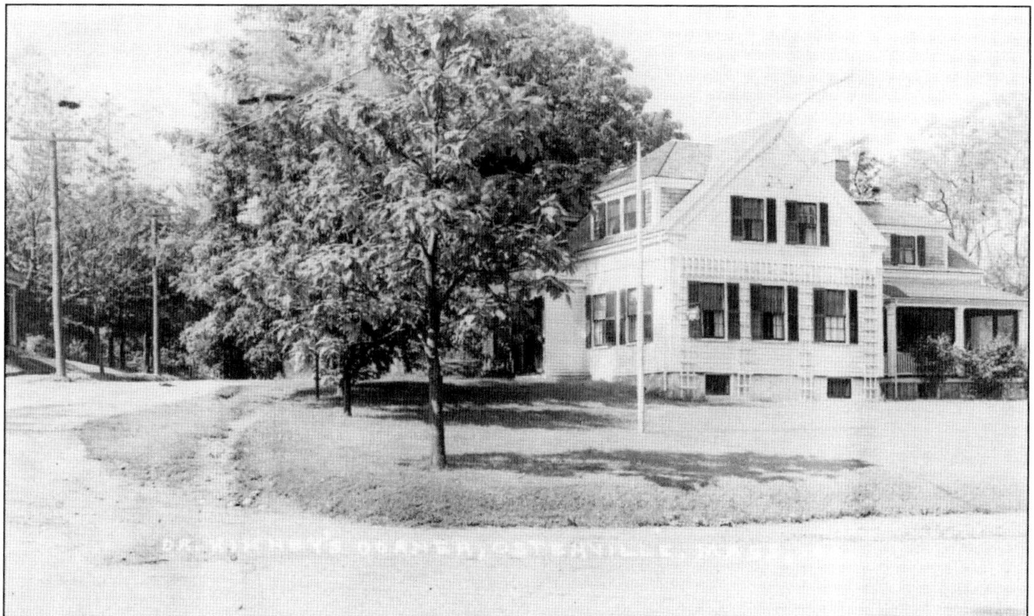

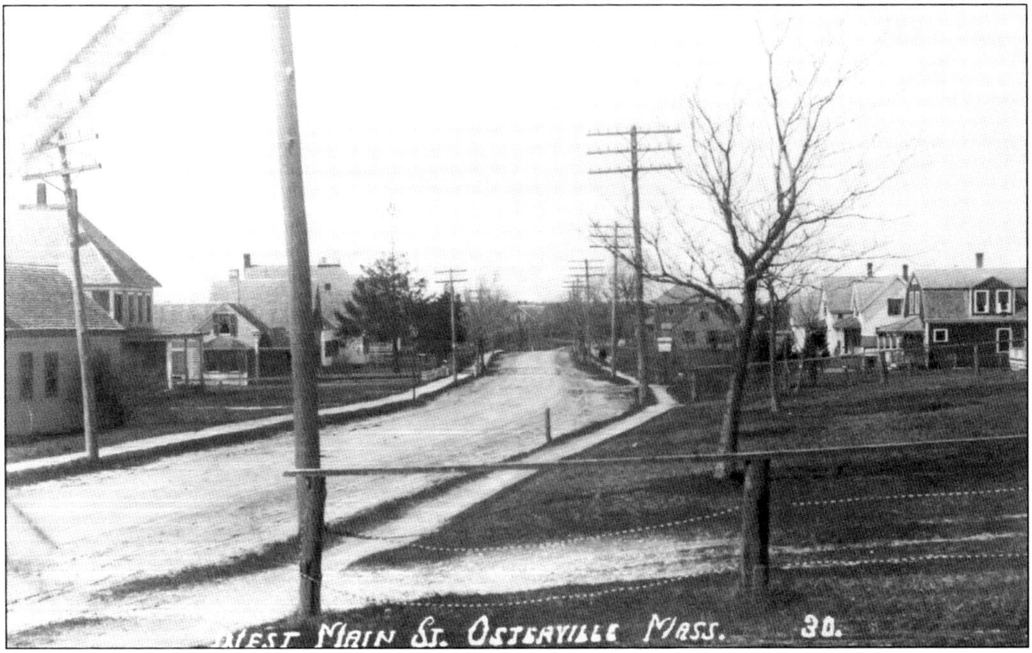

This postcard is looking west on Main Street heading out of the village. In the distance on the left is the Henry Foster Lewis house, which later became the site of the Midway Garage. It can be identified by its widow's walk. The house burned in 1921, but the barns are still in use today as inspection bays for Midway Garage.

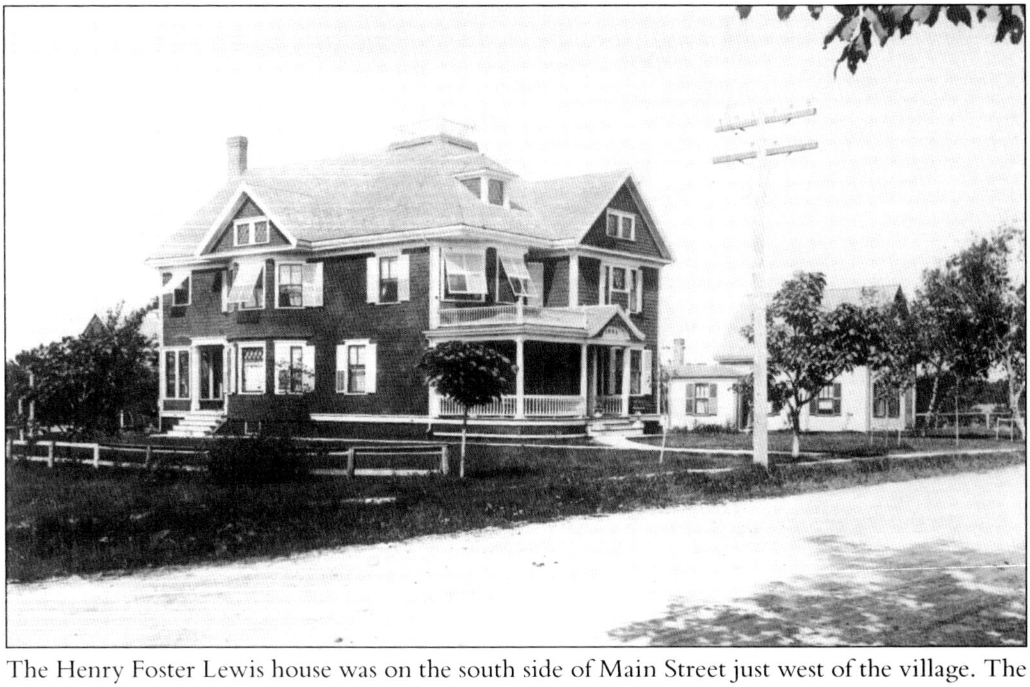

The Henry Foster Lewis house was on the south side of Main Street just west of the village. The barns behind the house were used as the stables for Capt. Daniel Bursley's stagecoach, which would pick up passengers at the West Barnstable train station. The barns also housed the first fire equipment for the village. The house to the right would later become the site of the fire station.

Two

The Churches

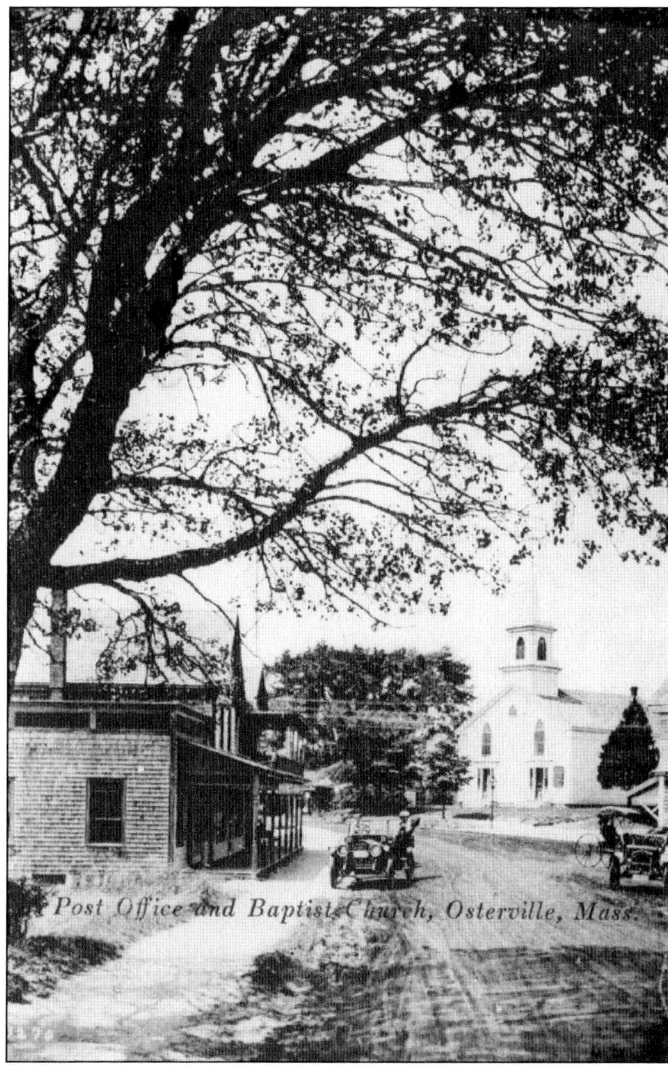

Families of the Hyannis Baptist congregation, including the Halletts, Lovells, Smalls, Childs, Hinckleys, Cammetts, and Blounts, founded the Osterville Baptist Church in 1835. The construction of the Greek Revival structure was completed in 1837, and the exterior of the building looks very much the same today. In 1889, the interior of the church sanctuary was outfitted with plush red speaker's chairs and matching cushions for the worshipers. The church is a central landmark in many Osterville postcards and photographs. The former location of the post office is on the left. In 1987, the church was added to the National Register of Historic Places.

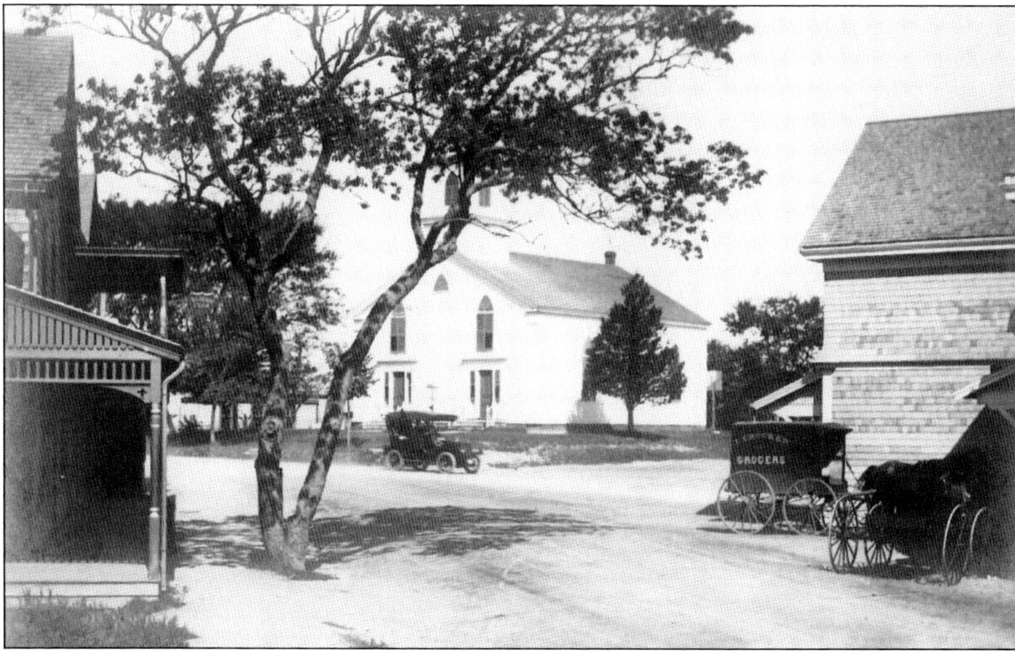

Next to the Osterville Baptist Church was a watering trough for horses. The weather vane visible at the top of the steeple in the postcard below was replaced in 2003. The original was donated to the Osterville Historical Museum. The weather vane in the shape of a feather quill represents the power of the written word of scripture.

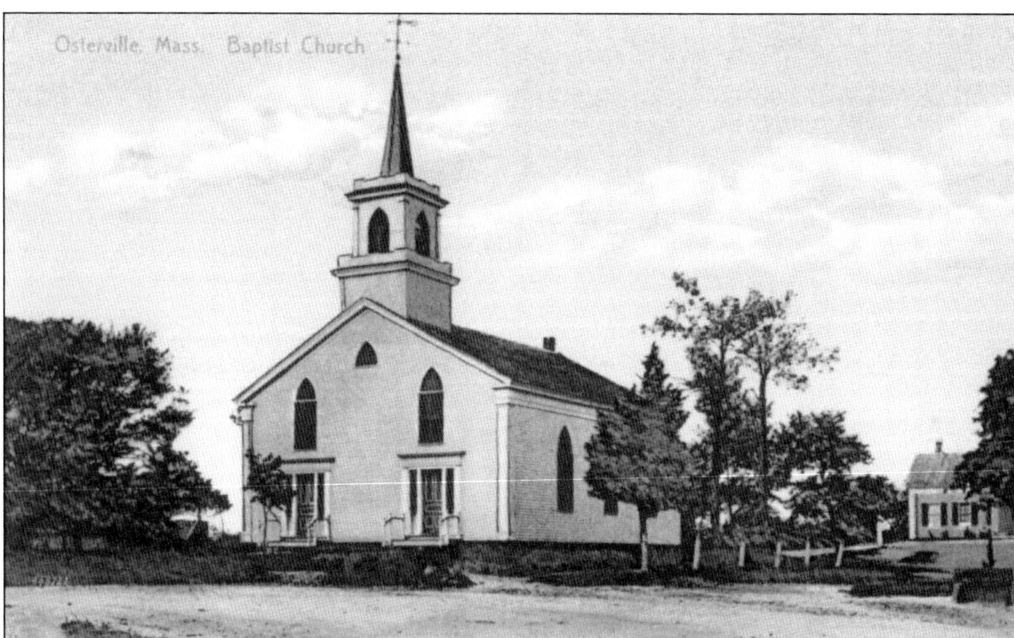

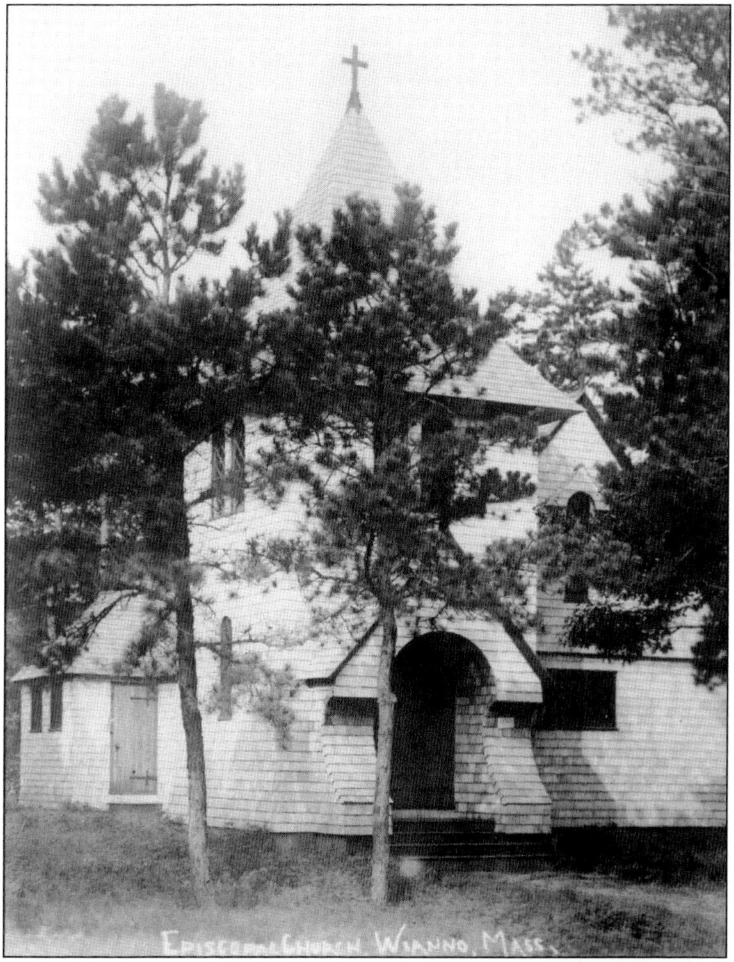

St. Peter's Episcopal Church is located on Wianno Avenue and was established in 1903 as a summer chapel. It was designed to seat 115 and cost $3,000 to build on land donated by Thomas Gaff and Gordon Shilitto. In 1969, summer services began being held at Crystal Lake. In 1975, the facilities were expanded and the church became a year-round parish. Another expansion was completed in 2012.

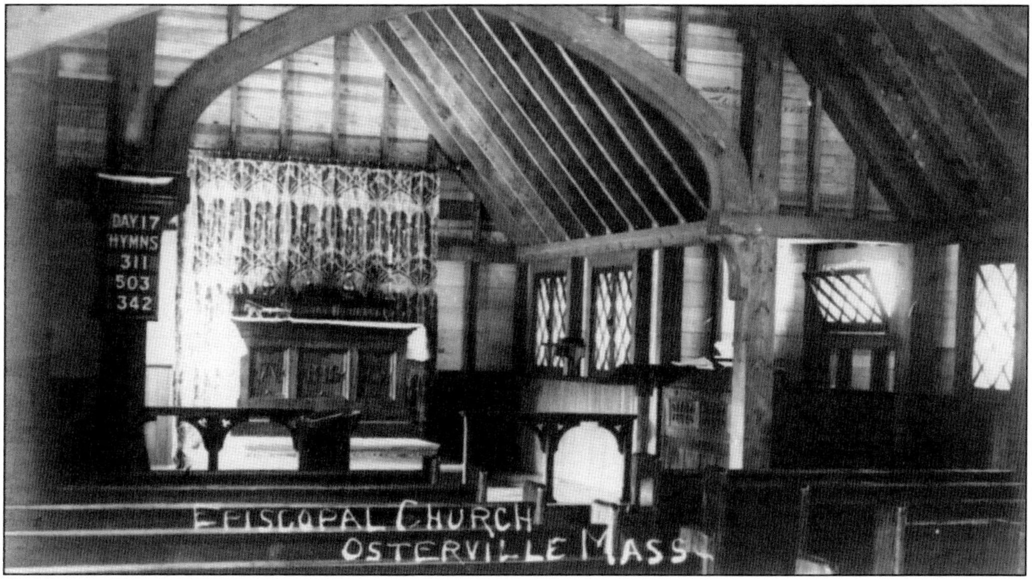

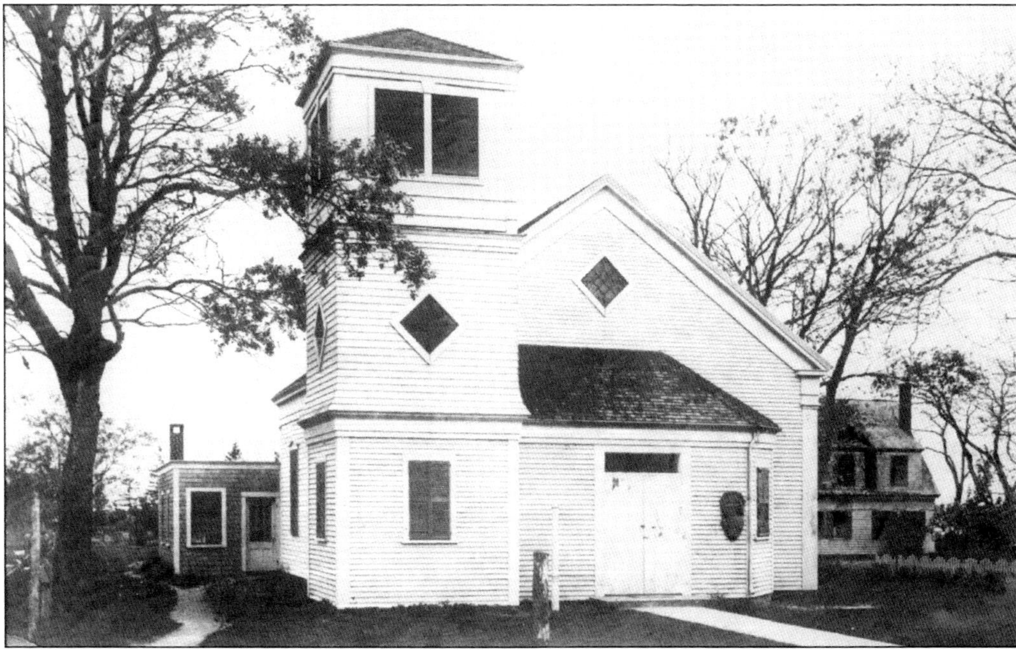

The Methodist Church was originally located on Main Street. The church was formed by Oliver Hinckley in 1829, and the building was completed in 1847. In 1970, a new church was built on Pond Street to accommodate a growing congregation. The original spire and bell were moved. Today, a retail space, Checkerberry House Interiors, occupies the building, but the original diamond-shaped windows are still visible above the door.

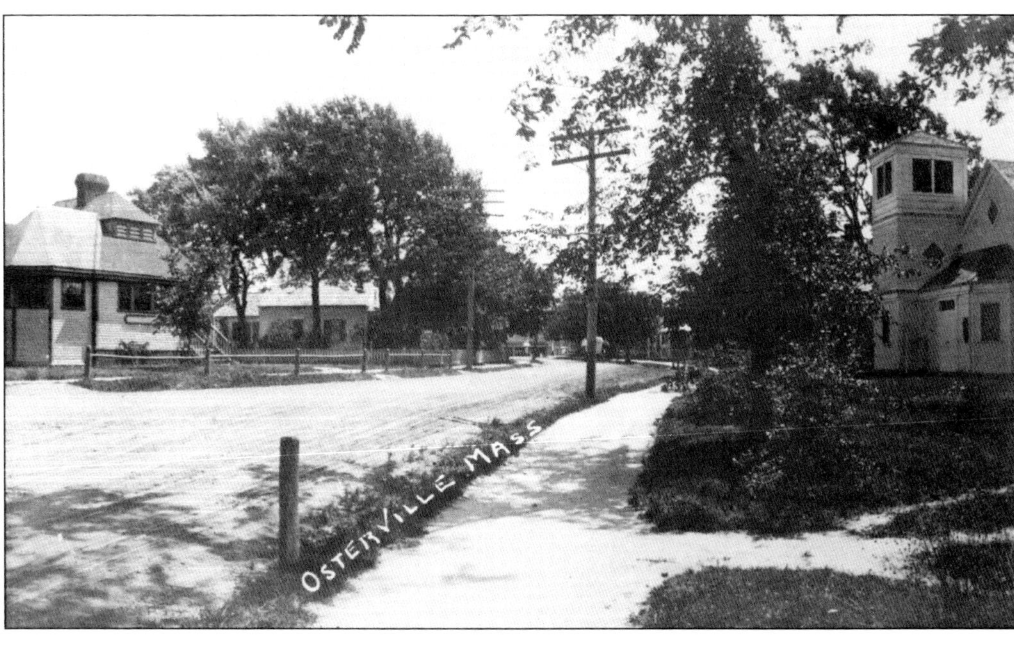

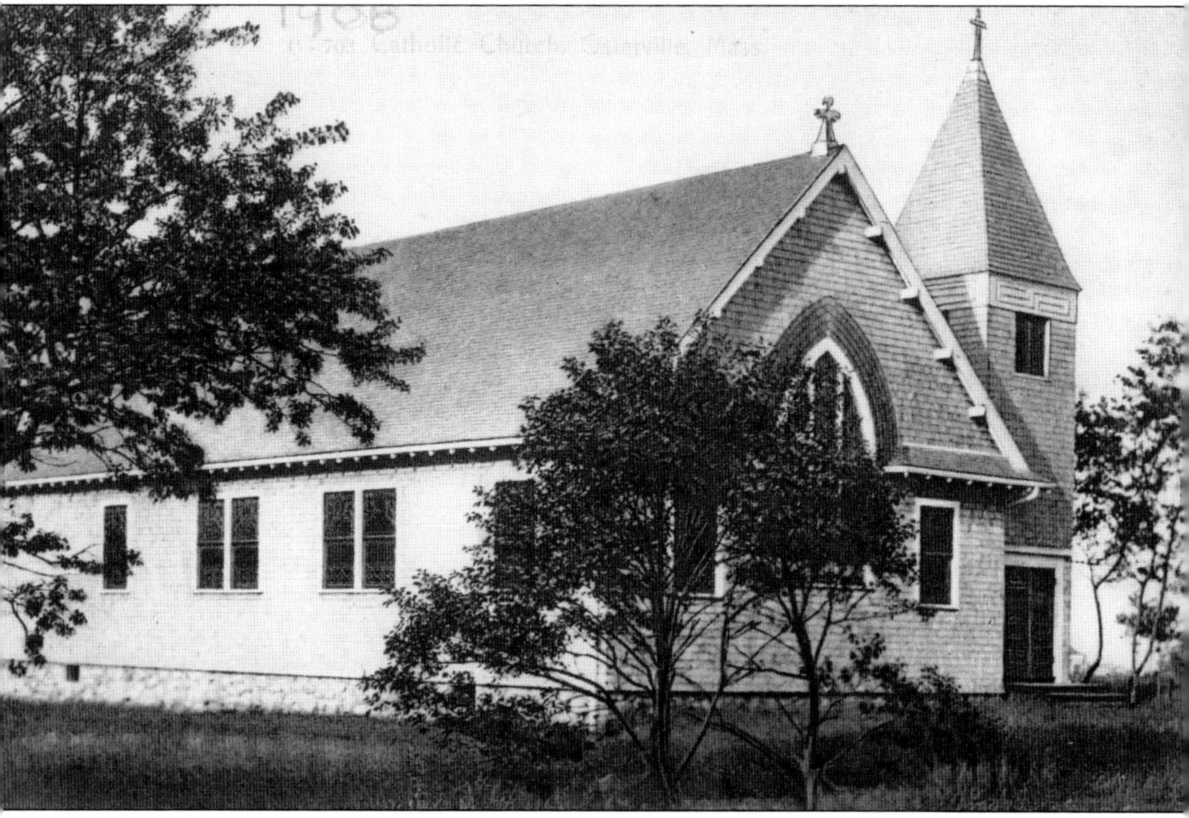

Our Lady of the Assumption Catholic Church was built in 1905; its name was taken from the patroness of the diocese—St. Mary of the Assumption. The congregation actually began years earlier, in 1882, as a mission of St. Francis Xavier in Hyannis. The Masses were held in the village in Union Hall until the Diocese of Fall River bought the land on Wianno Avenue in 1903 for $400. Early parish families included the Beaumonts, Daniels, Hansberrys, and Shieldses. Bishop William Stang dedicated the church. Mass was celebrated every other week. The building was expanded in 1916 and 1926 and again in 1960. The image in this postcard, postmarked in 1908, shows the first half of the nave of the present church.

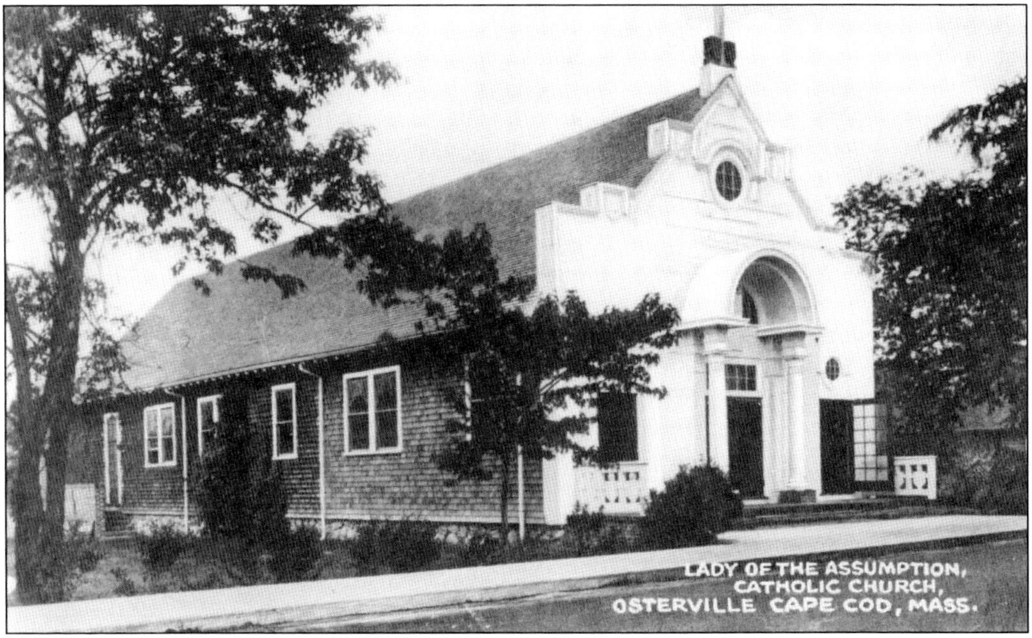

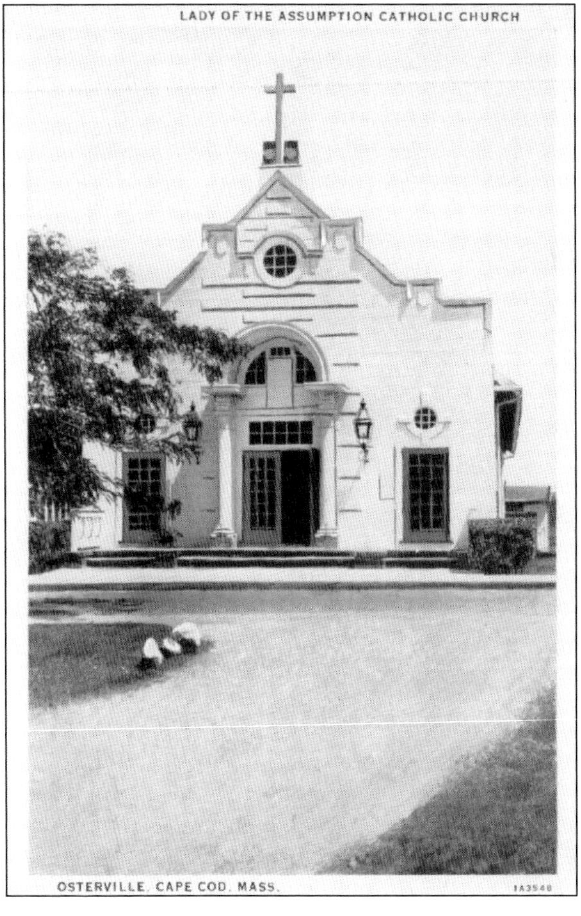

There have been several changes to the front of Our Lady of the Assumption Catholic Church. The most involved renovations happened in 1960 when a new facade and sides were added, giving it the shape of a cross. Additional renovations took place in 1966. There is also a rectory and a parish activities building on the grounds. Both images shown here are before the side additions were added. The image on the left shows the front facade from the driveway of the house across a paved Wianno Avenue.

Three

East Bay Lodge

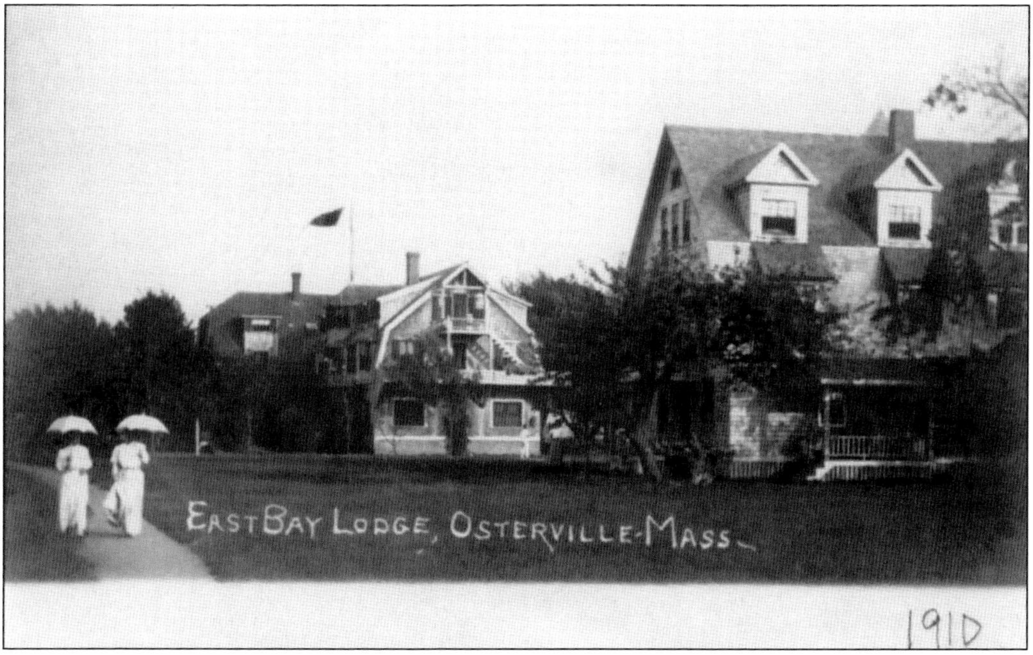

The East Bay Lodge, located on East Bay Road, was built in 1886 by retired sea captain Nelson H. Bearse Jr. According to author Shirley Eastman, the "East Bay Lodge dominated Osterville's seaside landscape during its glory years in the early 1900s. On a sunlit summer day, the view from the tree-lined driveway next to the lodge was magnificent. Visitors called it one of the choicest resorts on the New England shore." In June 1904, a Sunday dinner served at East Bay Lodge from 1:30 to 2:30 p.m. cost 75¢. Through the years, East Bay Lodge changed owners until it was demolished in the late 1990s to make way for condominiums. Many Cape Cod families remember staying at the lodge, celebrating weddings there or enjoying a traditional Sunday brunch.

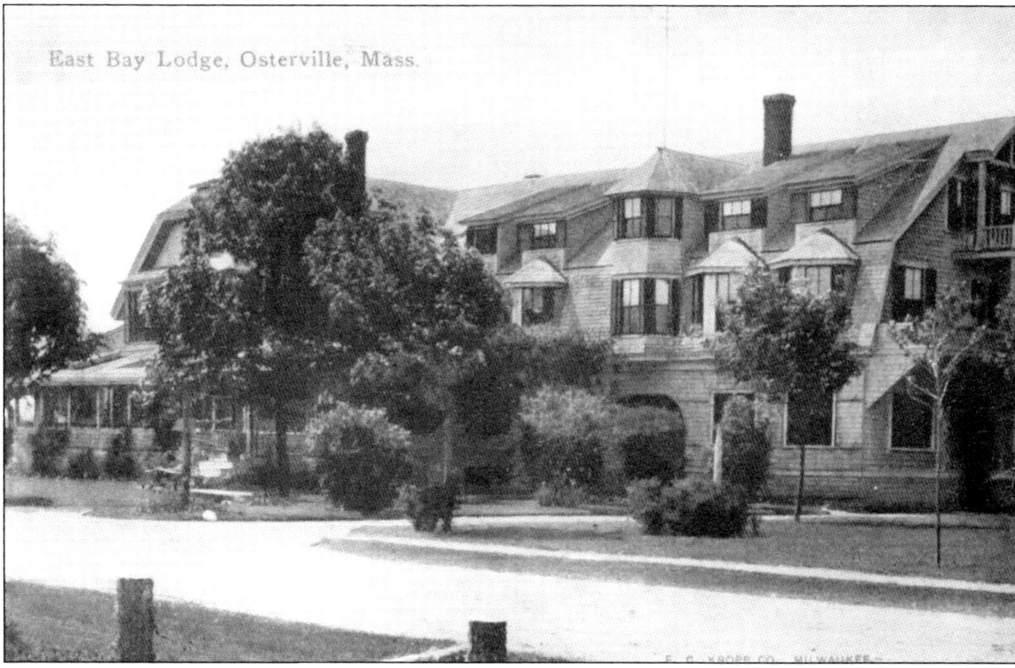

Nelson H. Bearse Jr. sent the postcard above with a 1¢ stamp to confirm a reservation for a guest from St. Johnsbury, Vermont. "Dear Sir, Will reserve room for you from Sept. 16. Yours Truly, N. H. Bearse, Sept. 8, 1910." It is postmarked September 8, 1910, at 3:00 p.m.

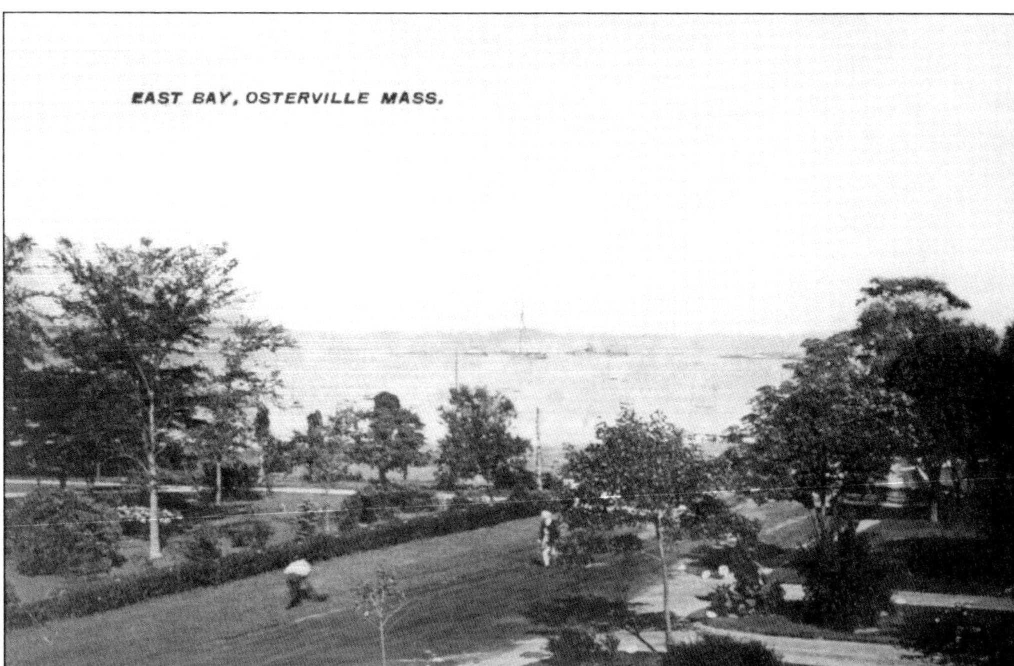

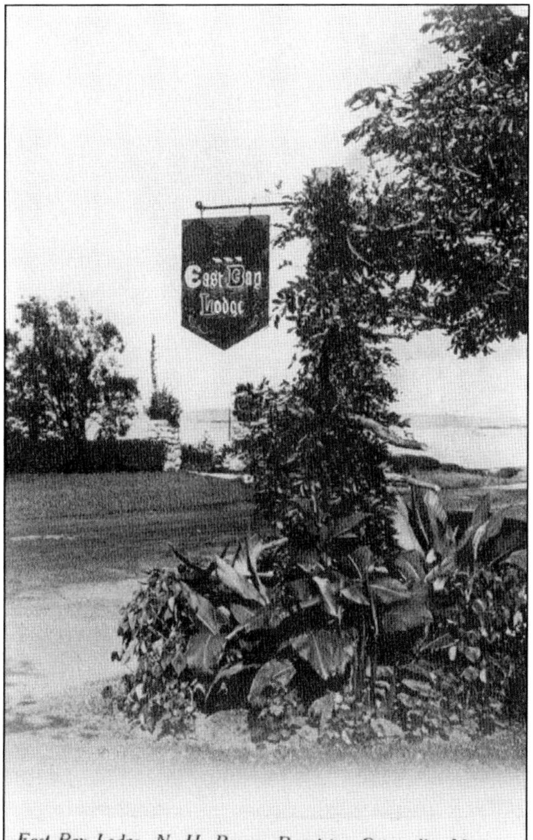

East Bay Lodge, N. H. Bearse, Proprietor, Osterville, Mass.

The following is from a 1930 advertisement for East Bay Lodge: "A perfectly appointed hotel conducted on the American plan with cuisine and service unexcelled. Every room with private bath or running water. Golf, clock golf, tennis, croquet, bathing, boating, fishing, saddle horses. Magnificent shore, country views, drives and walks. Charles H. Brown, proprietor."

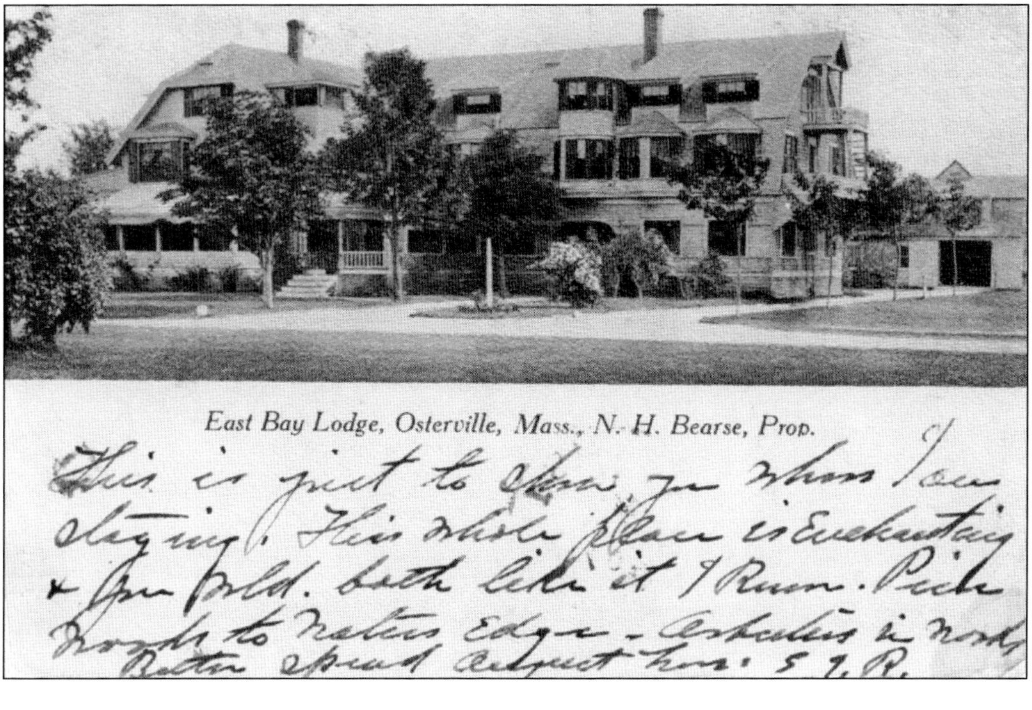

East Bay Lodge, Osterville, Mass., N. H. Bearse, Prop.

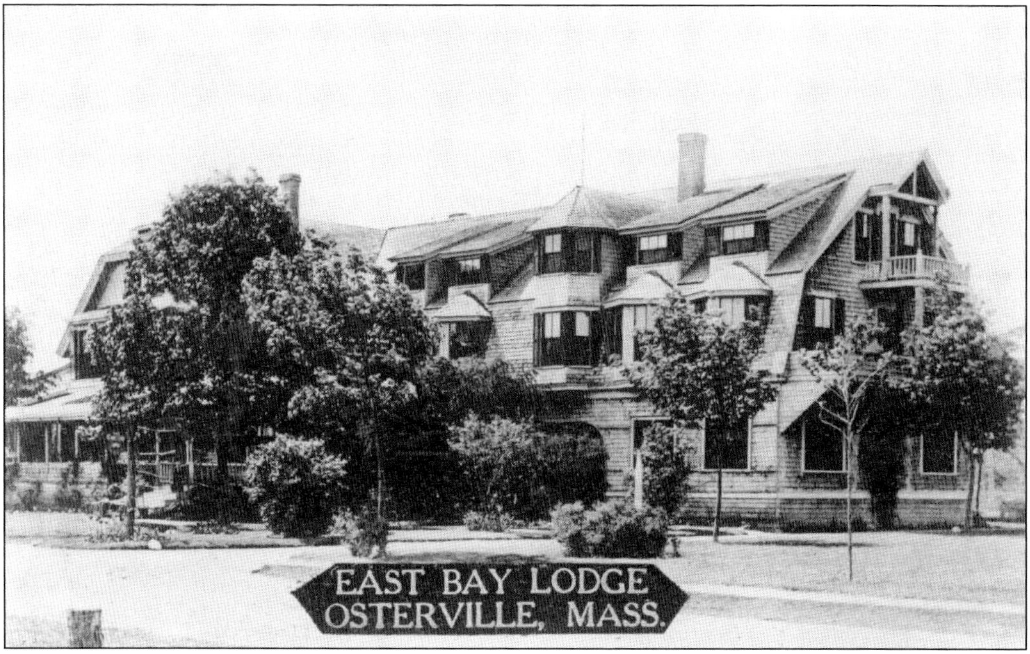

East Bay Lodge boasted 75 rooms and included multiple buildings, such as the main lodge and the annex. Captain Bearse's home was the starting point of the lodge. It was added onto and expanded greatly. The annex, seen in the postcard below on the right, was built over the Josiah Ames house, and a tower was constructed in 1911 to house the staff.

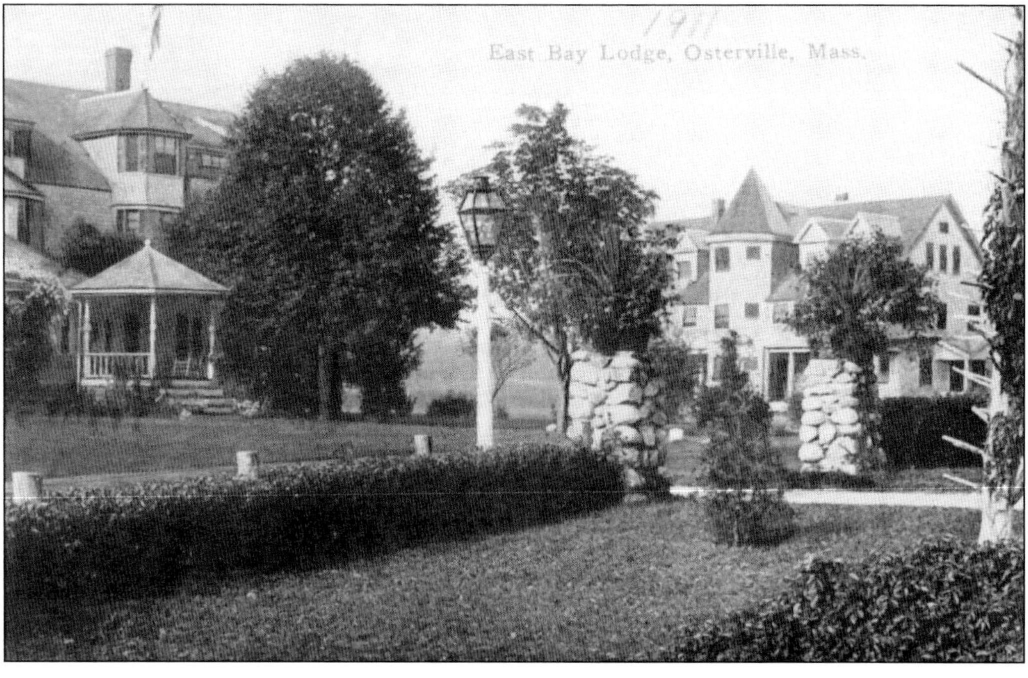

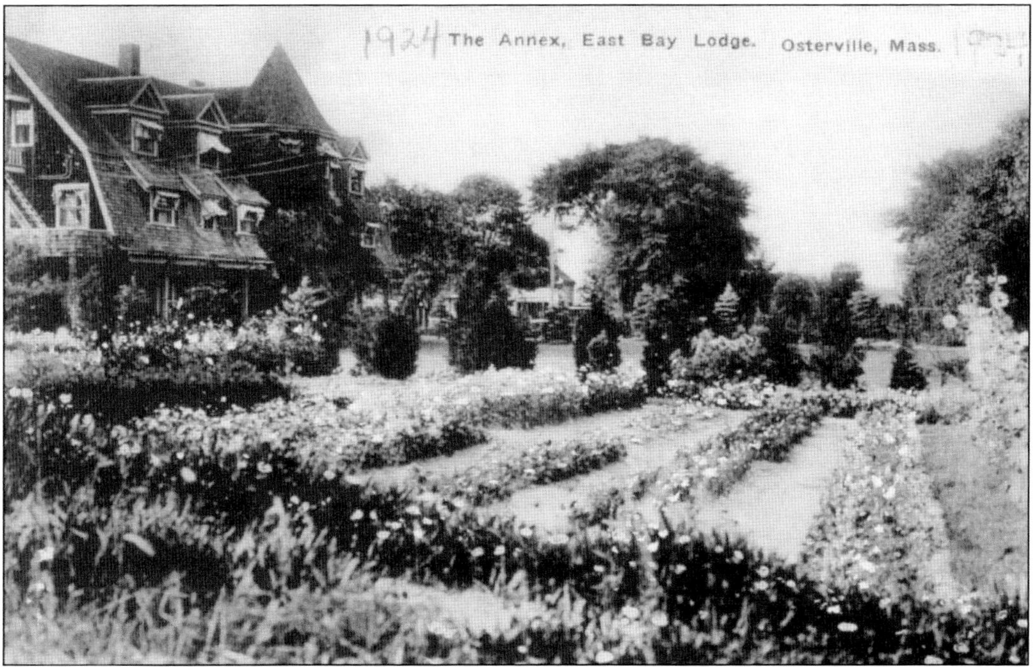

The lovely formal gardens by the annex and the heavily wooded landscape offered guests many opportunities to enjoy the grounds. The postcard below refers to "a Cozy Nook" at East Bay Lodge. Guests stayed at the lodge not for a day or two, but for weeks or sometimes months at a time. It was intended to be a home away from home for extended respites by the sea.

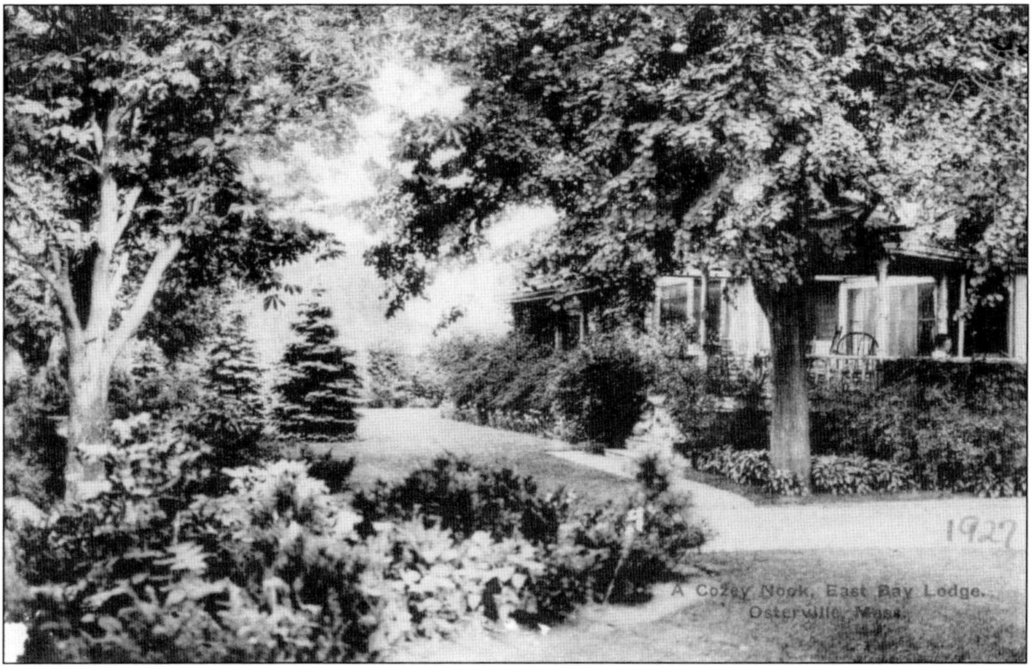

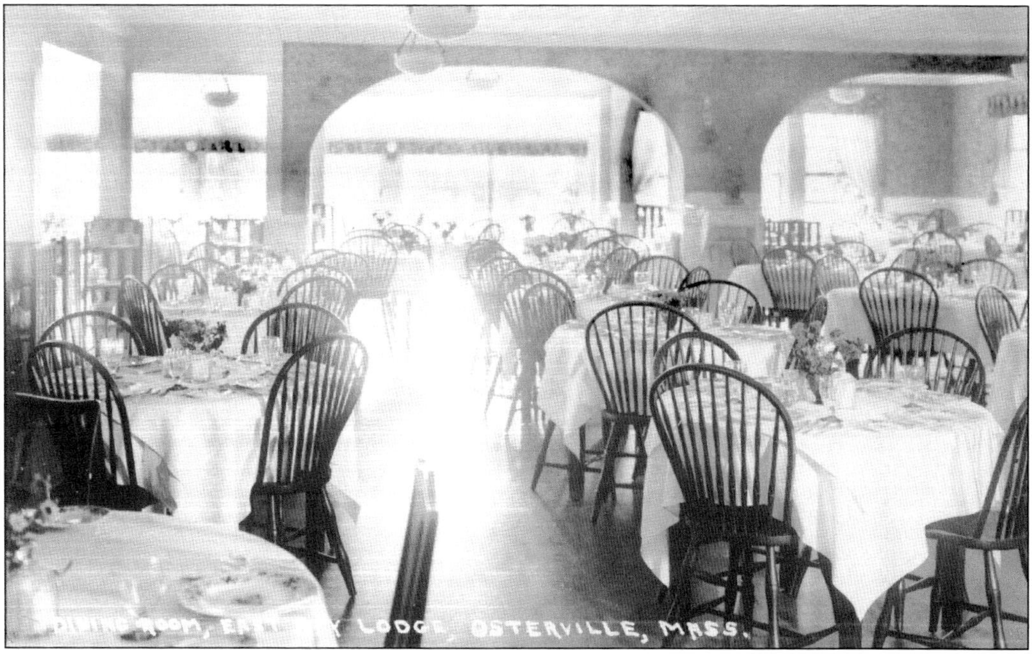

The interior furnishings of the East Bay Lodge were lavish for the day. Oriental rugs covered the wooden floors, and upholstered and wooden furniture decorated the main rooms. The dining rooms were set with white tablecloths, fine china, and silver. Despite closing in 1998, the china and silver are still highly collectible, as are advertisements and matchbook covers, and occasionally memorabilia can be found in Cape Cod antique shops.

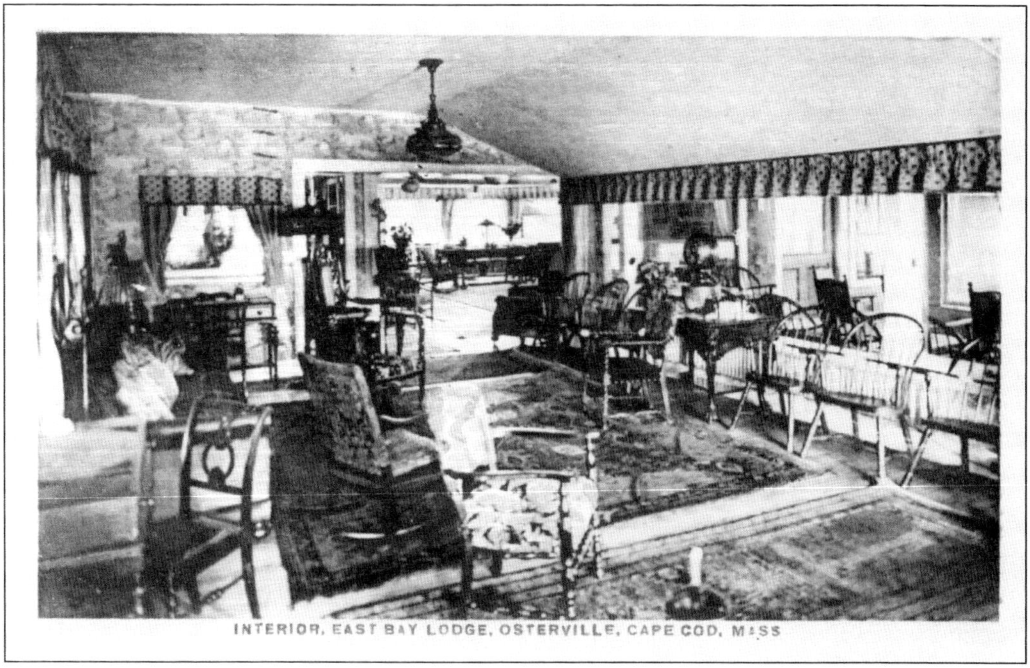

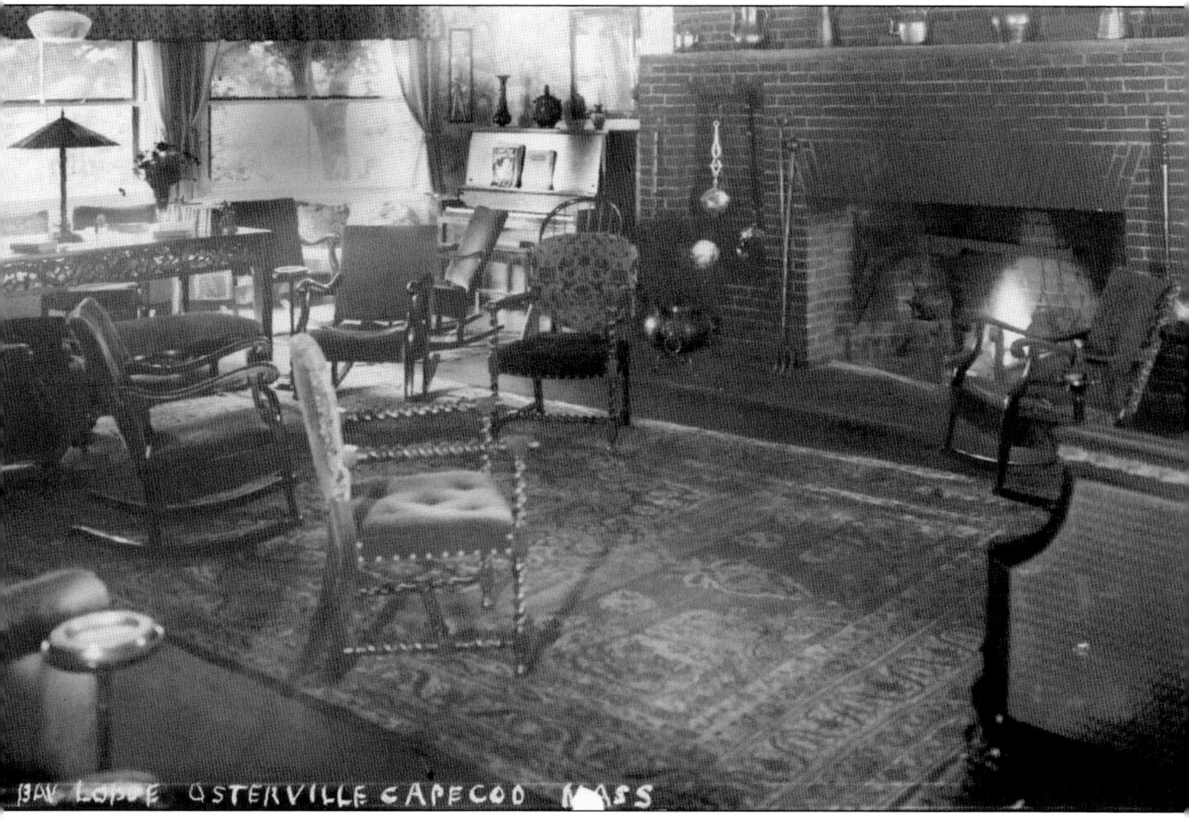

A writing desk, piano, comfortable chairs, and roaring fire grace this interior view of East Bay Lodge. Fire was a great threat to these large wooden structures. There was in fact a fire at East Bay Lodge in May 1923, but luckily, it was contained with no real damage. West Bay Inn was not so lucky. It was destroyed by fire in 1935.

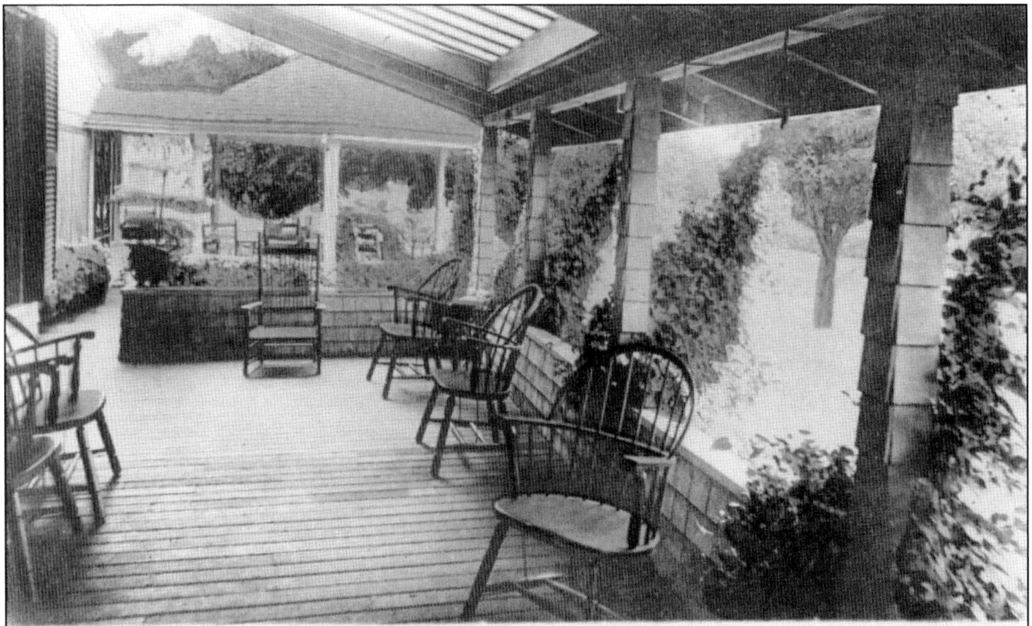

VERANDA, EAST BAY LODGE, OSTERVILLE, MASS.

Guests were welcome to use the inviting porches as well as the grounds. The breezes coming in off the nearby bay cooled the open-styled verandas. The image below shows East Bay Lodge on the right looking south to East Bay. Families that lived in the houses that lined East Bay Road on the right included the DeWitts, the Lovells, and the Hodges.

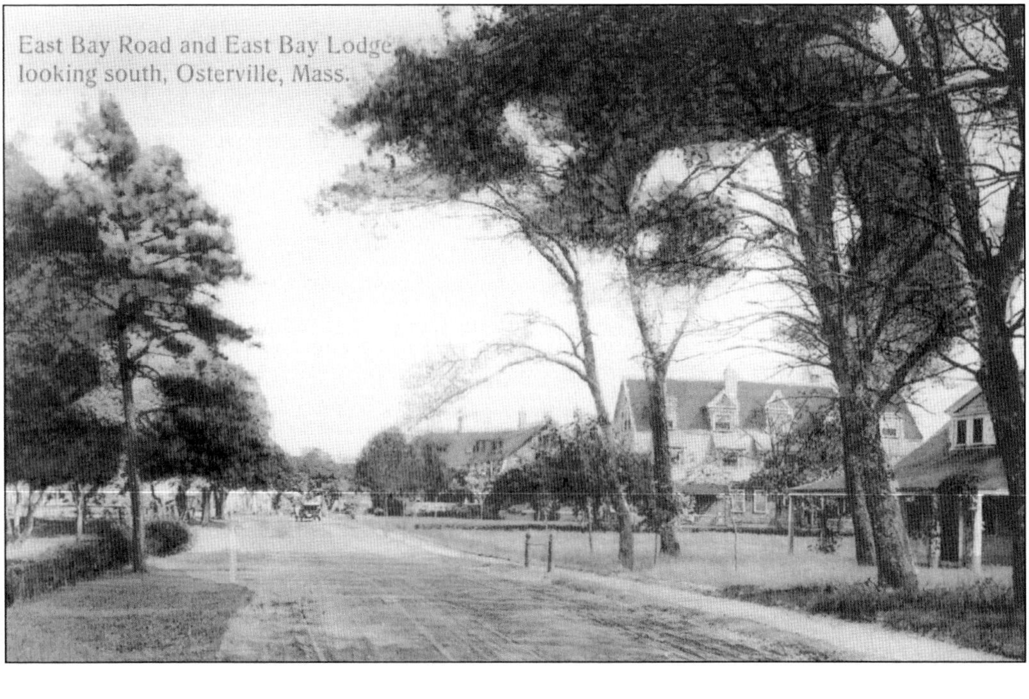

East Bay Road and East Bay Lodge looking south, Osterville, Mass.

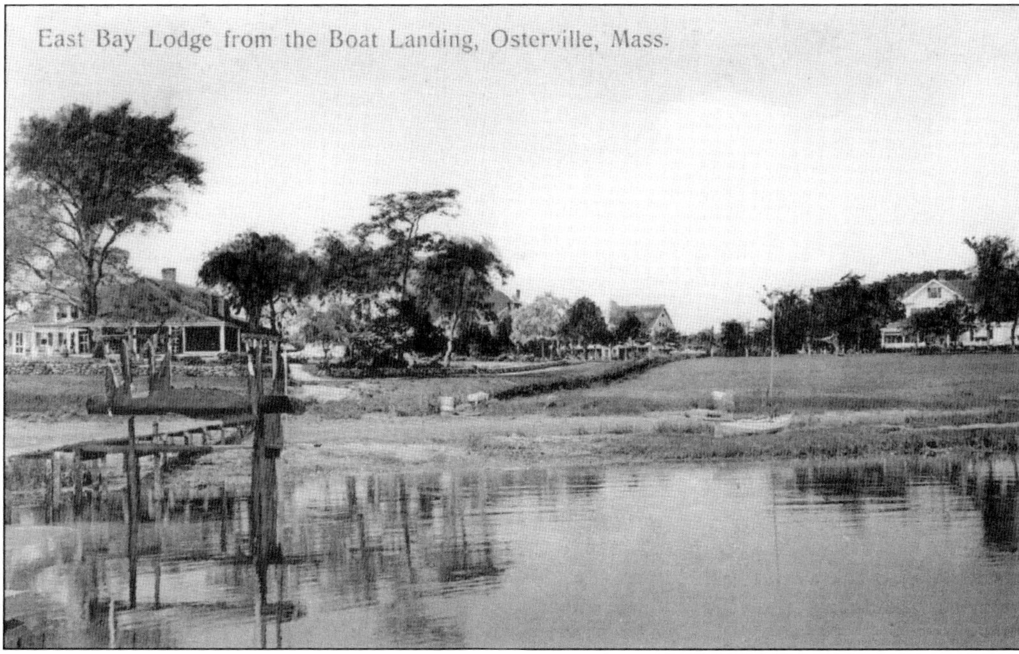

Travel to Osterville was usually by train from Boston to the West Barnstable railroad station. The author of the postcard above writes, "Dear Mother, Am writing this on the train and will mail it in Springfield. Left Boston at 2:00 p.m. The Gardners left this morning at eleven. It's fine weather to travel." The card was postmarked in Springfield, Massachusetts, at 5:00 p.m. on August 20, 1912. Train service was also available at the time to neighboring Hyannis.

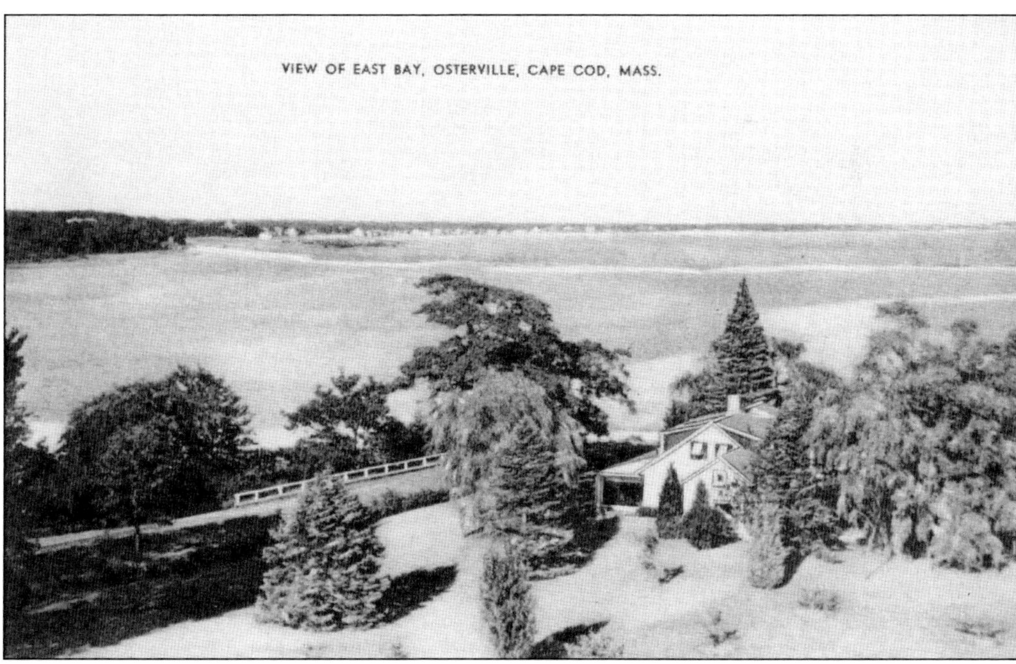

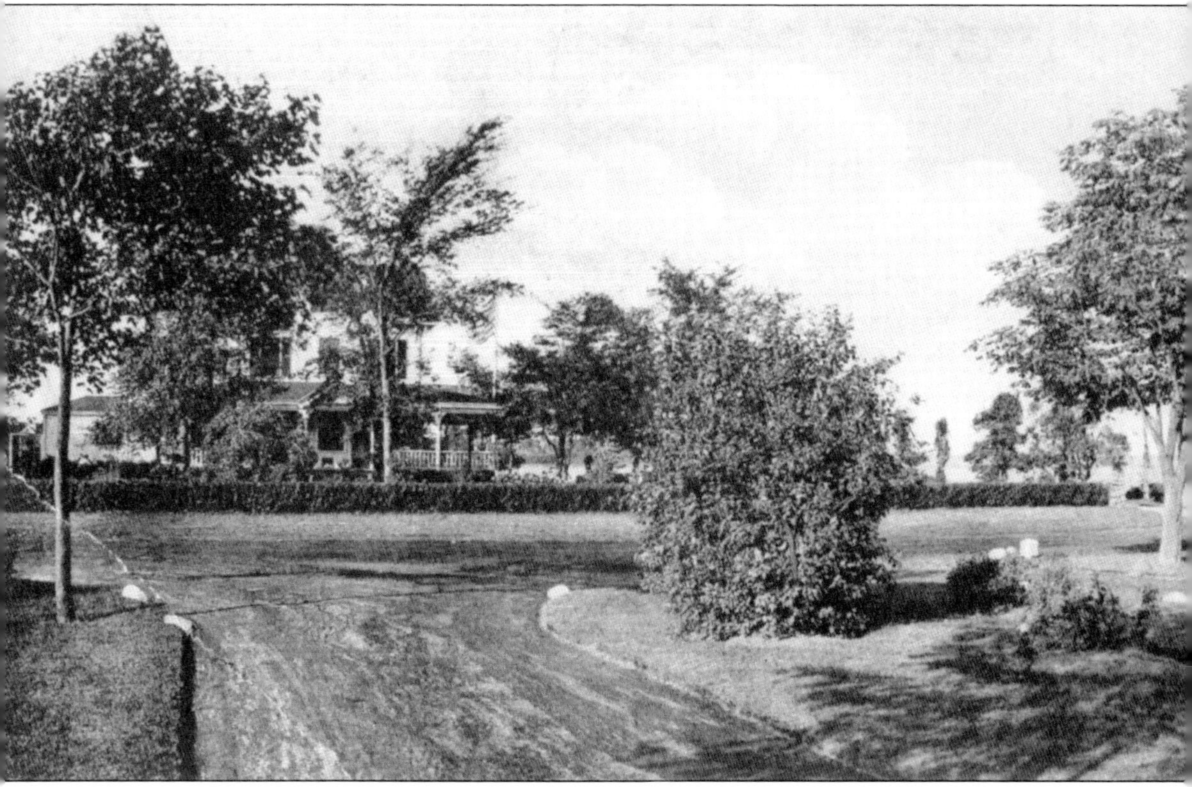

Many pathways throughout the property enabled an easy morning stroll to view East Bay or, as in the case in the image above, even a child's bicycle ride. An advertisement by Nelson H. Bearse Jr. proclaimed the following: "East Bay Lodge and Homestead are situated very near to the shore of East Bay, a beautiful sheet of water flowing in from Vineyard Sound, giving to

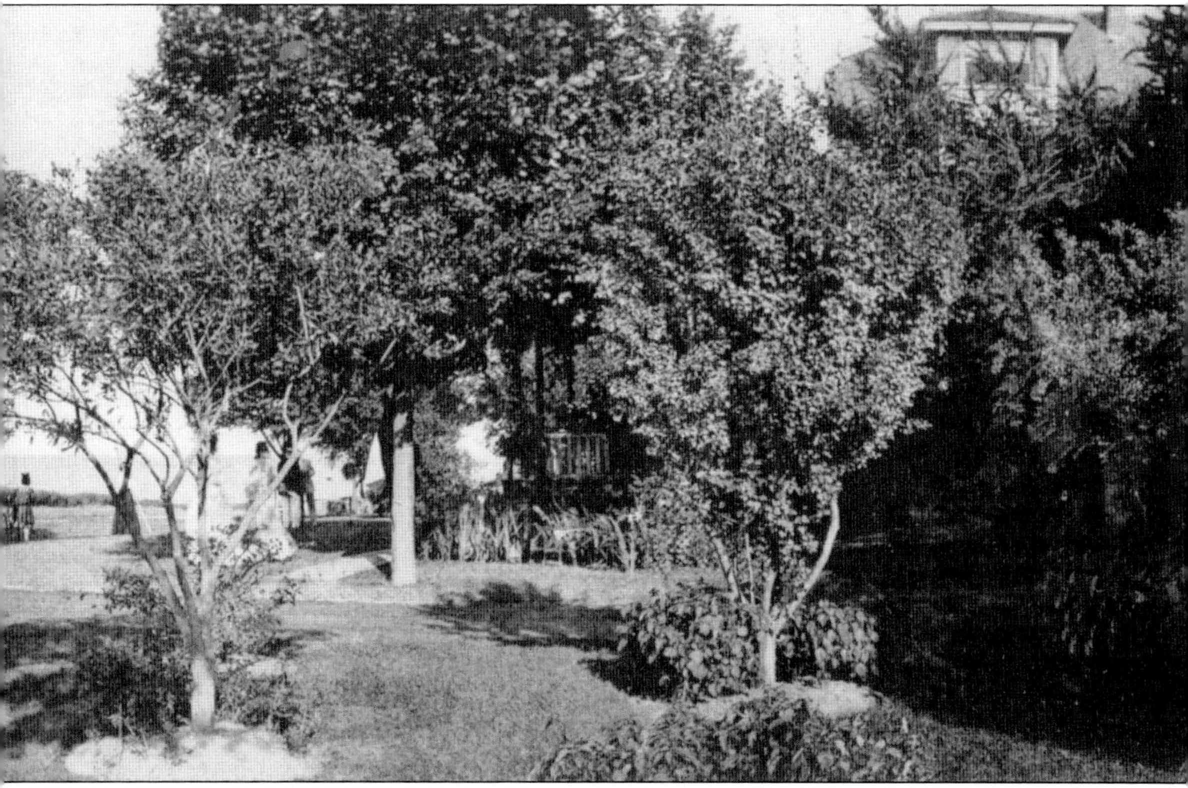

the guests of either house a view rarely surpassed, and making it particularly convenient and attractive for boating. The Lodge has recently been awarded the first prize as the most attractive and best-kept place in Osterville."

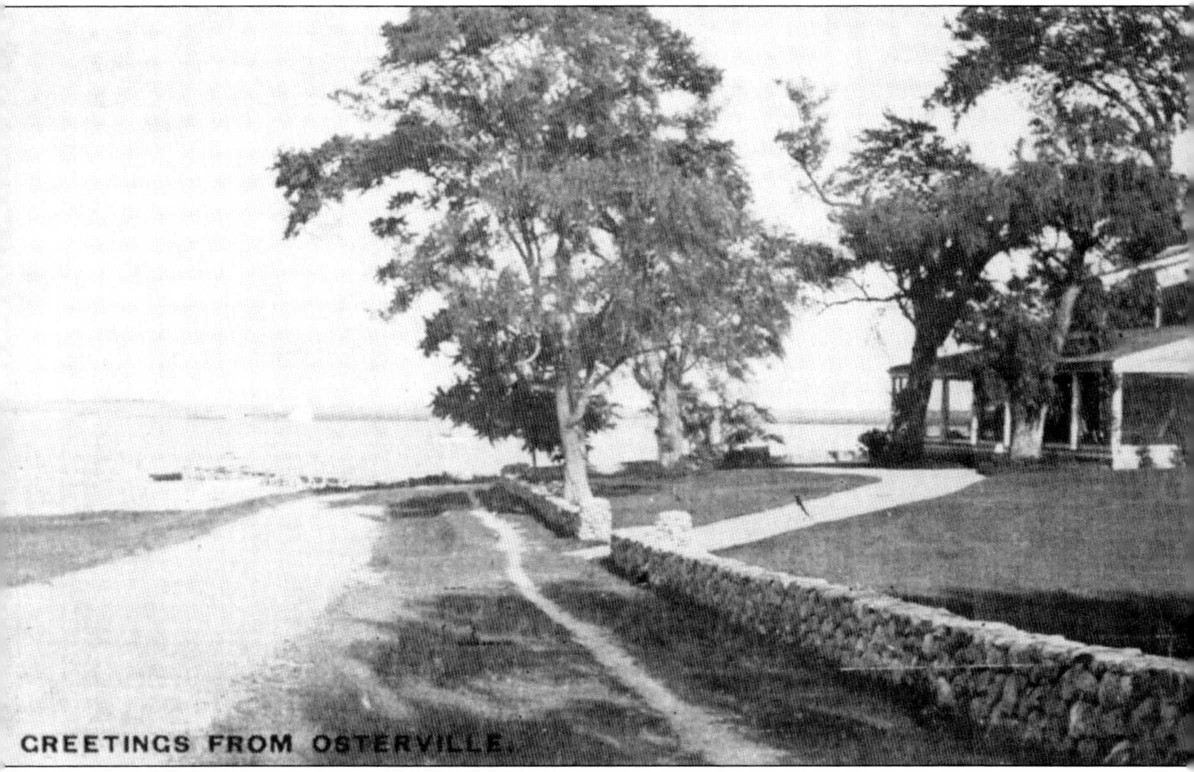

This view is looking southeast from East Bay Lodge. In the early 1800s, the waters of East Bay were used for a saltworks. Windmills pumped saltwater into a series of descending large covered vats. As the water worked its way to the lowest vat, it evaporated, producing natural sea salt. It became a booming business as the salt was used for, among other things, curing fish. To the right in the photograph is the Seth Goodspeed house. His family was one of several prominent Osterville families, including the Lovells, Scudders, Hodges, and Ames, who lived on East Bay Road. Goodspeed was both a shipbuilder and salt manufacturer. He also served in the state legislature from 1838 to 1839.

Four

West Bay Inn

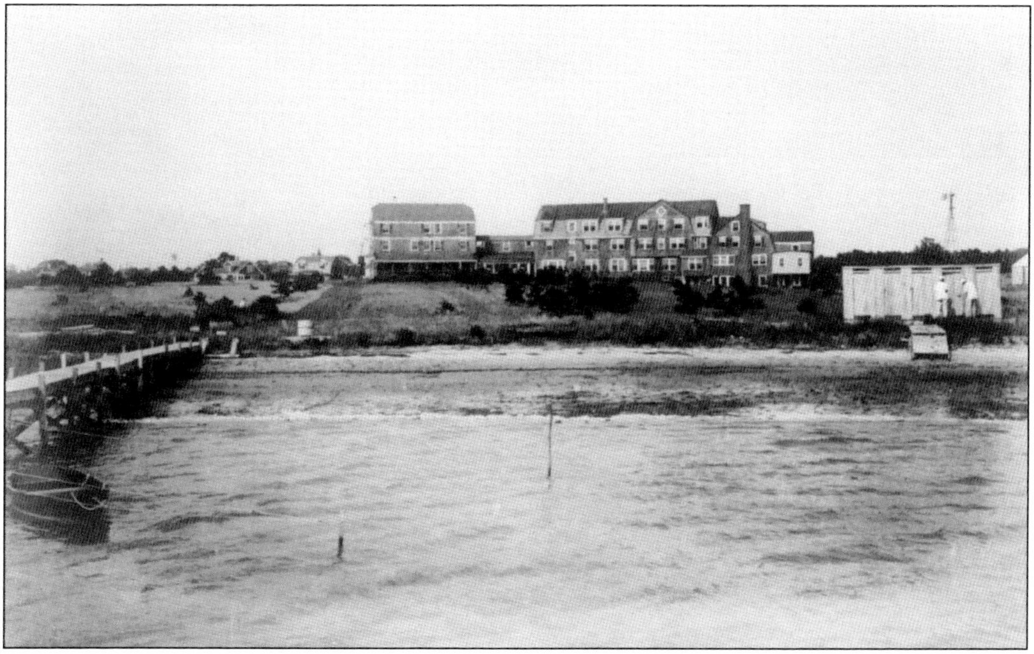

The West Bay Inn was located directly on the waters of West Bay off Eel River Road. An advertisement in the July 11, 1914, edition of the *Boston Evening Transcript* states the following: The West Bay Inn is a "modern Hotel, directly on the water, open until October 1. Always cool, fine bathing beach on property. Cuisine the best on Cape Cod. Seafood a specialty. Reduced rates for September. Special prices to Clubs. Send for booklet. E.S. Crocker, Proprietor."

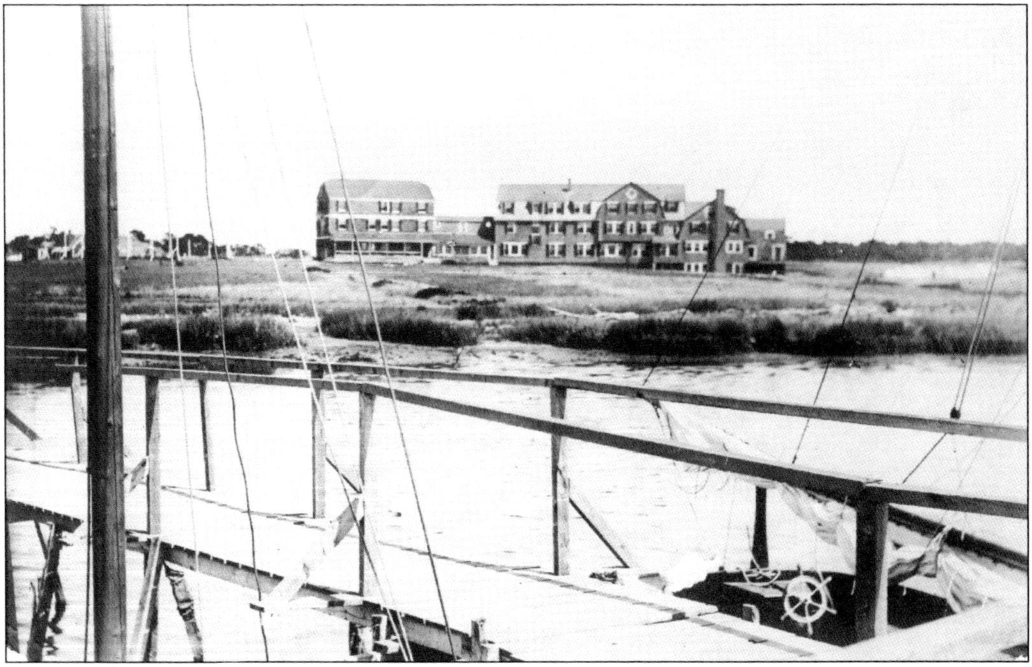

The West Bay Inn was built in 1905 and, like most inns in Osterville, offered easy access to boating and a bathing beach. In the bad weather, the sender of this postcard notes the following other activities to do in the village: "Glad you are having such a good time. Everything is the same here except for the cold weather. We had movies last night." The Star Theatre was located in the Pattison Block on Main Street.

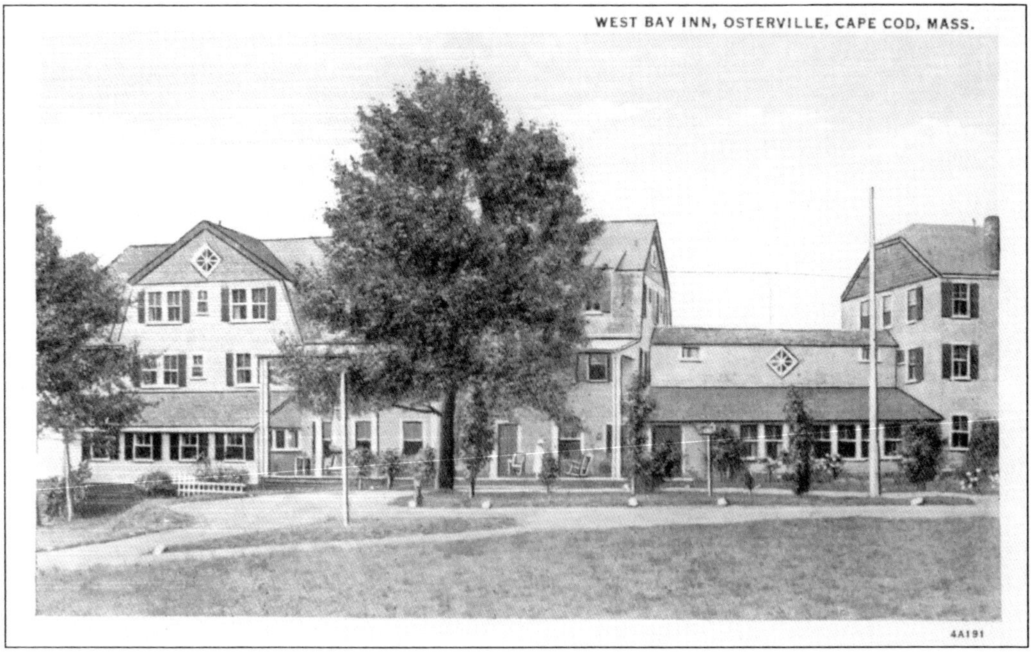

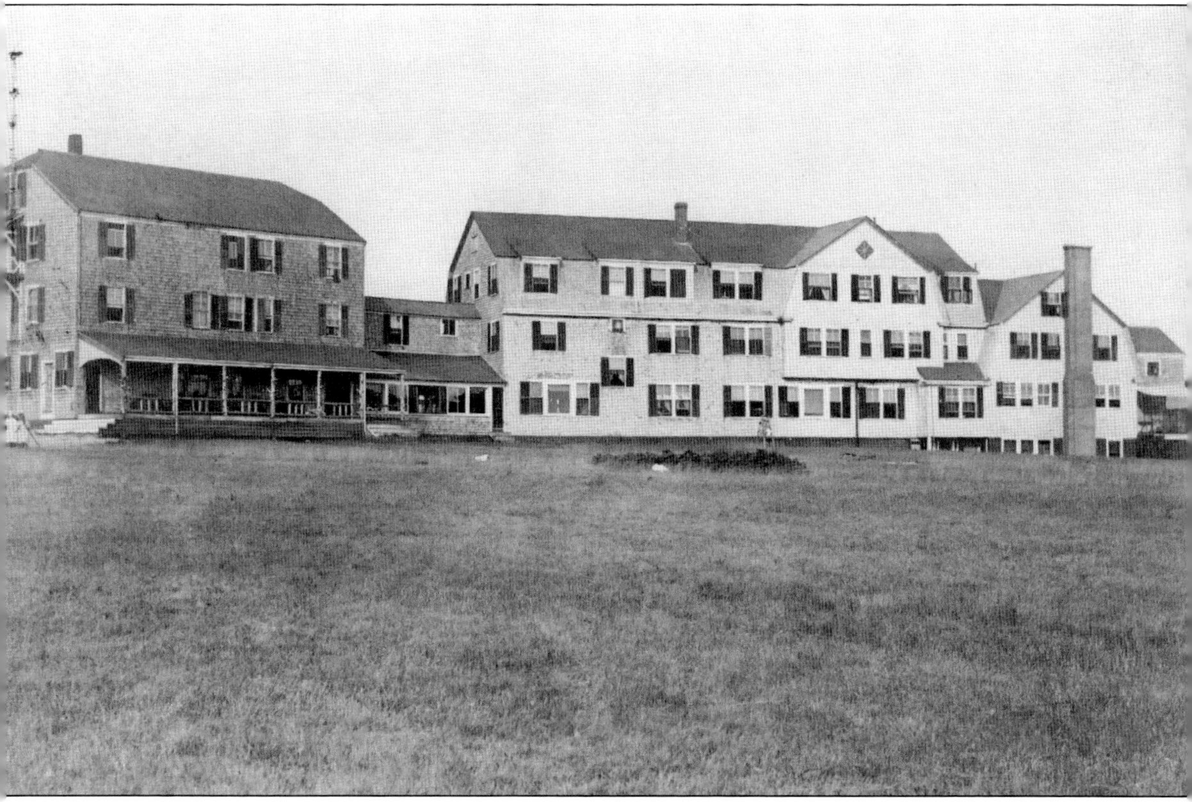

Boasting 65 rooms, the West Bay Inn was a very popular destination. In October 1935, a massive fire broke out one evening. Despite the response from the Centerville-Osterville Fire Department and help from the villages of Hyannis and Cotuit, the building was a complete loss. At the time, damages were estimated at $50,000; in today's figures, that would be almost $1 million. There was no wind that night, so buildings nearby were not damaged. Thousands of people came to watch the massive glow from the inferno. The inn had been unoccupied for two weeks, according to owner Edward S. Crocker. The property had been advertised for sale. It was only partially covered by insurance.

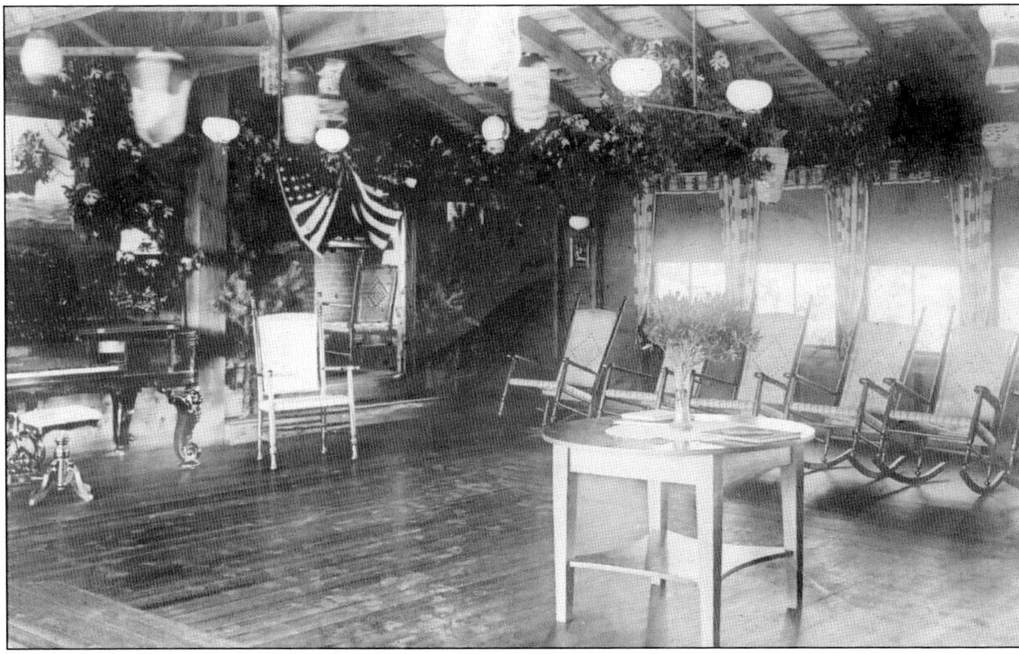

The interior furnishings of the sun parlors at the West Bay Inn are shown in these two images. The patriotic bunting, along with the rocking chairs, created a space that encouraged guests to gather and socialize. A common event was the "community sing." The event was open to the public and would have been held in these rooms with special music arranged and played on the piano, as seen in the above left. The inset in the image below shows another pastime at the West Bay Inn—baseball. The golden age of baseball was taking off in the 1920s with players like Babe Ruth, who began as a pitcher for the Boston Red Sox.

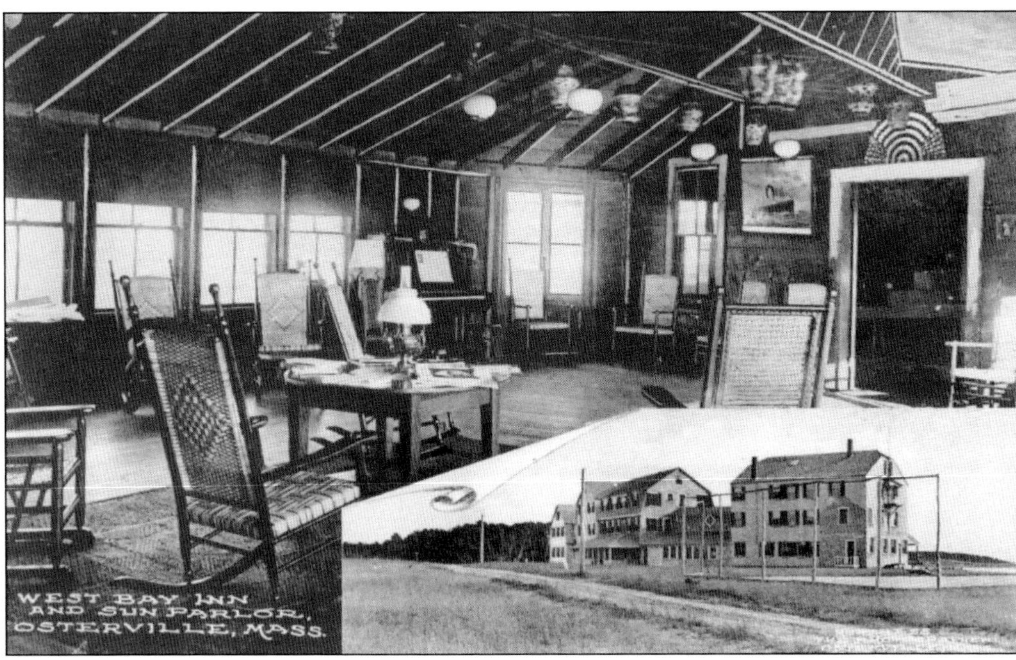

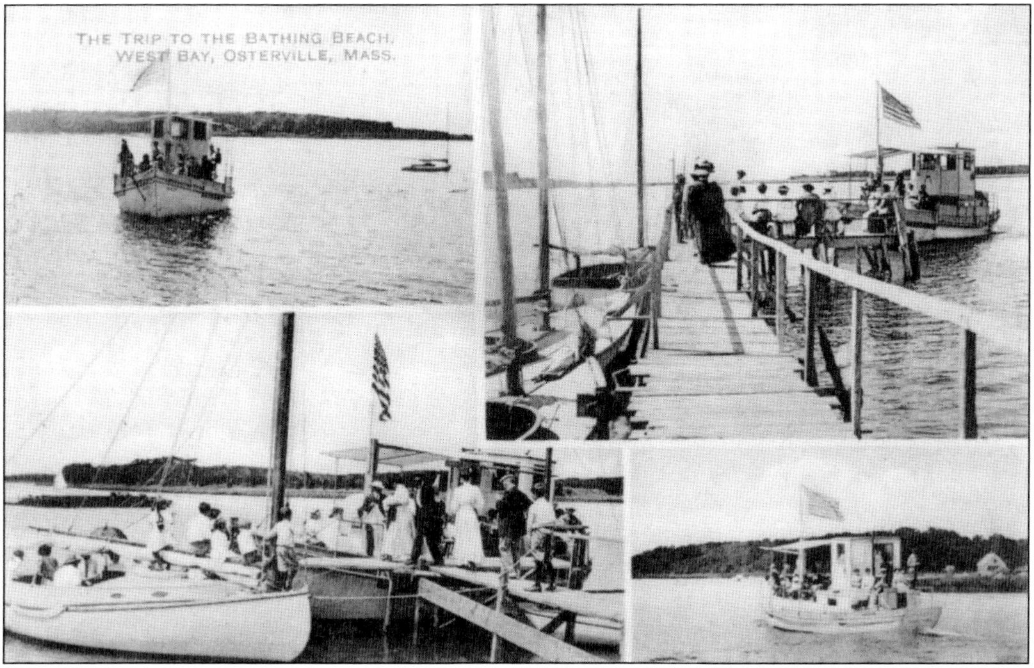

These images show a "Trip to the Bathing Beach" on West Bay. Note the long dresses and fancy garb of the guests out for a sail to the beach. There are several Crosby catboats docked at the pier. Note that *Hooker* was the name of Joe Crosby's vessel. This boat took tourists around the bays to Dead Neck. In October 1898, the West Bay Cut was approved by the Massachusetts Legislature. When it was completed around 1900 and improved upon in 1908, boats could directly access West Bay and the Crosby boat shops without having to sail through Cotuit.

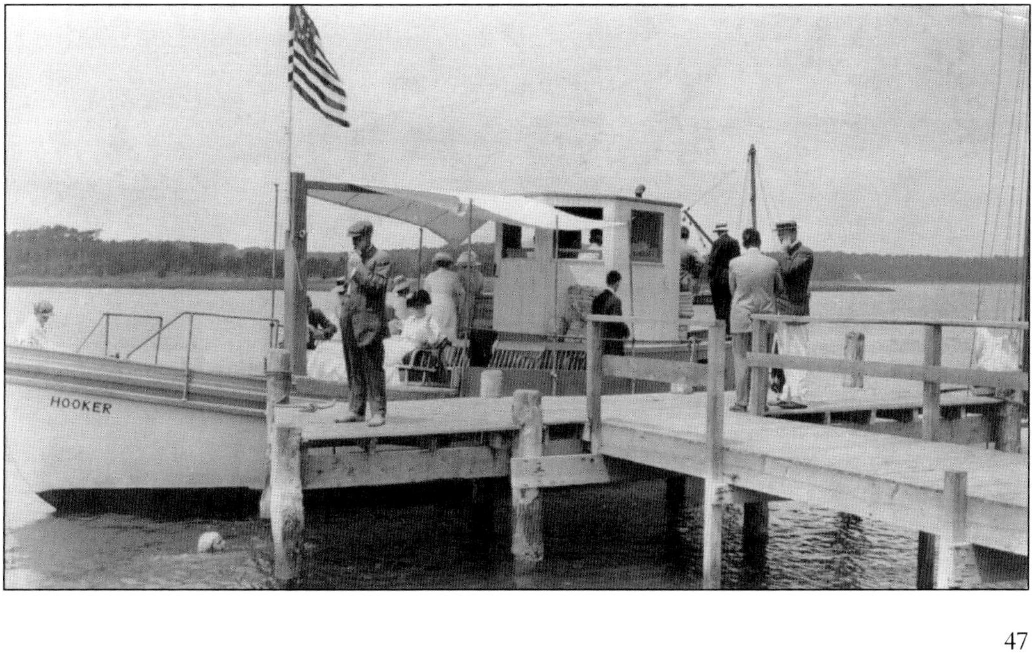

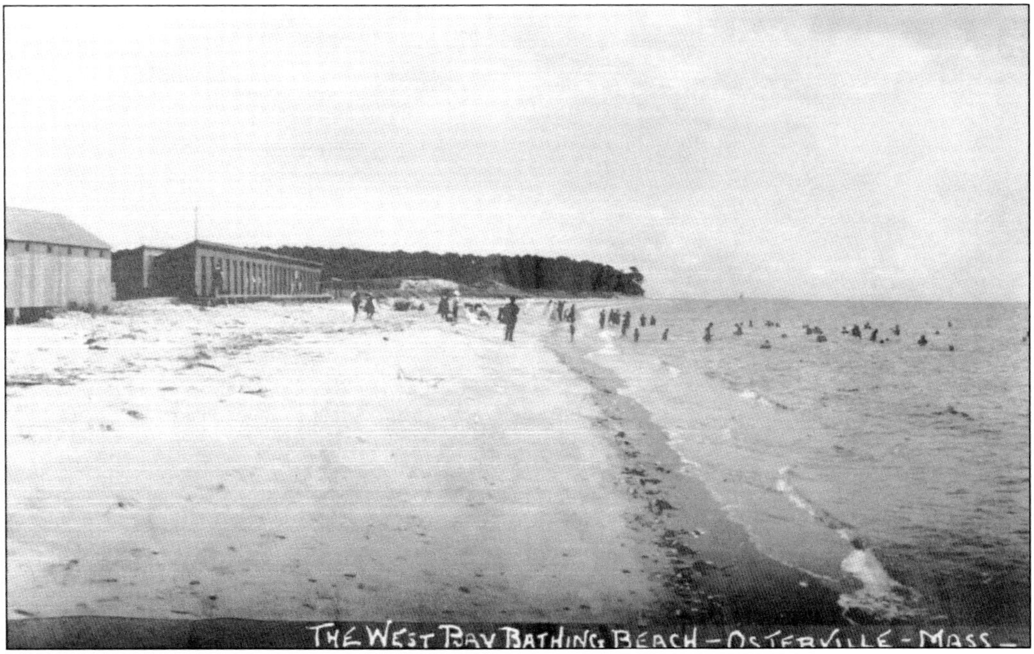

Guests set sail in a Crosby catboat at the West Bay Inn pier. The Crosbys built more than 3,000 catboats over the decades. The postcard below, addressed to a Mr. Walter E. Fisher of Winchester, Massachusetts, says, "Your mother stands a chance of learning to swim before you do. She is just like a duck in the water. Acts as if she belongs there. Lovingly, Lillian." Whether sailing or swimming, this love of the water kept hundreds returning to these beloved inns by the sea every summer.

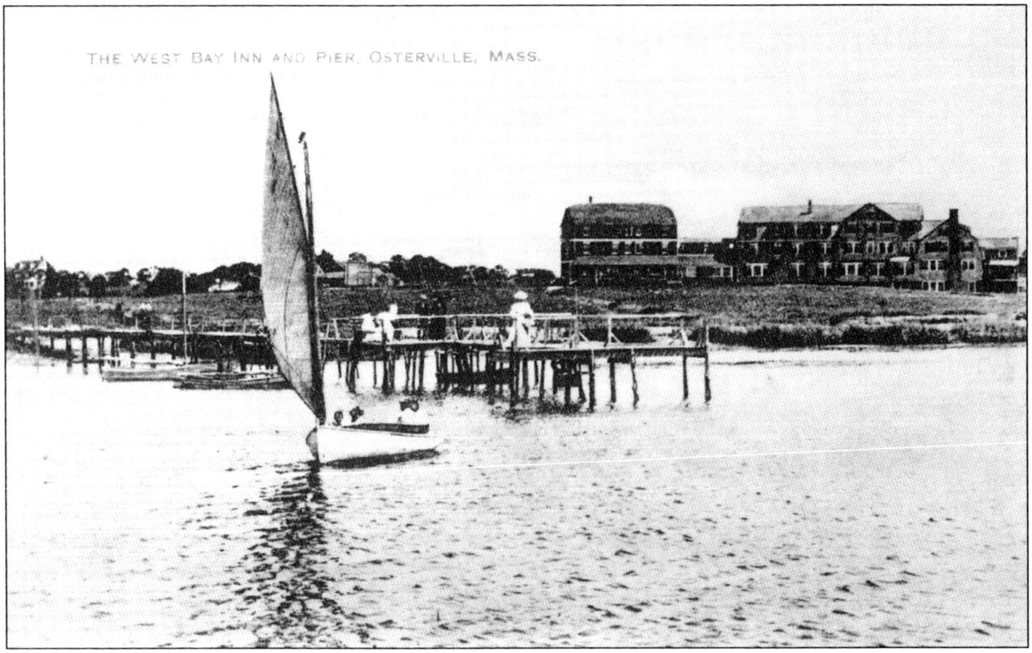

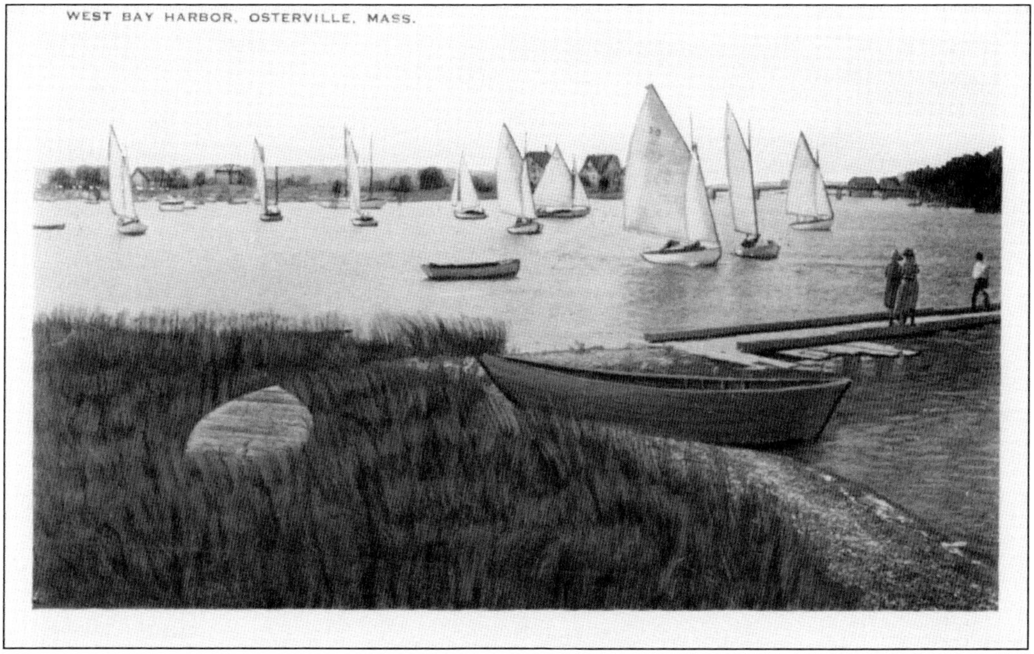

A fleet of catboats sets sails in the inner West Bay harbor in the image above. The owner of the West Bay Inn sent the postcard below in 1912 as an early direct mail piece. The reverse of the card states, "Greetings from West Bay Inn. The Proprietor would be pleased to reserve rooms for you. An early reply will oblige, Yours truly, E.S. Crocker."

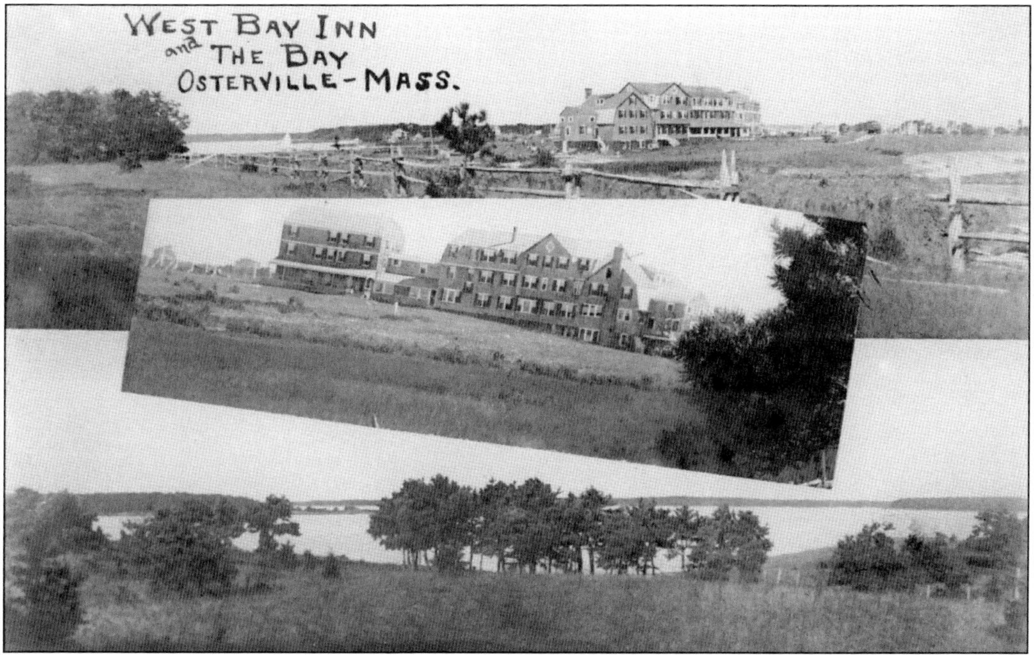

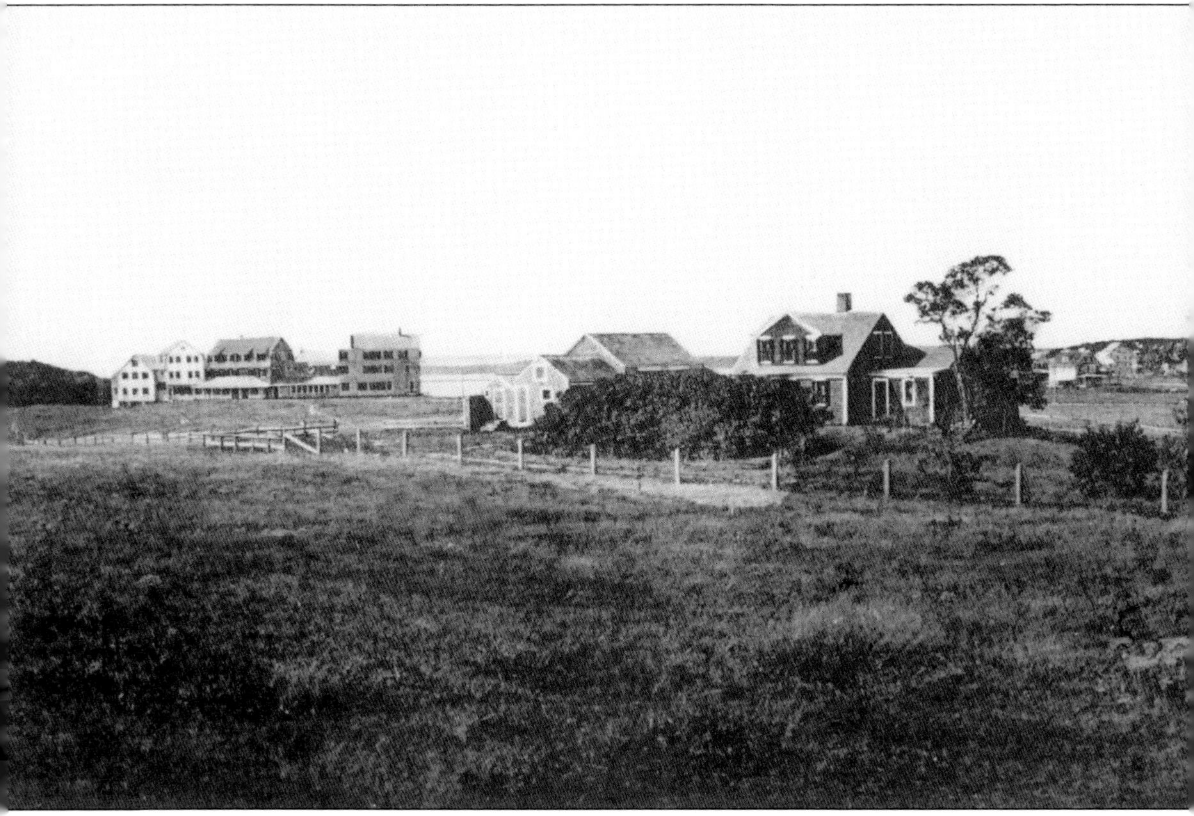

Osterville-based Louis Huntress took the photograph in this rare panoramic postcard. The card itself was printed in Germany. A number of Osterville postcards are works of Huntress, sometimes known as "the photographer of Osterville." He had a summer studio in the village at the corner of Bay Street and Parker Road. During the rest of the year, he took photographs all

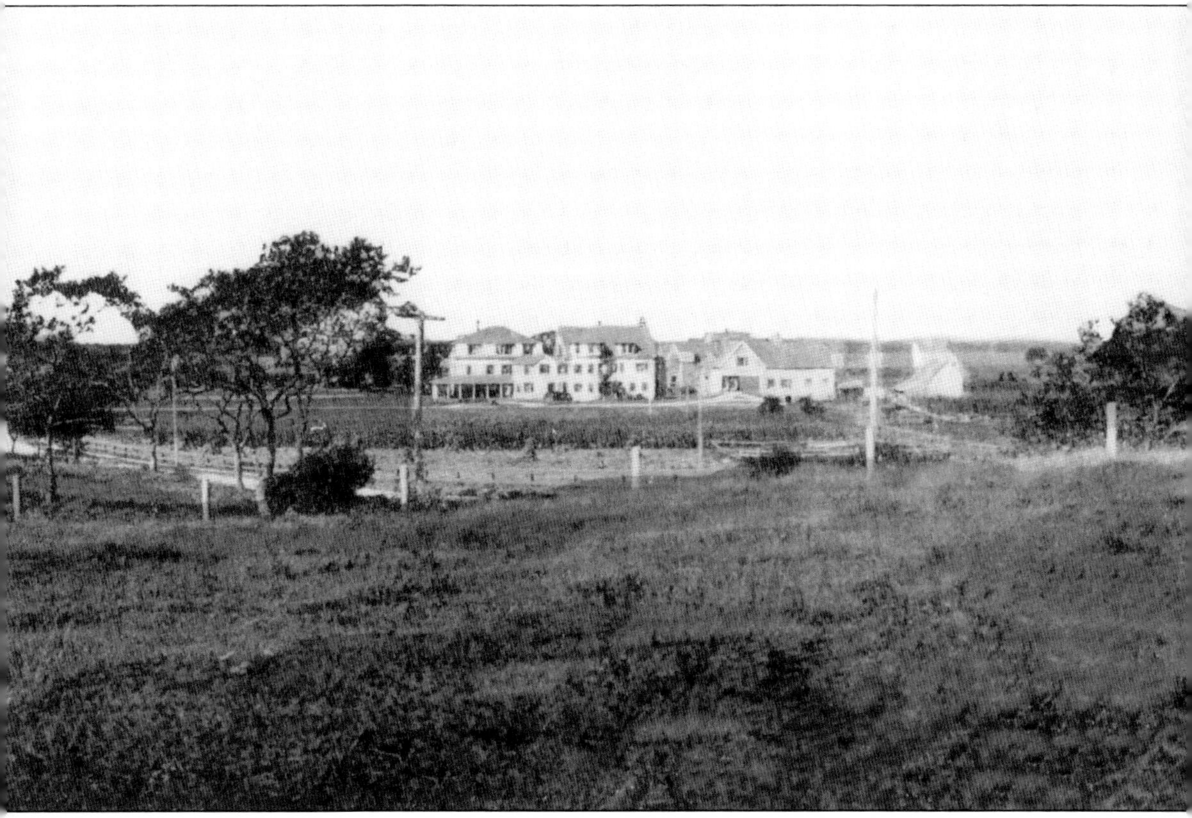

over the East Coast of the United States. Seen in this image, West Bay Inn is on the far left, the Benjamin Crocker home and barn are adjacent on the right, and on the far right is the Crosby House, another smaller hotel for summer guests.

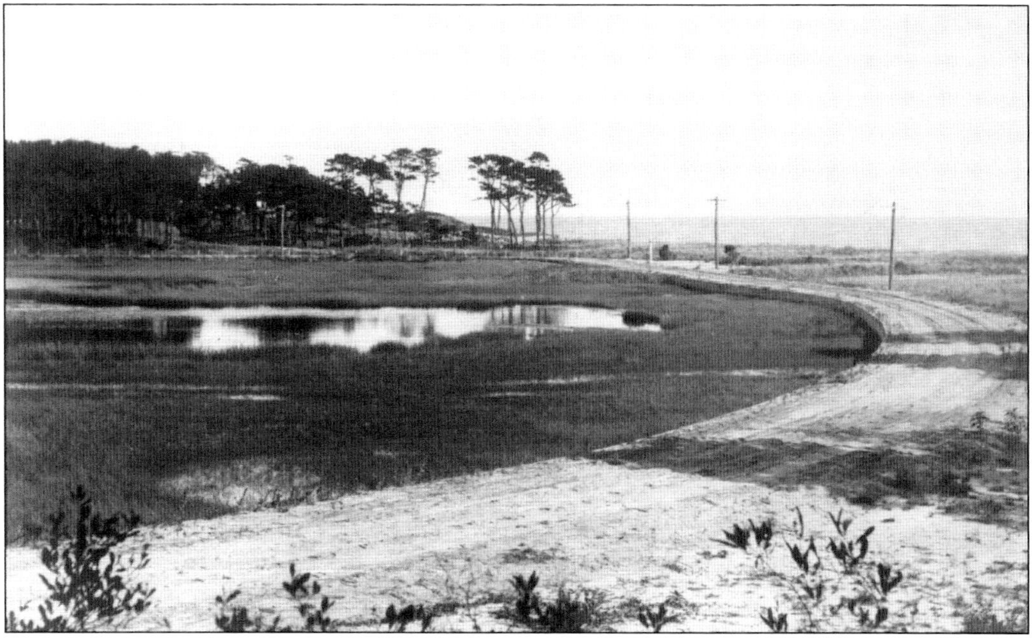

These two images show Eel River at Seaview Avenue. The postcard above shows Seaview Avenue at the foot of Eel River. The scene below is facing east with the head of Eel River on the left and Nantucket Sound on the right. The West Bay Inn was located off Eel River Road. The Wianno Yacht Club and the Wianno Club, formerly known as the Cotocheset House, were located on Seaview Avenue. The West Bay Inn faced the southwest and because of its location was able to take advantage of the prevailing ocean breeze. It was reported to be the coolest location in all of Osterville.

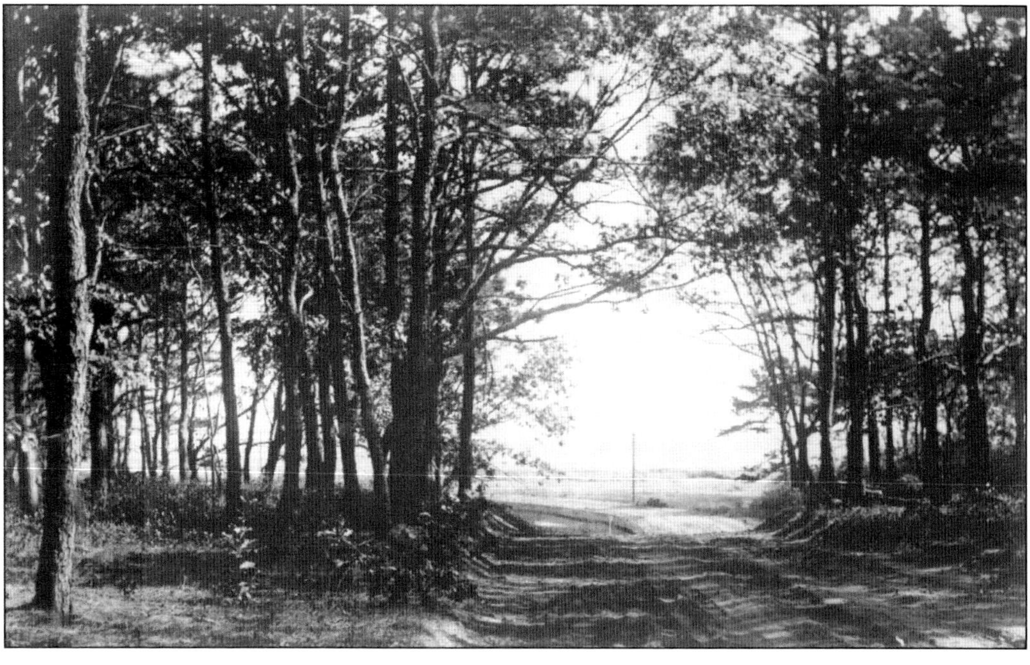

Five

Crosby House and More

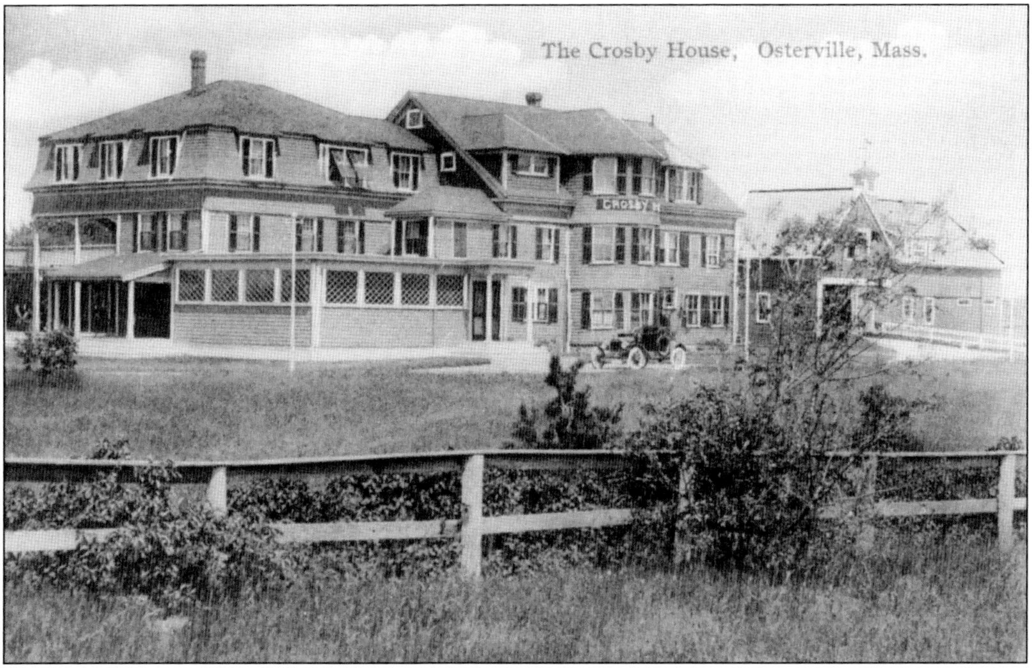

The Crosby House on West Bay Road was originally the home of Andrew and Tirzah Crosby. She was the one who conducted the séance that led to the birth of the Crosby catboats, as they are known today. Her son Horace and his wife, Lucy, opened the Crosby House as a hotel in 1860. Each year, they continued to add on to the house to increase capacity. At its height, the Crosby House could accommodate up to 50 guests.

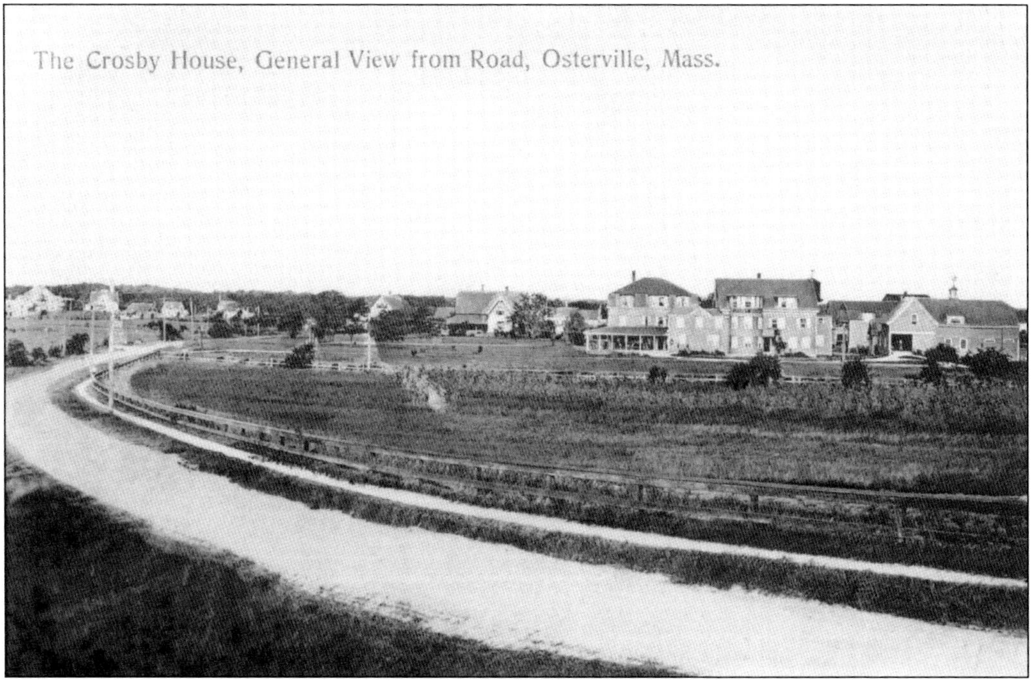

One can see the sweeping view in the postcard above. The Crosby House is on the right. In an August 18, 1891, newspaper article, the guests at the Crosby House reportedly enjoyed a "hop" (party) at one of the boat shops the previous Saturday night. The owners' grandson Harold Crosby eventually took over the Crosby House. Its reputation for being a hospitable place continued with a July 17, 1920, masquerade party, at which Harold Crosby was crowned king.

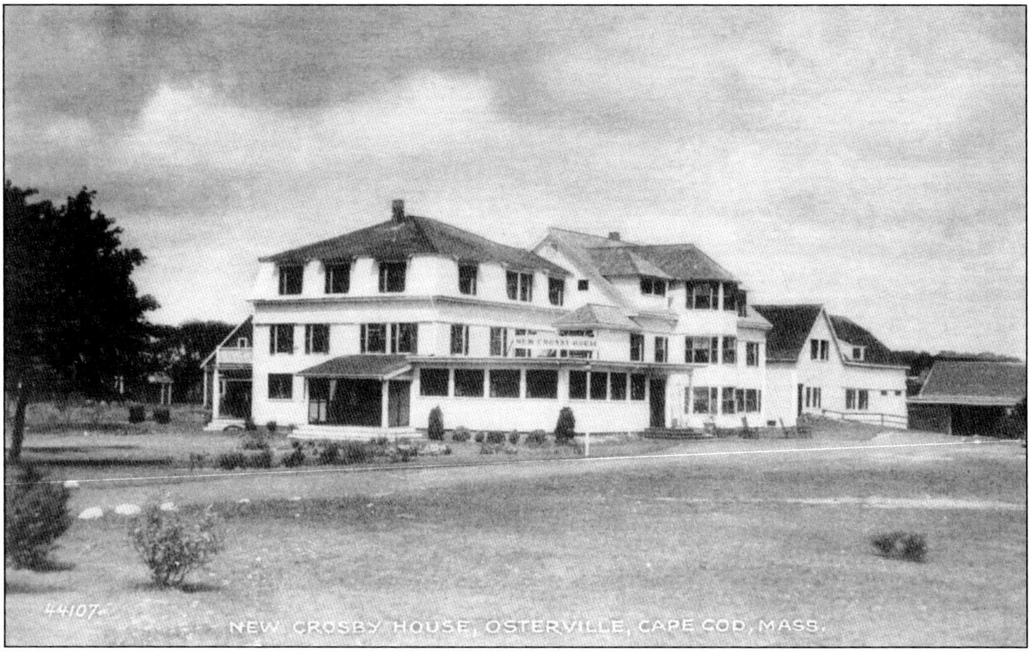

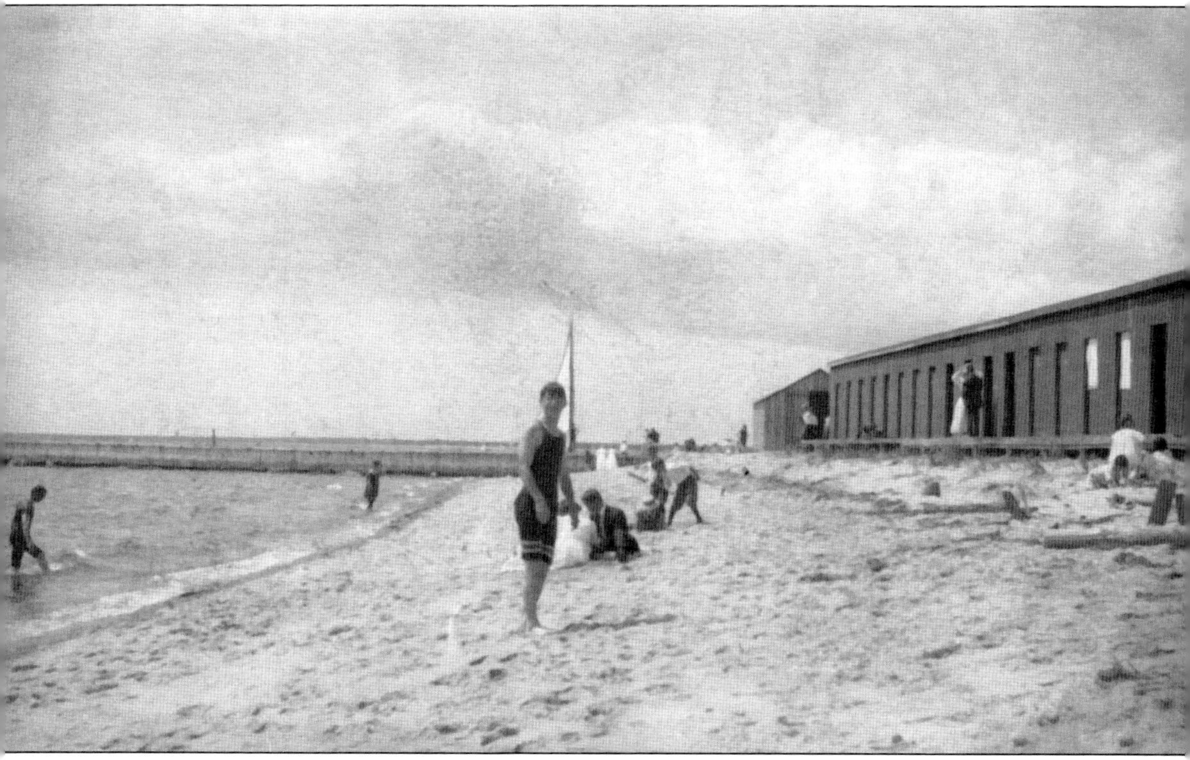

A guest at the Crosby House sent this postcard of the bathing beach at Wianno with its wooden bathhouses to the right. The sender wrote, "Am boarding at the Crosby House, Osterville, for all summer. Charlie and Helen coming here for August. Sallie going to Plymouth. Sorry I can not go and see you. Am having a fine rest. Boys love it. With love, Ethel." The card, sent to an address in North Weymouth, Massachusetts, is stamped July 24 at 7:00 a.m. The year has worn off. The benefits of a respite by the sea attracted many summer residents to Osterville.

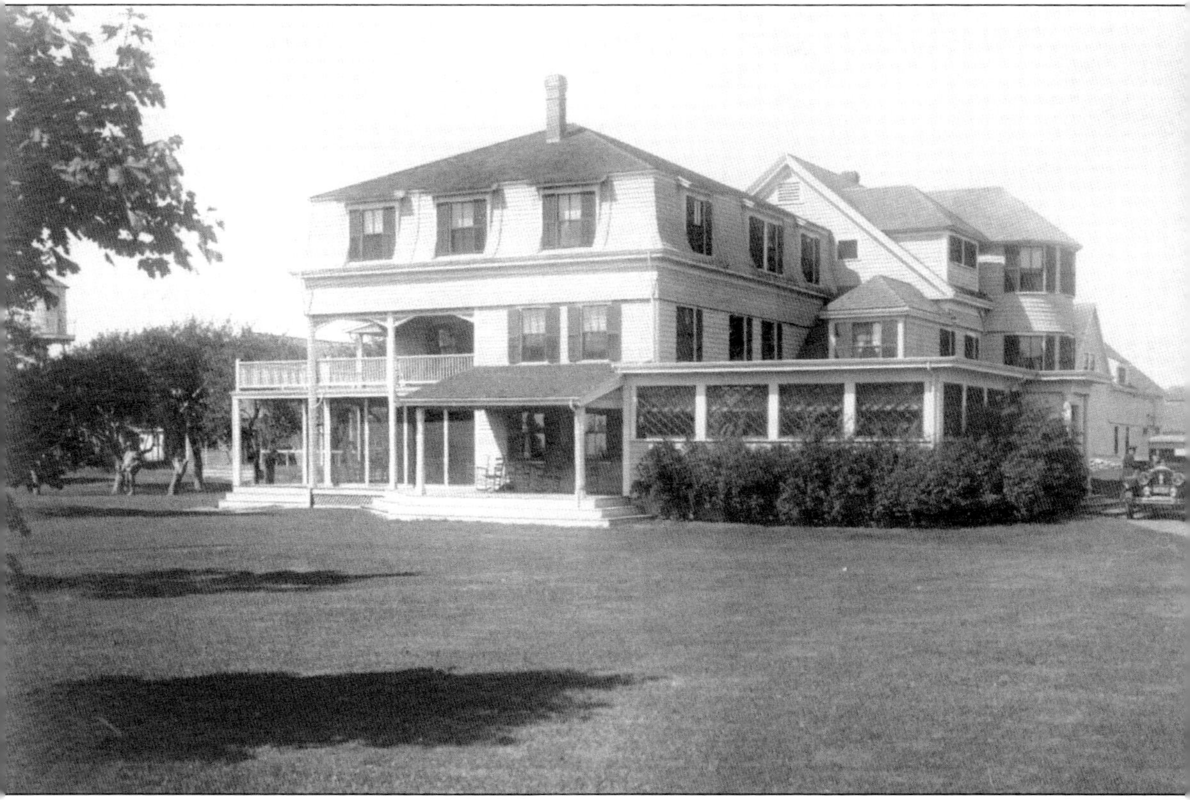

Another direct mail piece on a postcard beckons guests to stay at the Crosby House during the winter months. It stated, "Call Cotuit 196 and say that you are coming to spend a few days with us. The house is steam heated throughout, unexcelled table, moderate prices. Rates $6 per day, special weekly rates. Five golf courses within an hour's ride, excellent fishing, 15 miles of good shore bird shooting. Anticipating the pleasure of seeing you, I remain very truly yours, Laurence Welch, Manager, Leonard J. Bliss, Proprietor." The inn was sold in 1927 to Bliss, and it became known as Osterville Manor.

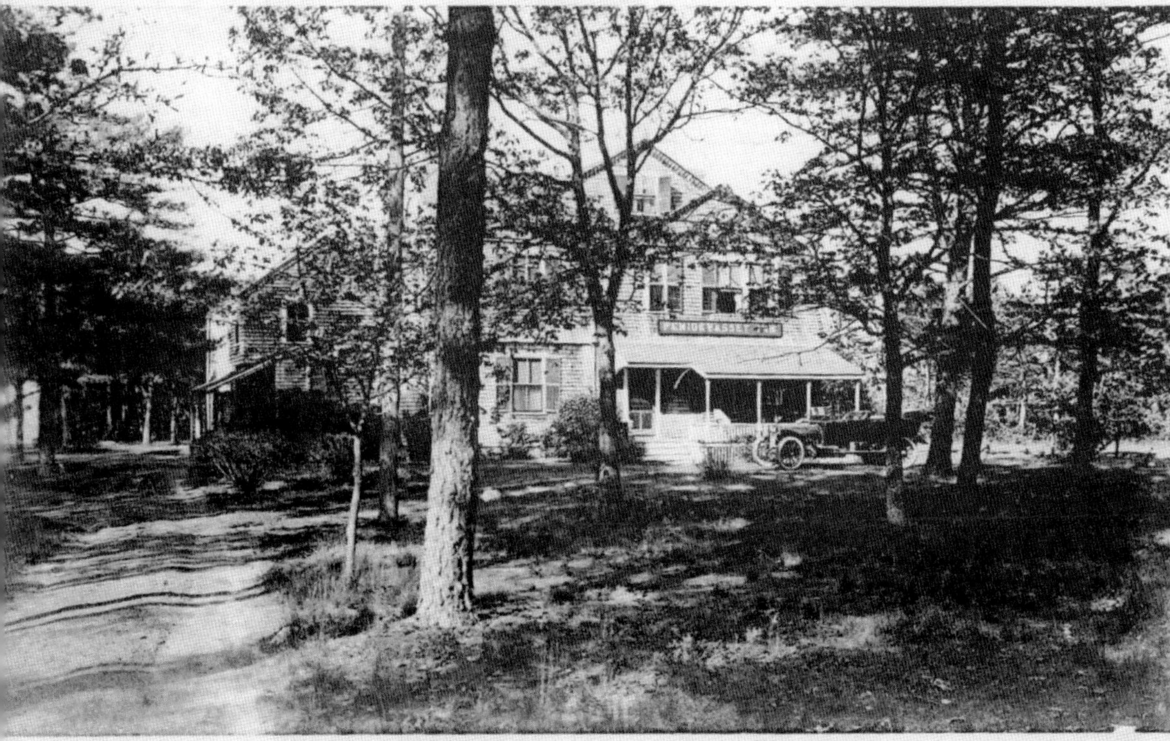

Pemigewasset Inn, Osterville, Mass.

Many smaller inns were located throughout the village. This postcard highlights Pemigewasset Inn, located on Wianno Avenue, with an early-model car in the front driveway. The Spruce Tree Lodge, located on Parker Road, was another small inn and was operated by Jeanette Bowes. It was previously the summerhouse of Josephine and Margaret Carret of Boston. That building was torn down in the 1970s to make way for condos.

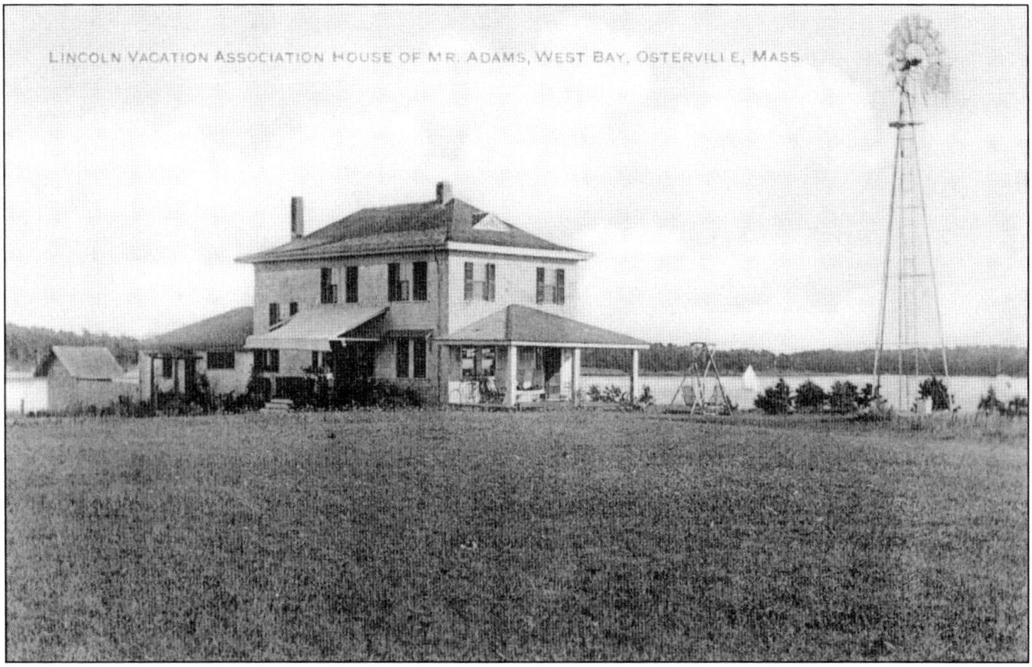

The Lincoln Clubhouse was located on Breezy Bluff just before the bridge to Oyster Harbors. In 1895, the Josiah A. Ames house began welcoming a large group of "fresh-air" boys, along with their teachers. The program brought children to Osterville for short vacations throughout the summer months. It was expanded to include young girls and mothers with babies. It was designed to give them "a chance to breathe the fresh, country air, and return to their work refreshed and strengthened."

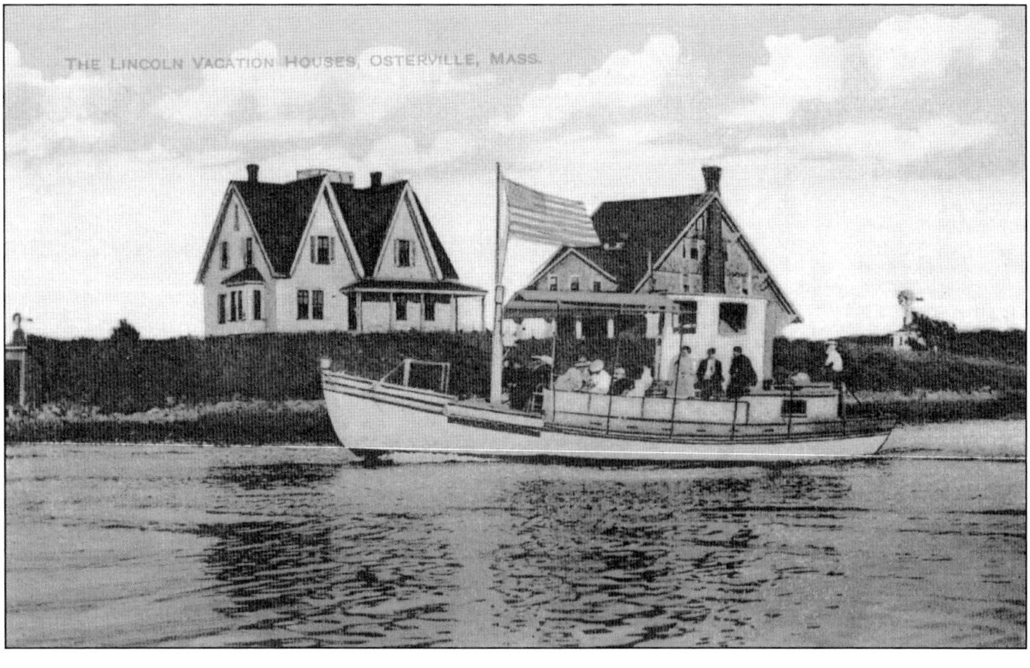

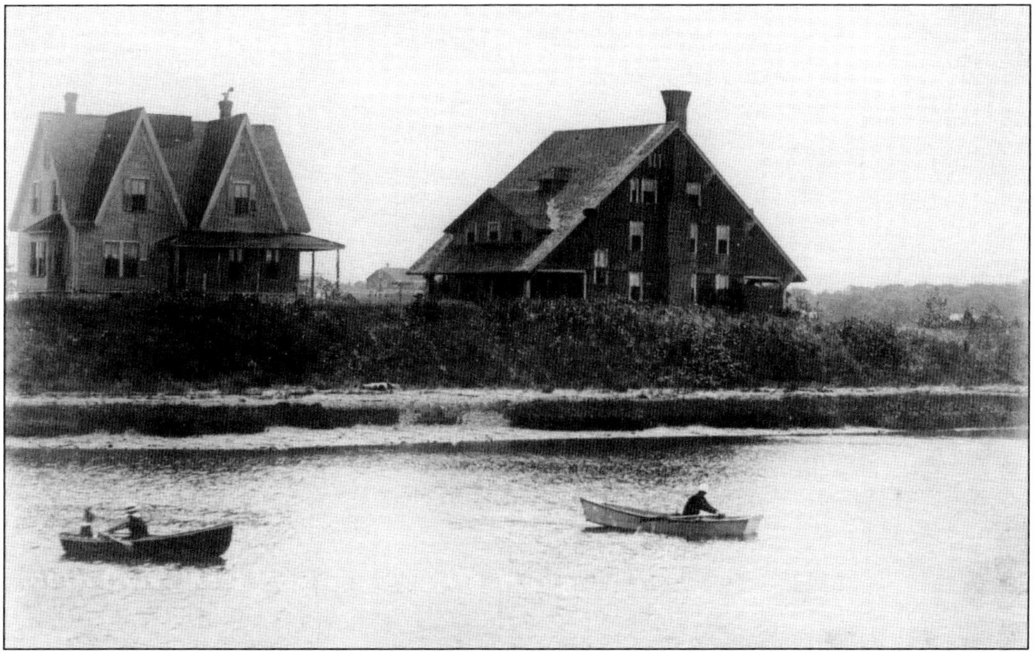

Due to the overwhelming demand for accommodations, the house on the left in the above photograph was added to the complex after the passing of the Ames family. Easy access to the water allowed for swimming and boating activities, as seen in the image above. The postcard below shows the bridge to Little Island, also known as Great Island, and Oyster Harbors at the left. The wooden drawbridge was completed in July 1891.

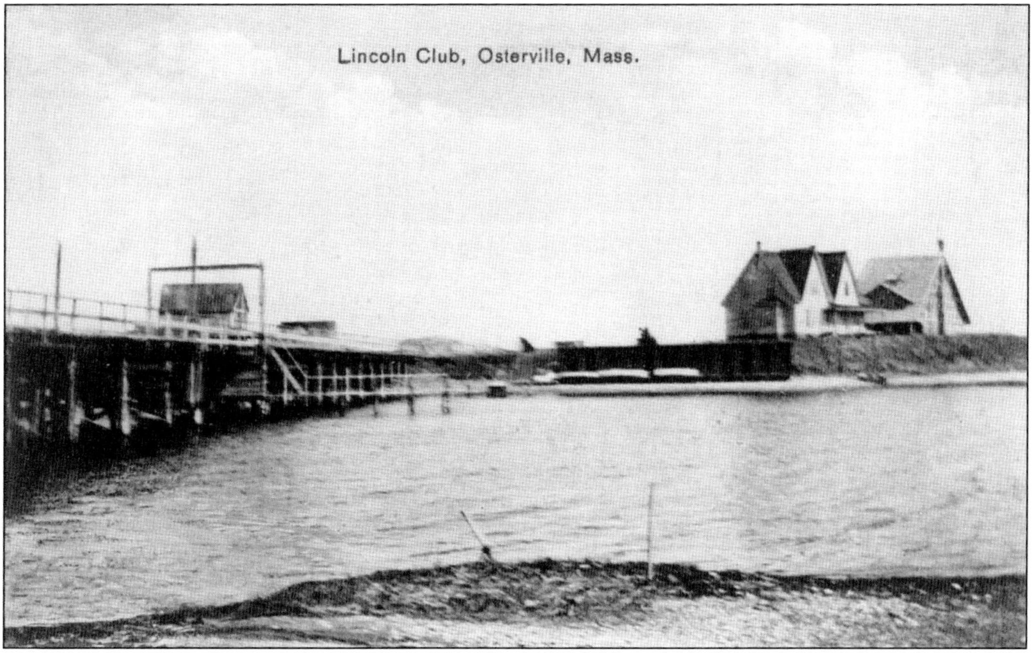

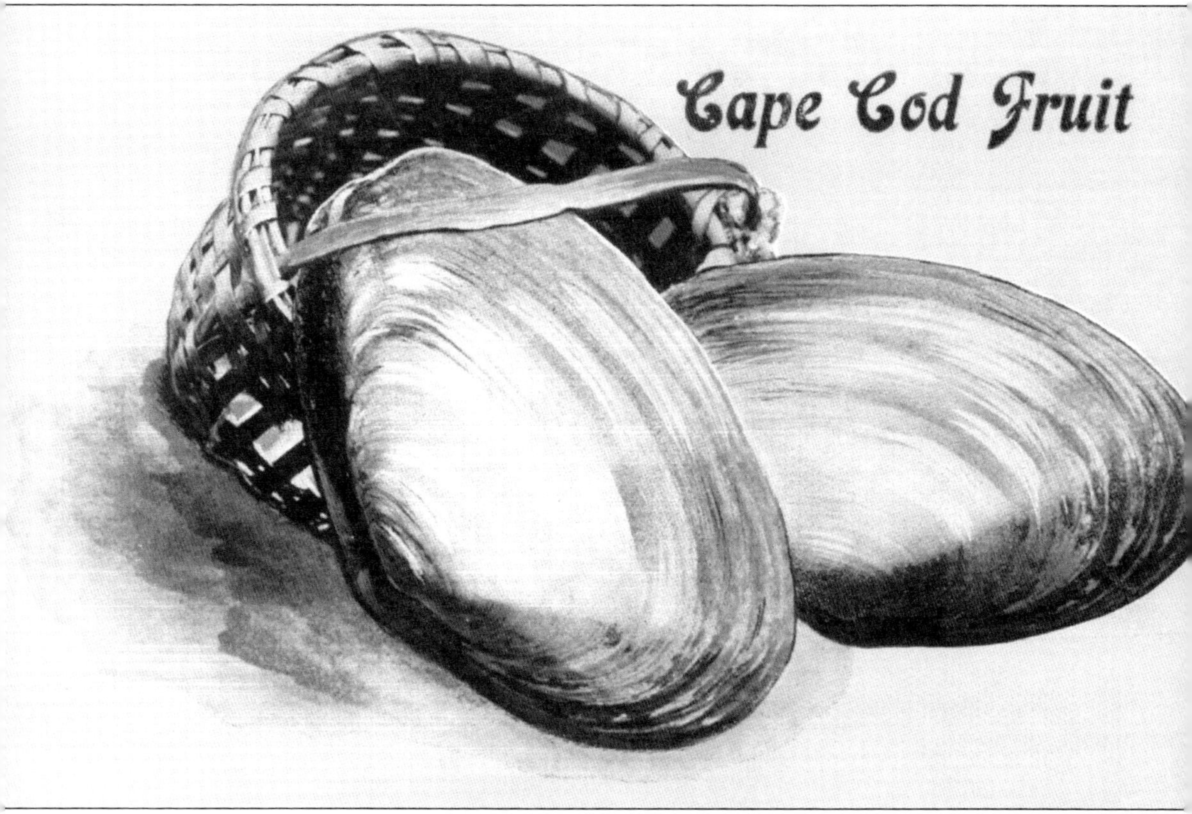

Clams were abundant in the waters off Osterville, and a number of summer visitors would spend their time clamming and enjoying the fruits of their labor. Clams (and oysters)62 are often referred to as the "fruit of Cape Cod," as this postcard indicates. The sender of the card wrote a note instructing the recipient to "have a chowder"—a fresh-from-the-sea meal found on the fine dining menus at all of the Osterville inns and lodges.

Six

The Wianno Yacht Club and Bathing Pavilion

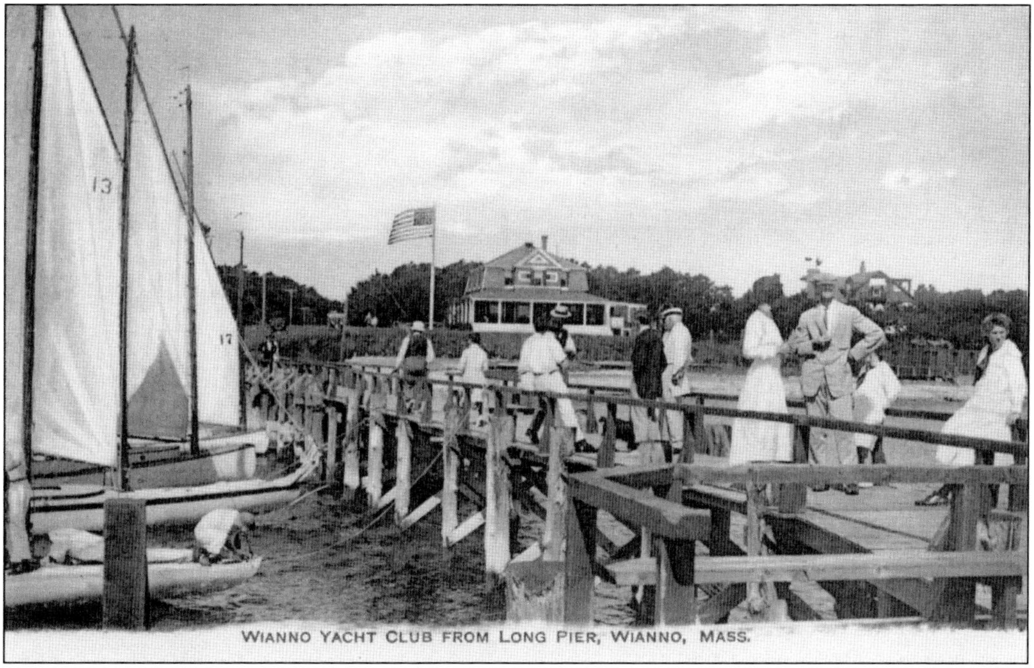

Here is a view of the Wianno Yacht Club (WYC) from Long Pier off Wianno Avenue. The boats are docked at the pier, and the members are dressed to the nines in suits and long dresses with petticoats to watch or participate in a day of sailing. By 1891, catboat races and, after 1914, Wianno Senior races were commonplace at the WYC. The American flag can be seen flying in the brisk winds off Nantucket Sound. The first annual regatta began in 1900 with a total of eight boats. The *Cicada*, a boat owned by the regatta chairman Francis Prescott, won. The first commodore of the WYC was William B.H. Dowse.

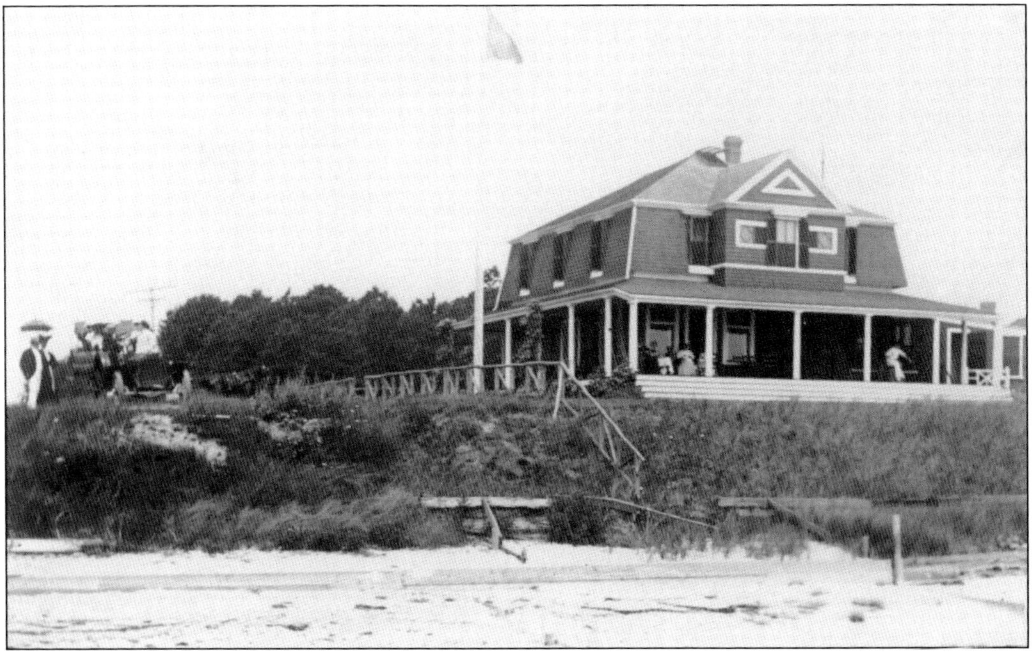

In 1916, members of the WYC formed the Wianno Club. The Wianno Club, located farther down Seaview Avenue, was connected to the WYC by the Wianno Pier and bathing beach and pavilion. For 30 years, the two were connected. In 1946, the two entities amicably split, and the WYC leased the Wianno Club's West Bay property, where it remains today. To this day, the two clubs fly the same original WYC burgee.

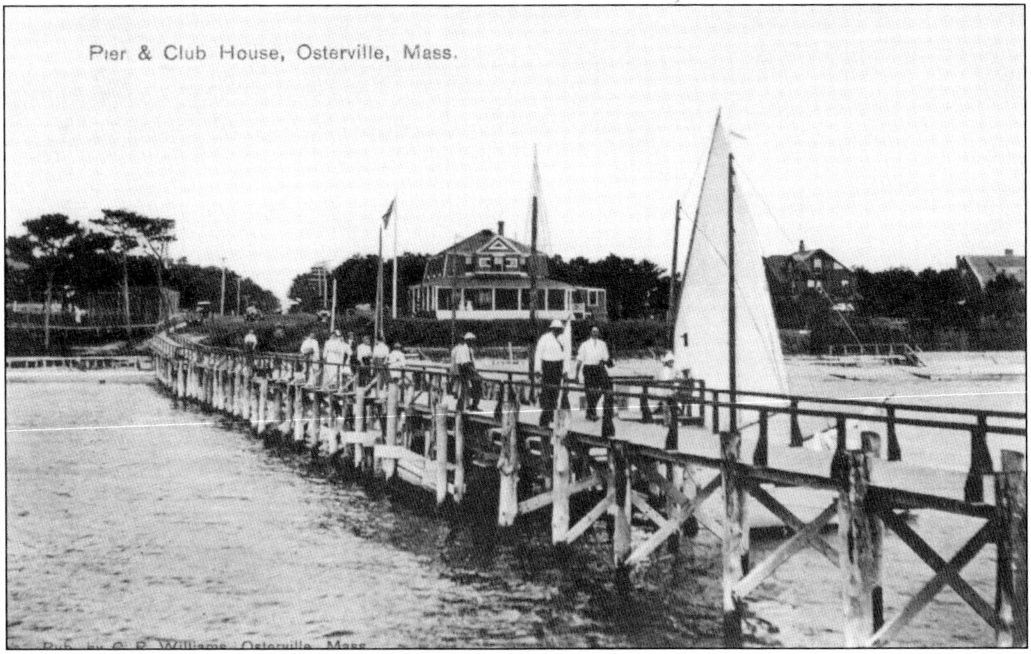

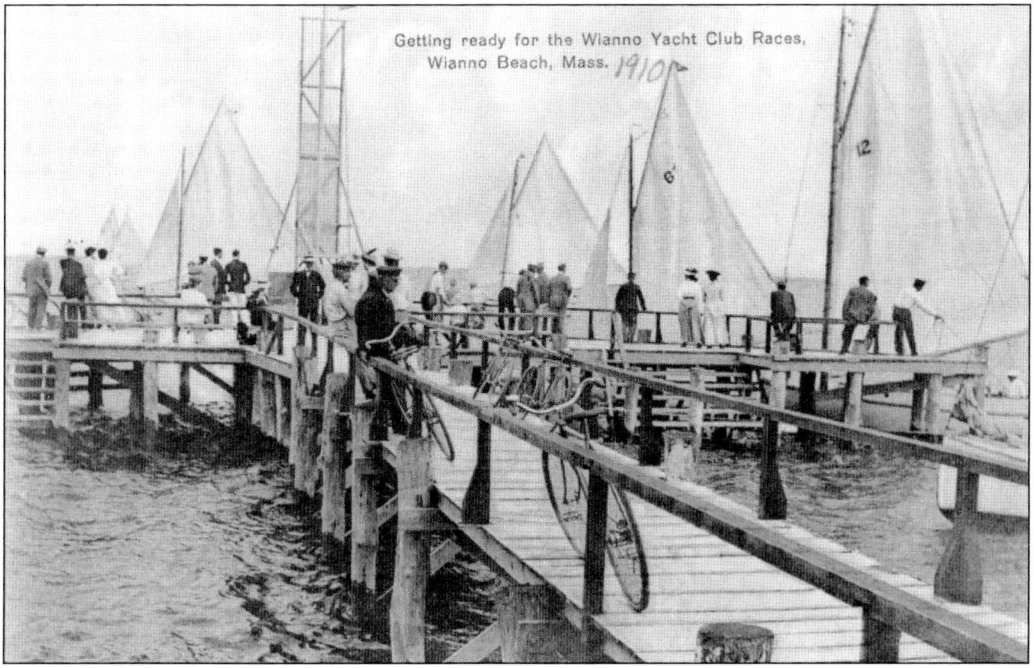

The building that housed the original WYC was located the end of Sea View and Wianno Avenues and was known as Mrs. Hill's Cottage. It was also affectionately referred to as the red onion with its red roof. In 1924, Wianno Senior races took place to the very popular Edgartown and Nantucket regattas. Edward C. Crossett became the second commodore during this time period (1916–1924). On July 4, 1931, the WYC officially opened its doors at its present location on Bridge Street on West Bay.

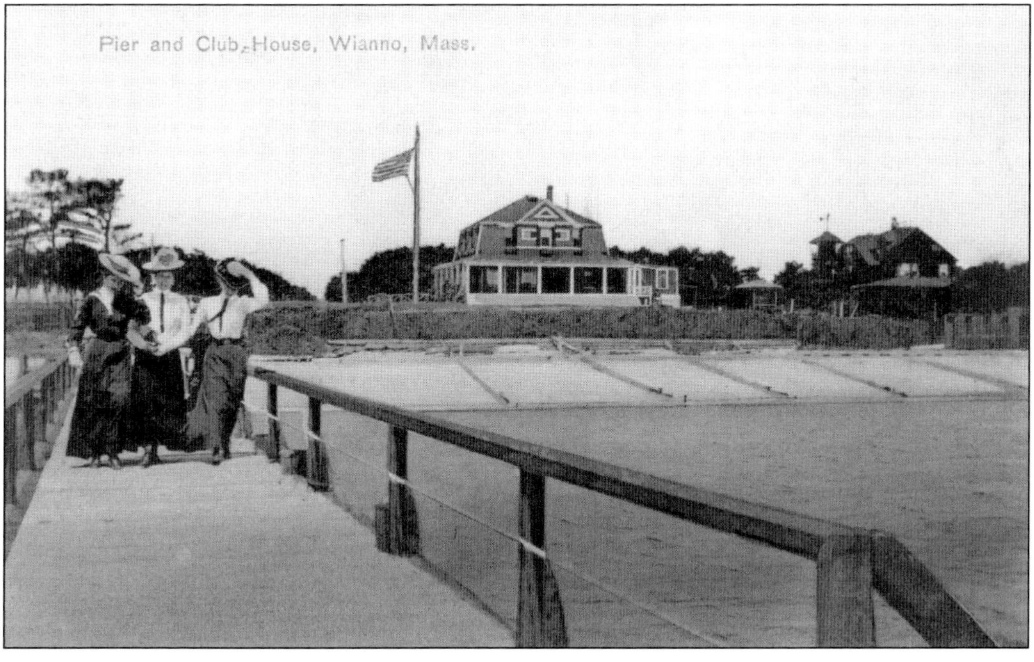

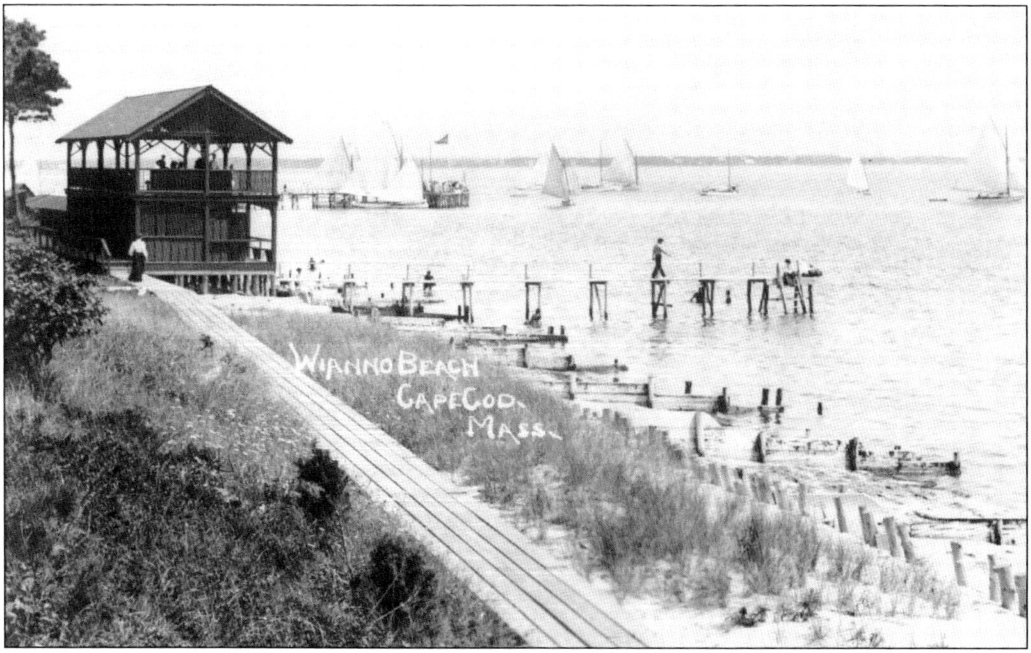

The Wianno bathing beach and pavilion were a buzz with activity. It was the draw to which many summer visitors flocked. The ideal vacation by the shore, with the healthy benefits of salt air, was something easily found here in Osterville. The wooden pavilion offered shade, and bathing houses lined the shore. From here, one could enjoy a swim or watch the catboat or Wianno Senior races from the adjacent Wianno Yacht Club.

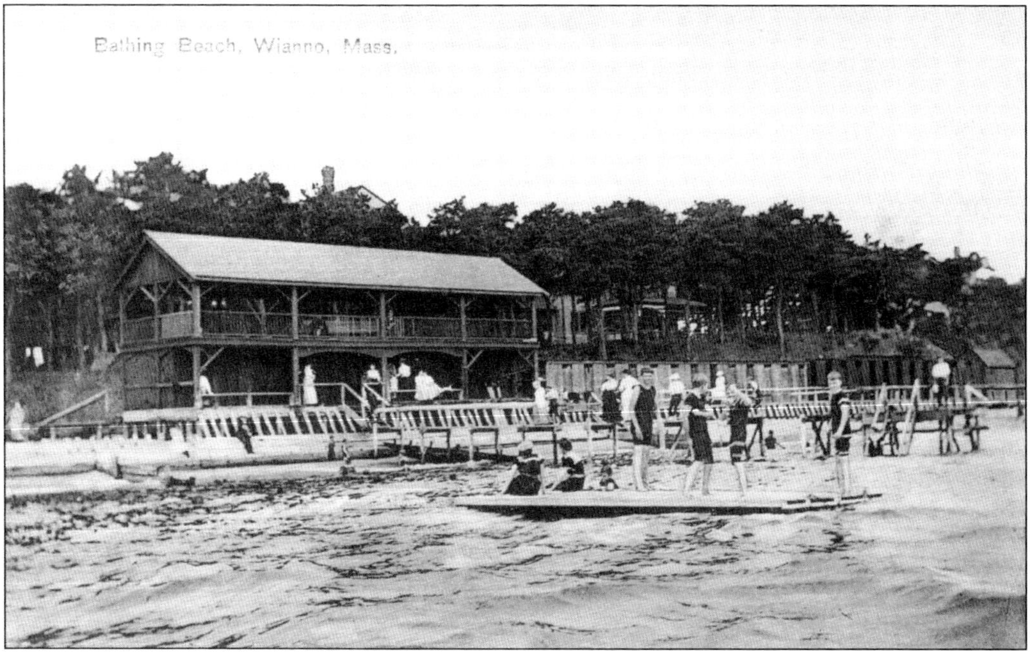

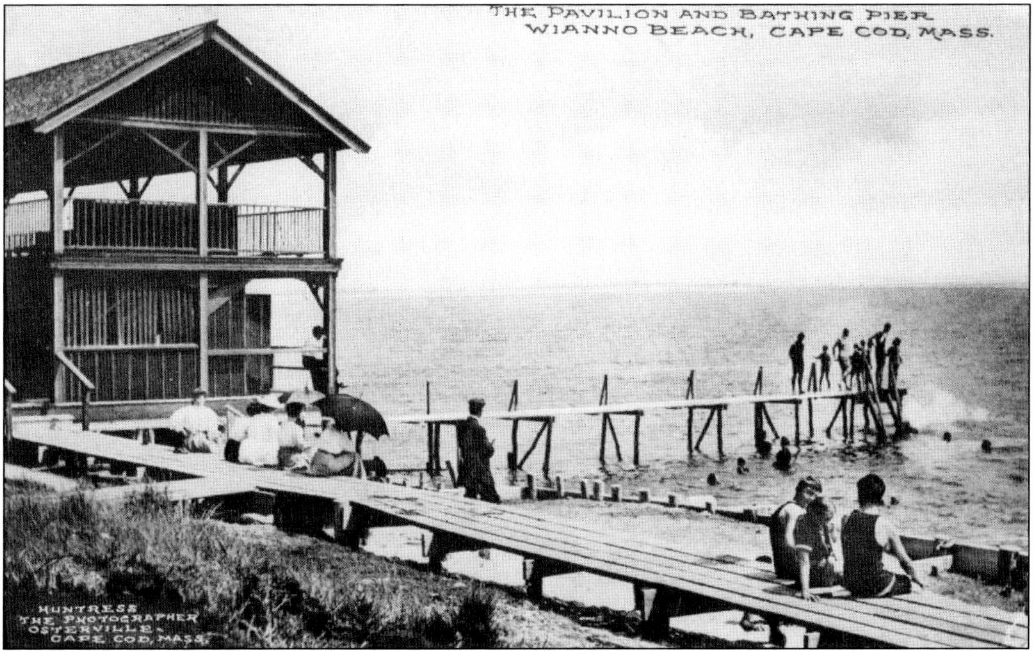

Swimmers enjoyed the cool ocean waters off the bathing pier in the postcard above. Meanwhile, in the postcard below, a race appears under way in the distance. In the foreground, a small group of ladies in long dresses with a parasol is going for a stroll along the boardwalk. They are headed in the direction of the Cotocheset House, soon to be called the Wianno Club.

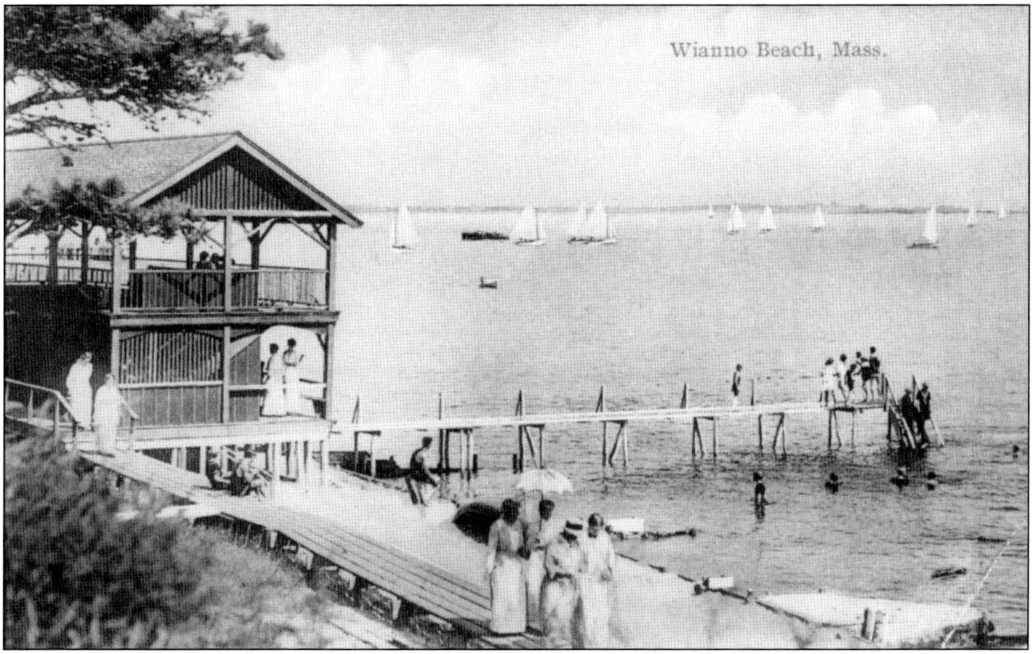

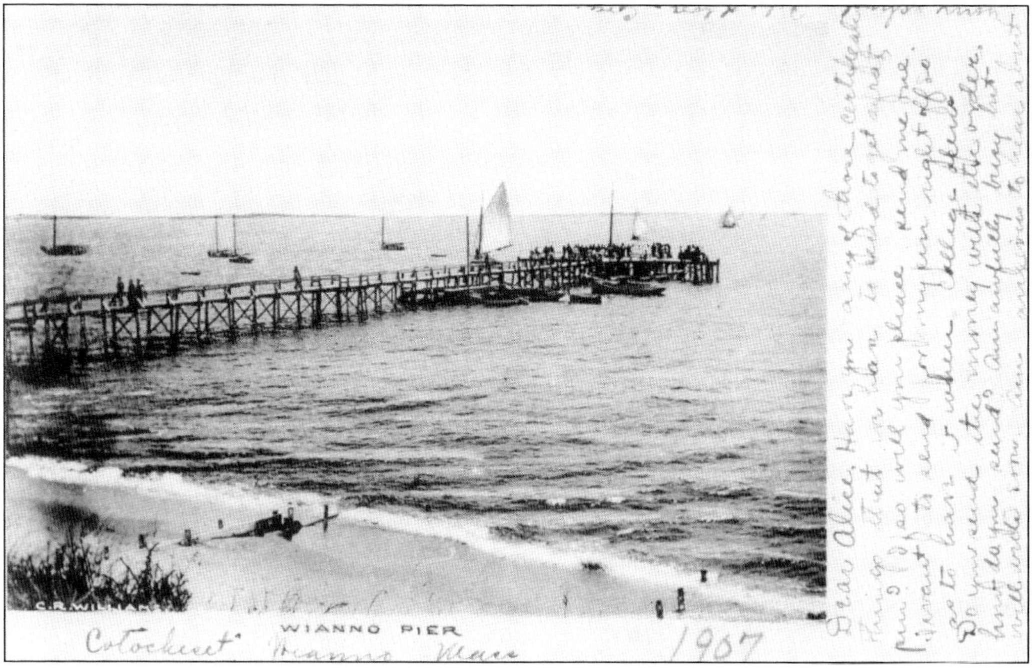

Here, the Wianno Pier overlooks Nantucket Sound. It was not unusual to find Capt. Nelson Bearse Jr., owner of the East Bay Lodge, sailing his catboat here. His daughter Molly also took an active role in the running of East Bay Lodge. When Molly died, she left a number of pieces of period furniture to the Osterville Historical Museum. This furniture is still on display in the museum today.

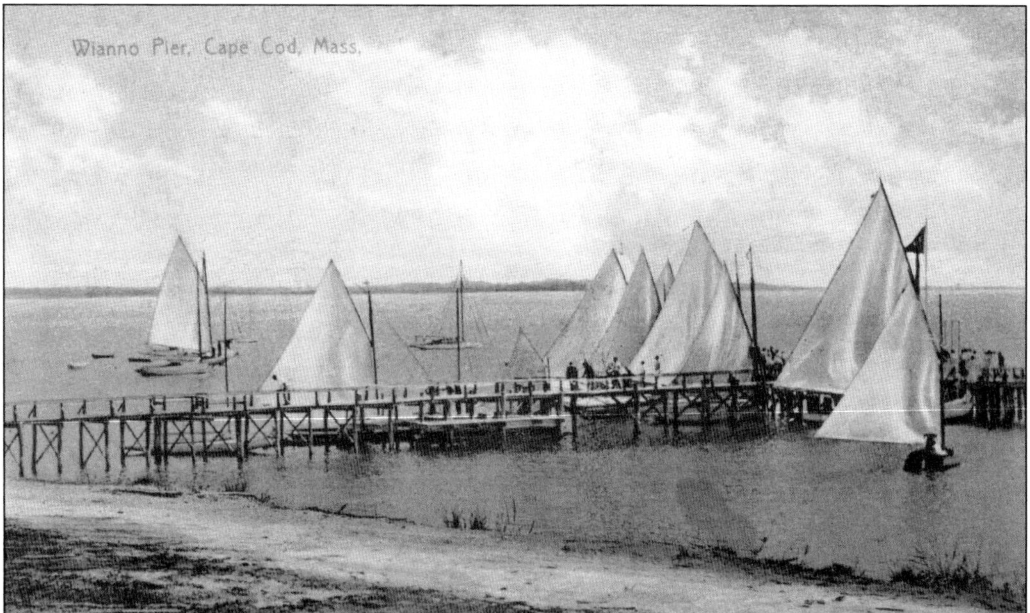

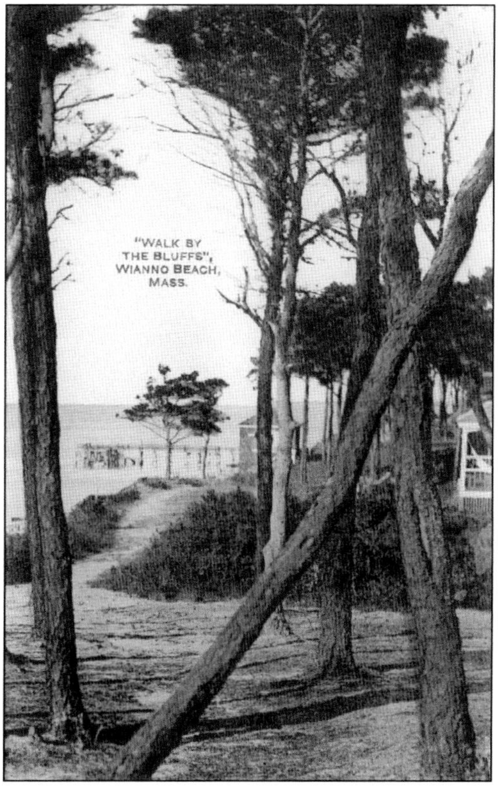

Along the ocean, there was a walking path known as the grove. These cedar tree–lined paths provided cool shade and offered a comfortable path for a morning or afternoon stroll with benches along the way.

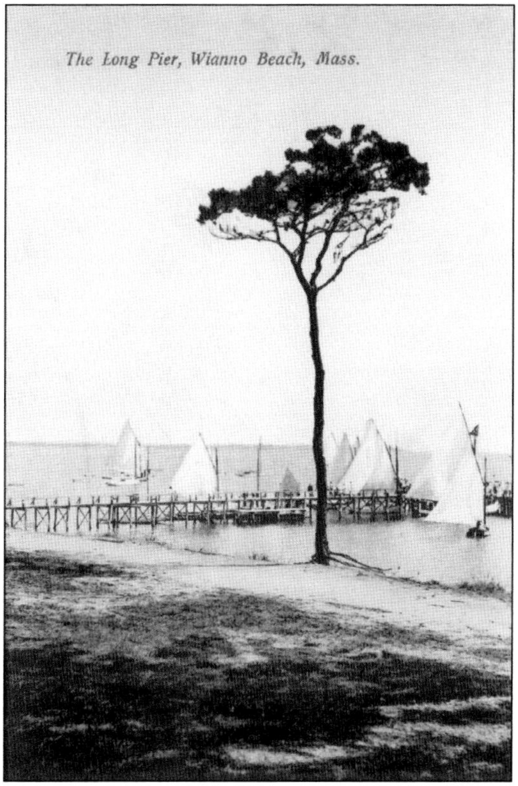

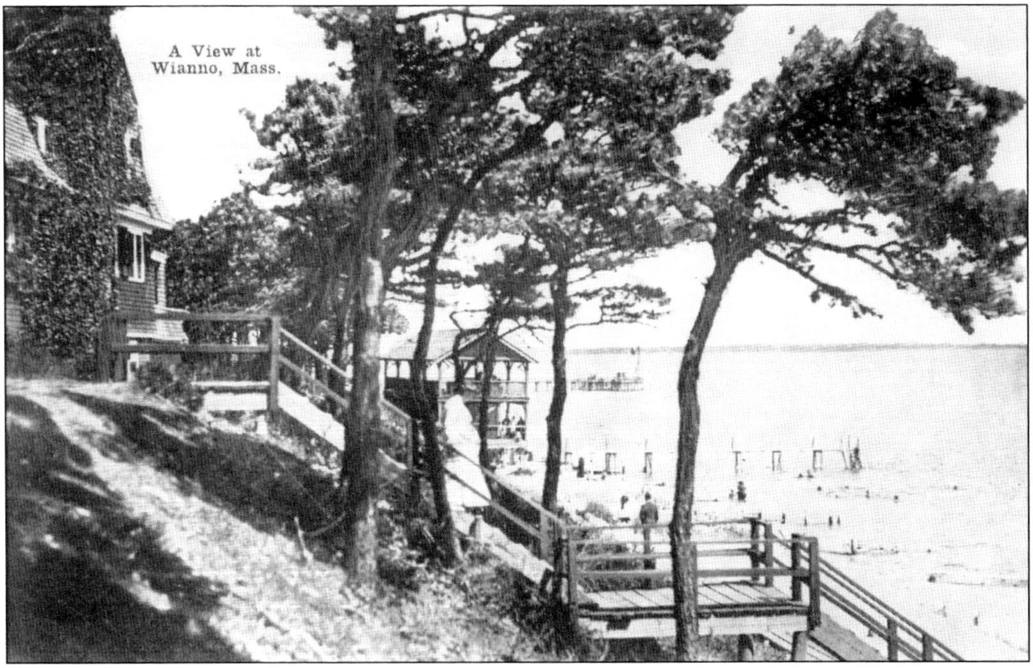

Another view of the bathing beach and pier from the staircase going down the steep bluff behind the Cotocheset House can be seen in the postcard above. In the hurricane of 1944, almost 40 feet of beach would disappear, causing significant erosion and loss of hundreds of trees lining the shore. The grove disappeared the night of that hurricane. In the postcard below, one can see the dirt road of Sea View Avenue. The Cotocheset House is ahead in the center, and Nantucket Sound is to the left.

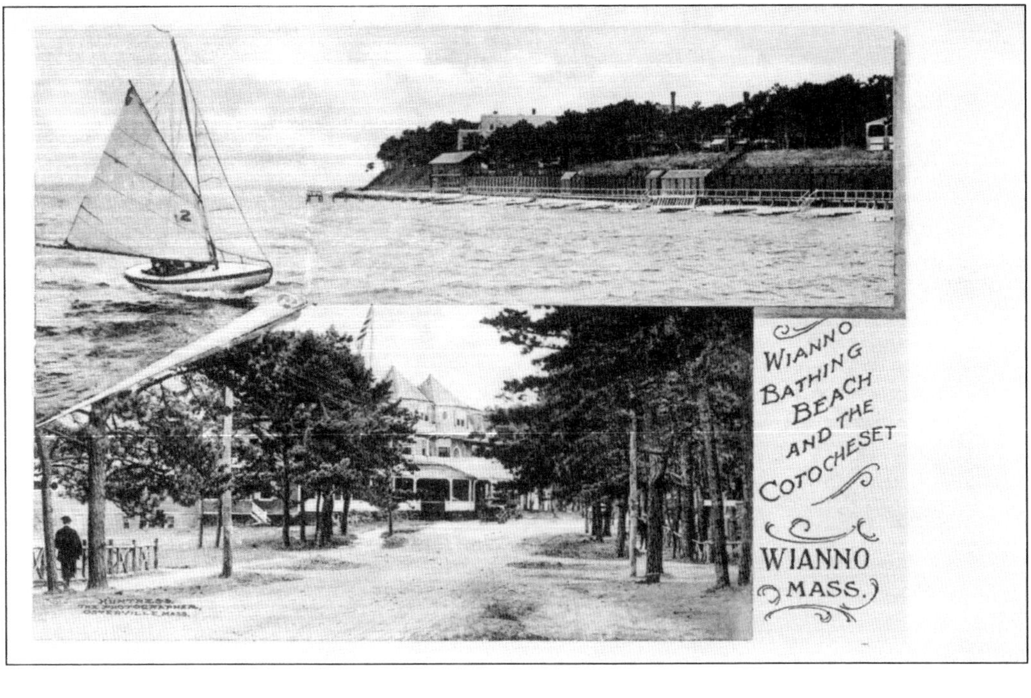

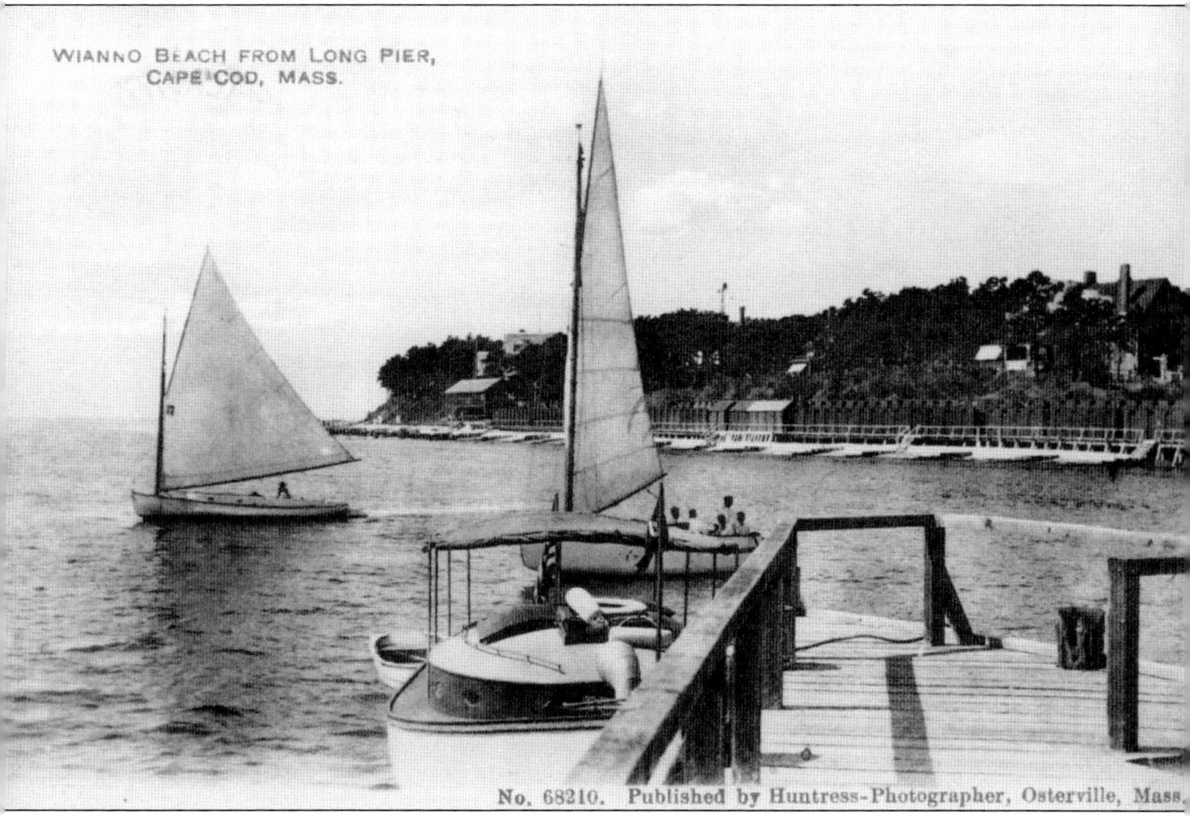

A catboat is at sail off the Long Pier at Wianno Beach. The Cotocheset is in the distance by the shore, and the bathing beach with wooden bathhouses can also be seen along the edge of the shore.

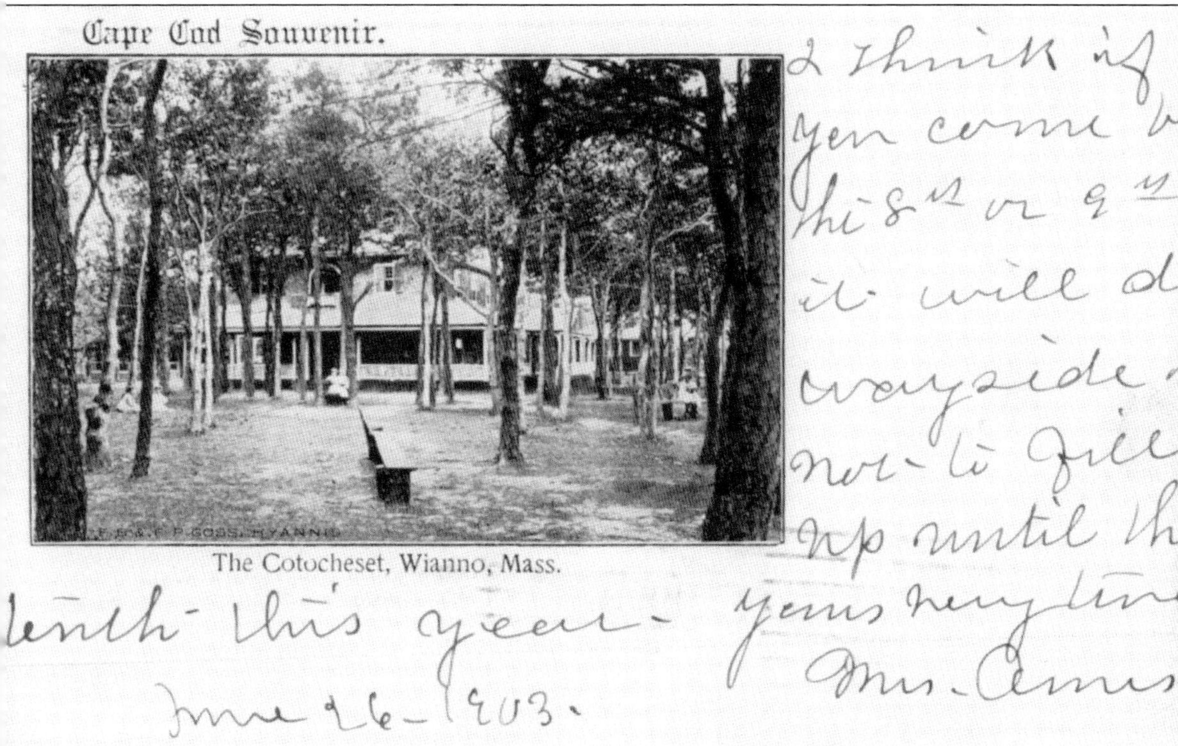

This postcard offers a clear look at the alley of trees forming the continuing grove along Sea View Avenue. A bench is seen in the center, and the Cotocheset is directly ahead. This card features a note written in 1903 and is signed by Mrs. Ames. Thankful Hamblin Ames was the manager of the Cotocheset at the time.

Seven

The Cotocheset House and the Wianno Club

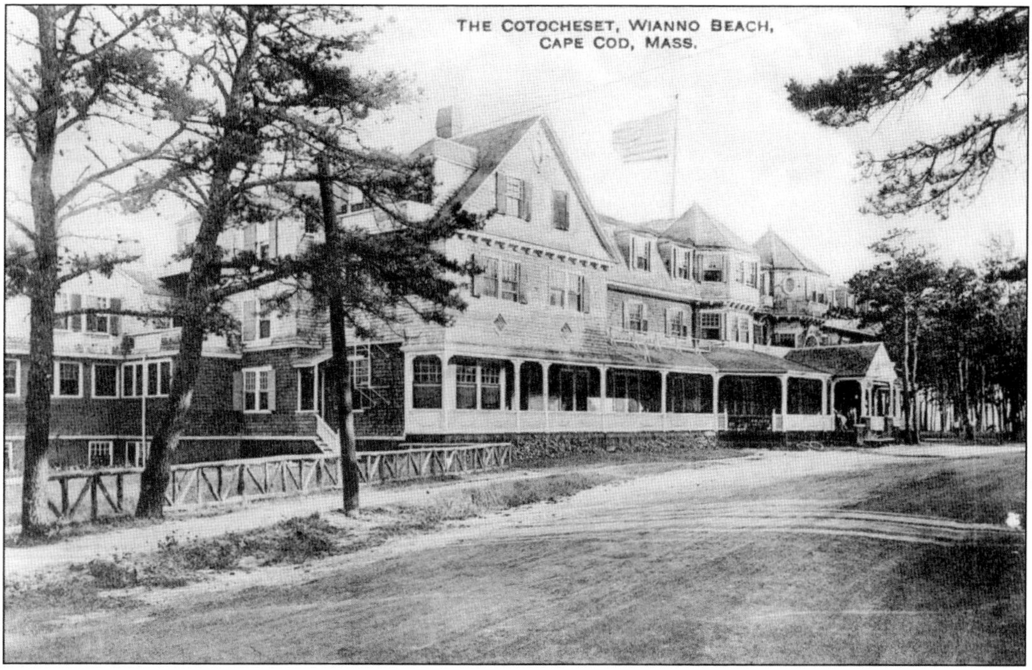

The grand Cotocheset House, located on Sea View Avenue, was the largest of Osterville's hotels. A group that included Scudders and Crockers, among others, built the original structure in 1873. It offered a number of amenities, including tennis courts, a bowling alley, a freshwater lake, and easy access to the beach, pier, and boardwalk. The original building burned in 1887 after two members of the staff, Lizzie Small and Hattie Lovell, discovered a fire on the third floor. Luckily, all of the guests were able to evacuate. They even had enough time to safely retrieve their belongings. Construction on the new building, seen here, began the next day.

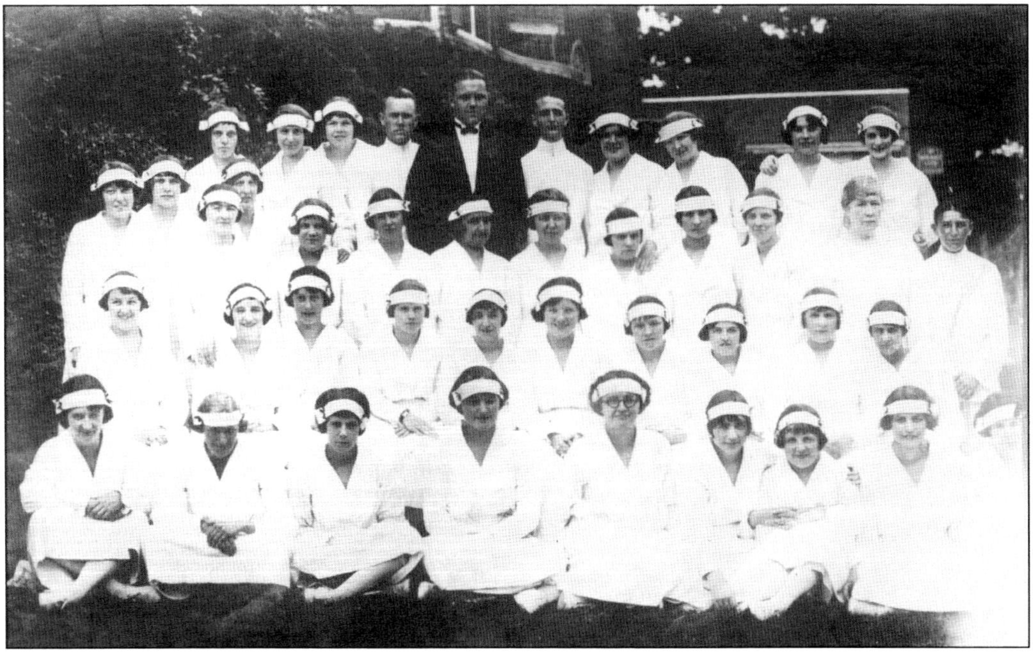

Pictured in the postcard above is the dining room crew from about 1924 to 1926. Included are a number of students from the Framingham Normal School, a teacher's college. In the postcard below, the interior of the main dining room can be seen. In 1916, the Cotocheset Company sold the property, and the private Wianno Club was established. The dining room layout and even the chairs remain the same in the Wianno Club today.

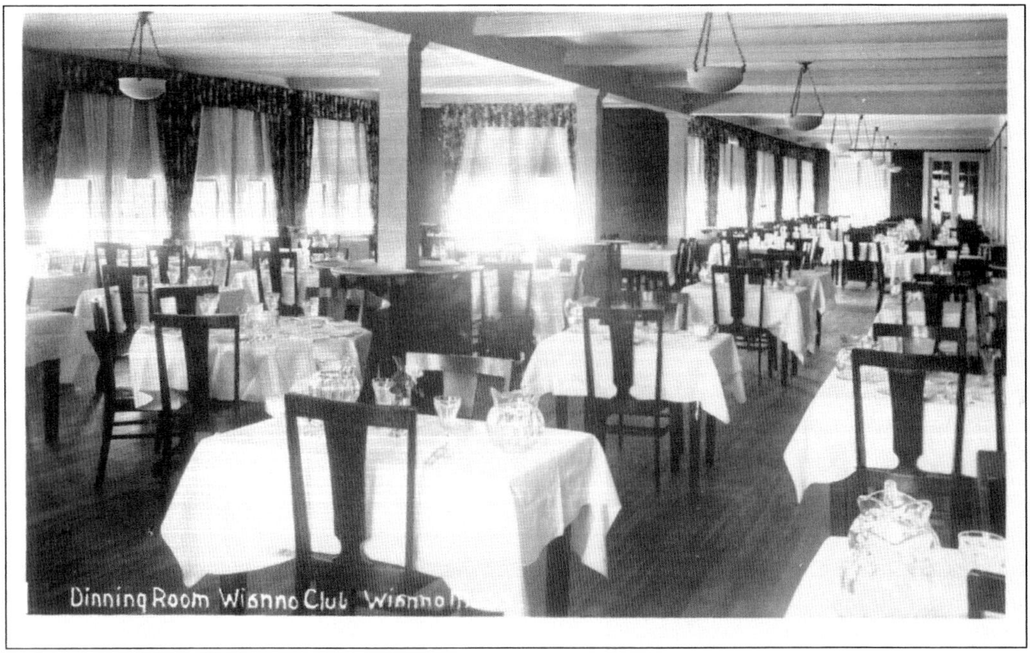

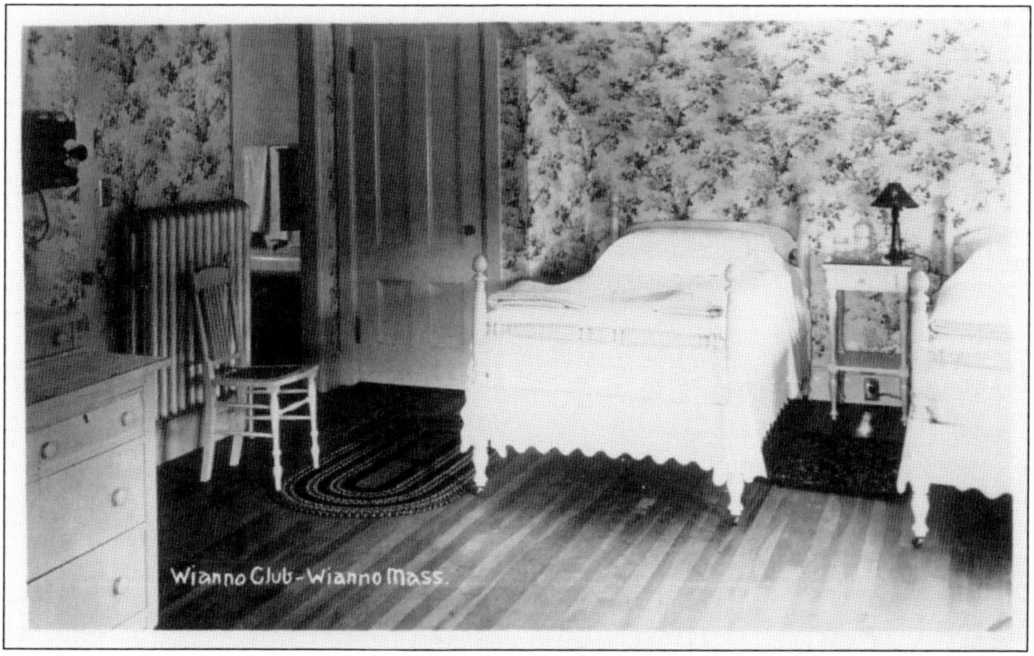

Interior images of a guest room and of a wicker-filled sunroom offer a glimpse at life inside the seaside resort. Due to its architectural significance, the Wianno Club was added to the National Register of Historic Places in 1979.

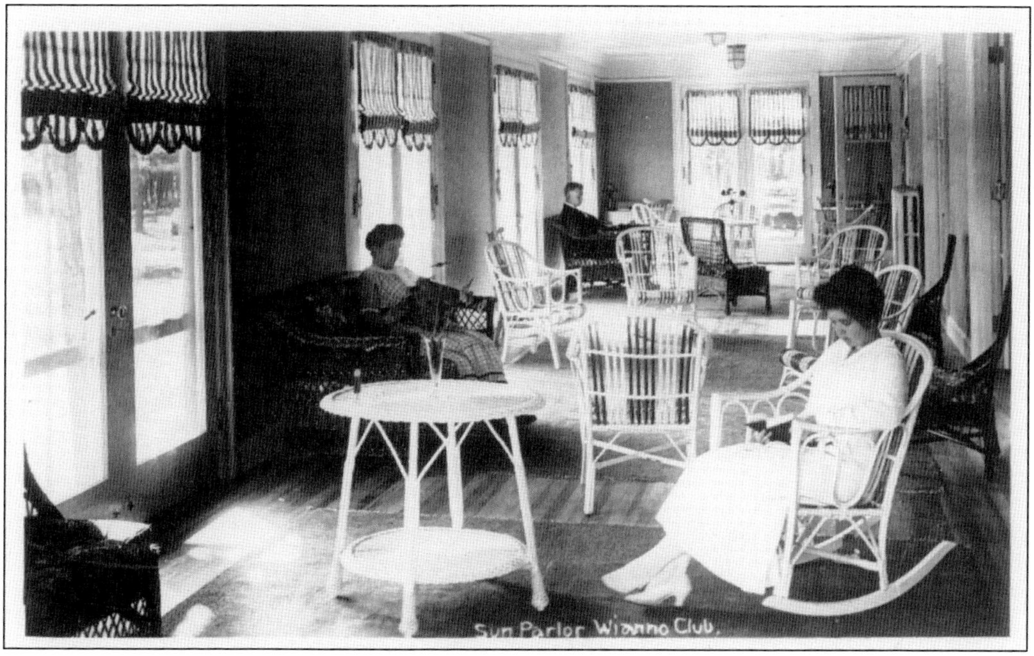

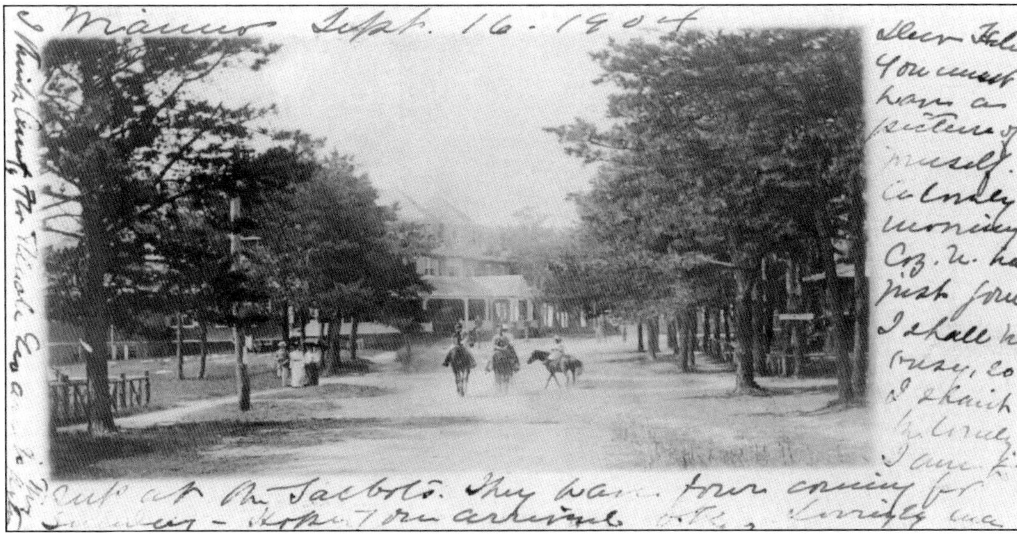

These two views are looking down Sea View Avenue with the Cotocheset House in the center. Sea View Avenue is still a dirt road here. The original stone foundation for the Cotocheset came from Daniel Webster's house in Boston. His mansion burned to the ground in 1872. The name Cotocheset came from the Native American who originally owned the land.

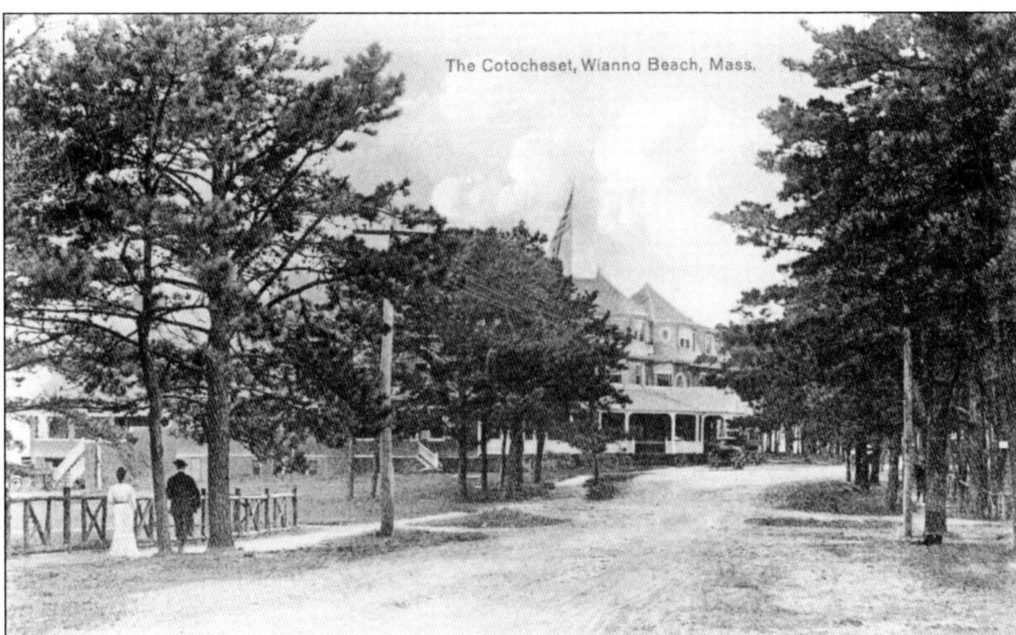

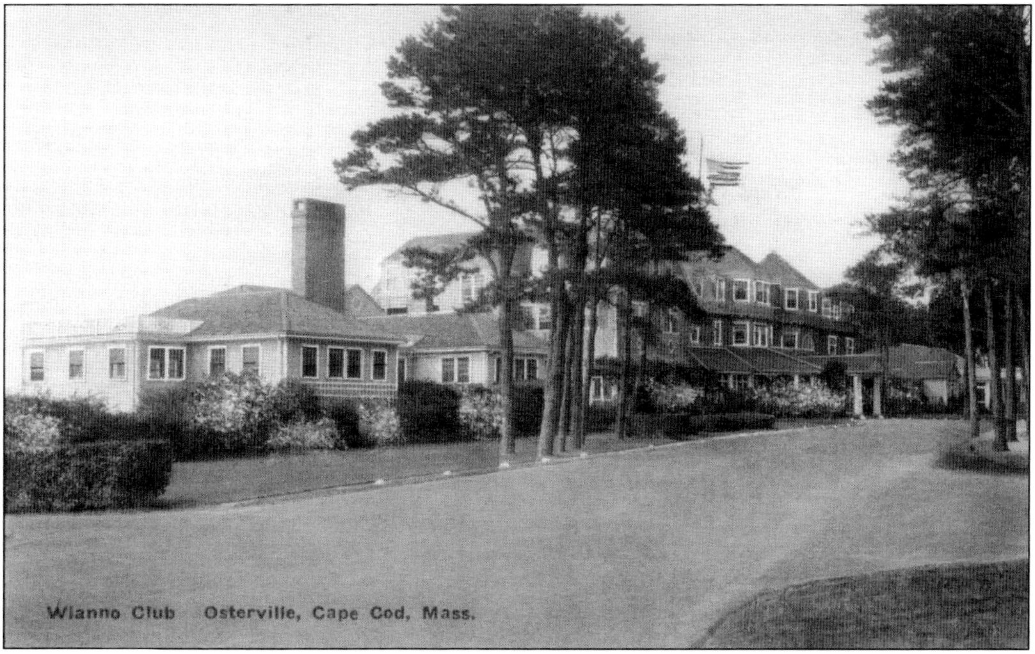

Two later views of the Wianno Club show Sea View Avenue with a paved surface. Wianno Yacht Club commodore William B.H. Dowse served as the first president of the Wianno Club from 1916 to 1927. A number of summer families and Wianno Club members began to build large homes during this time period up and down Sea View Avenue.

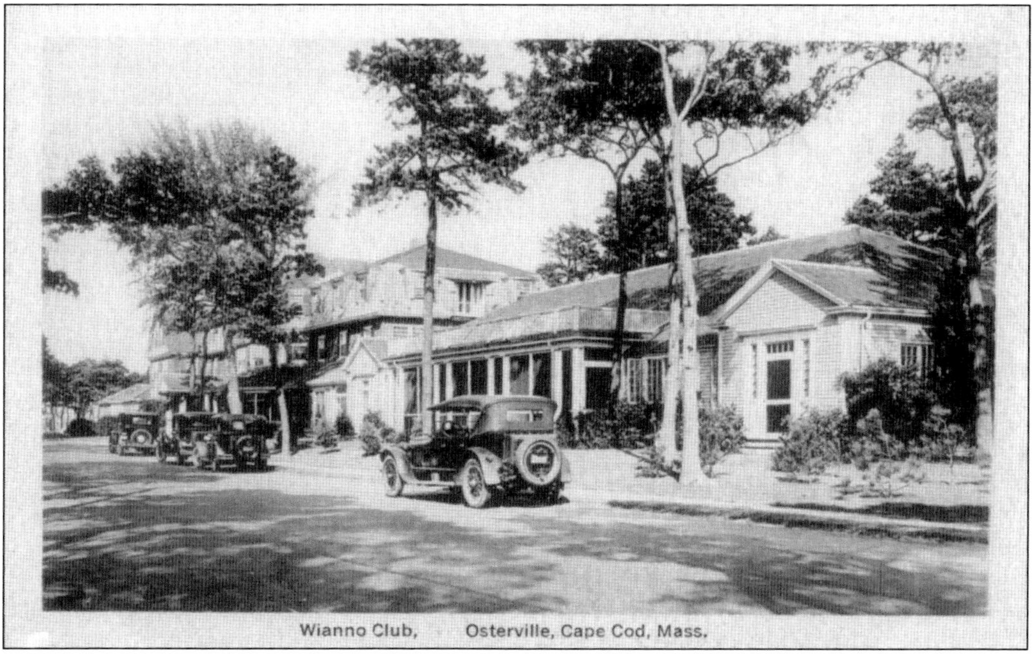

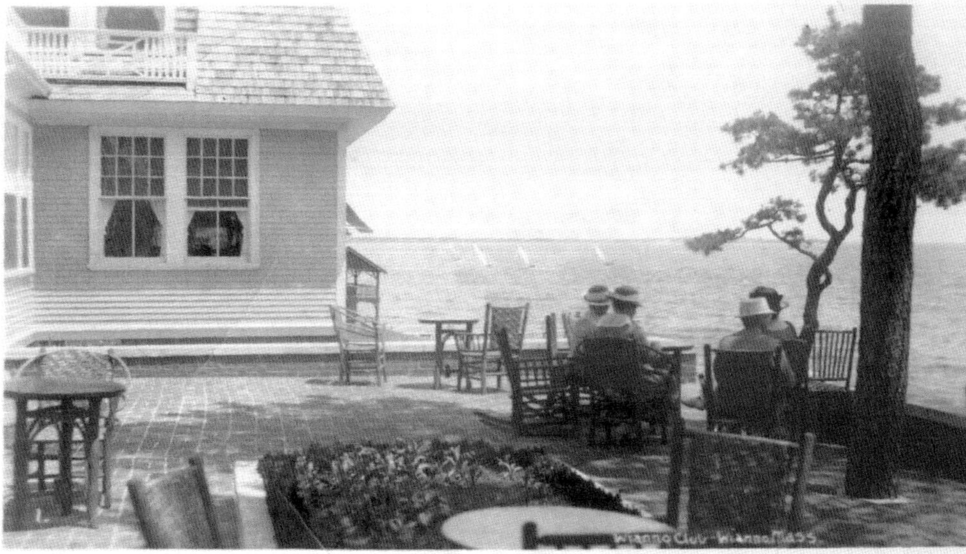

The rear of the Wianno Club with outside terraces and chairs can be seen in these two images. In the distance, one can see boats sailing in Nantucket Sound. There was no need to travel far from the Wianno Club. The club had its own stables and gas station nearby. Wianno also boasted its own post office, which was dubbed "the biggest little post office in the whole wide world." It was a seasonal post office, open from June 1 to September 30. Bertha West was its longest serving postmaster, retiring after 24 years and 8 months of service.

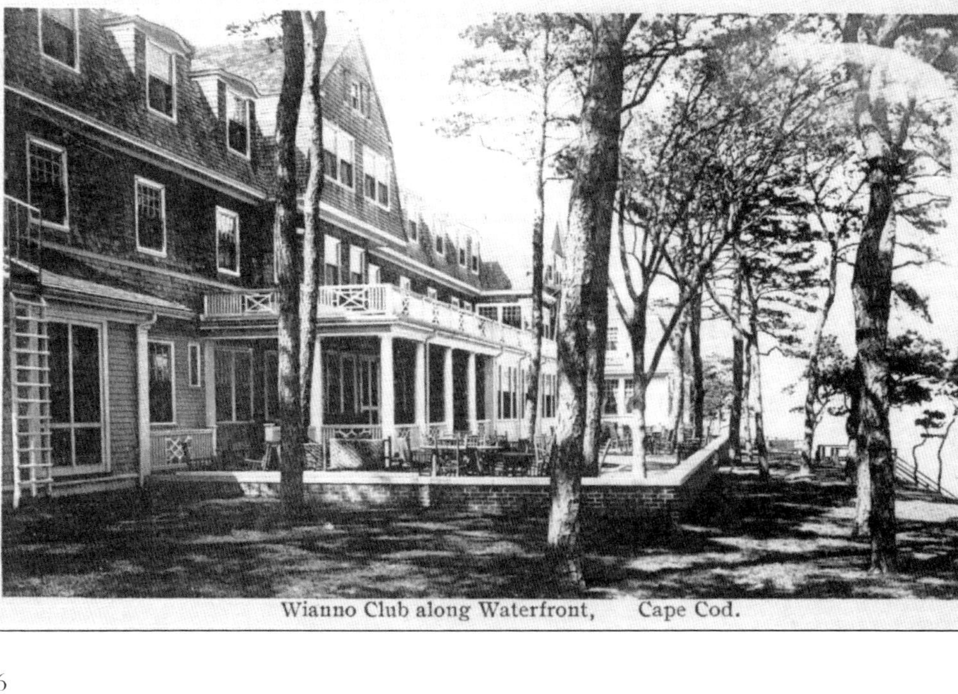
Wianno Club along Waterfront, Cape Cod.

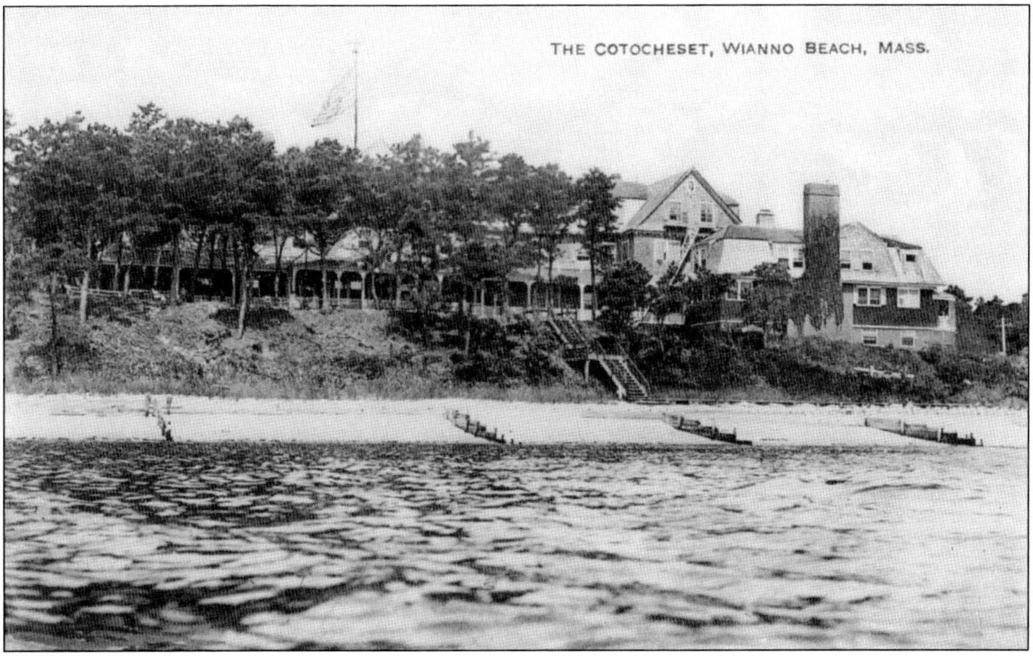

These two postcards offer a glimpse of the Cotocheset from the water. Wianno Beach is clearly visible, along with the stairs going back up the bluff to the grove promenade. Thankful Hamblin Ames, who lived on East Bay Road with her husband, Granville Ames, served as the proprietor of the Cotocheset House. The day following the fire at the Cotocheset, she served a full dinner under a tent to all of the guests. She was one of the first women to vote in Osterville after the women's suffrage amendment passed in 1920.

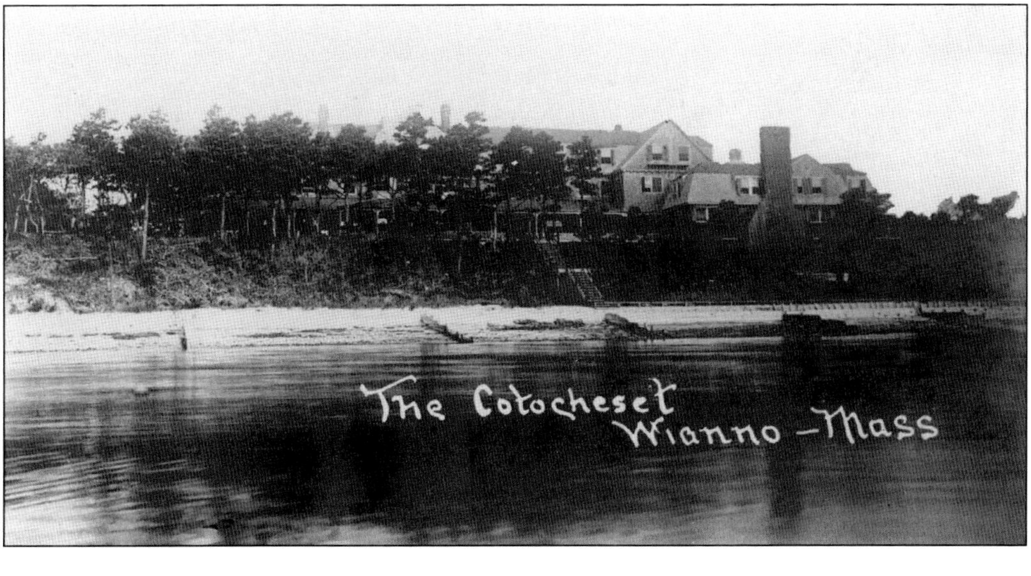

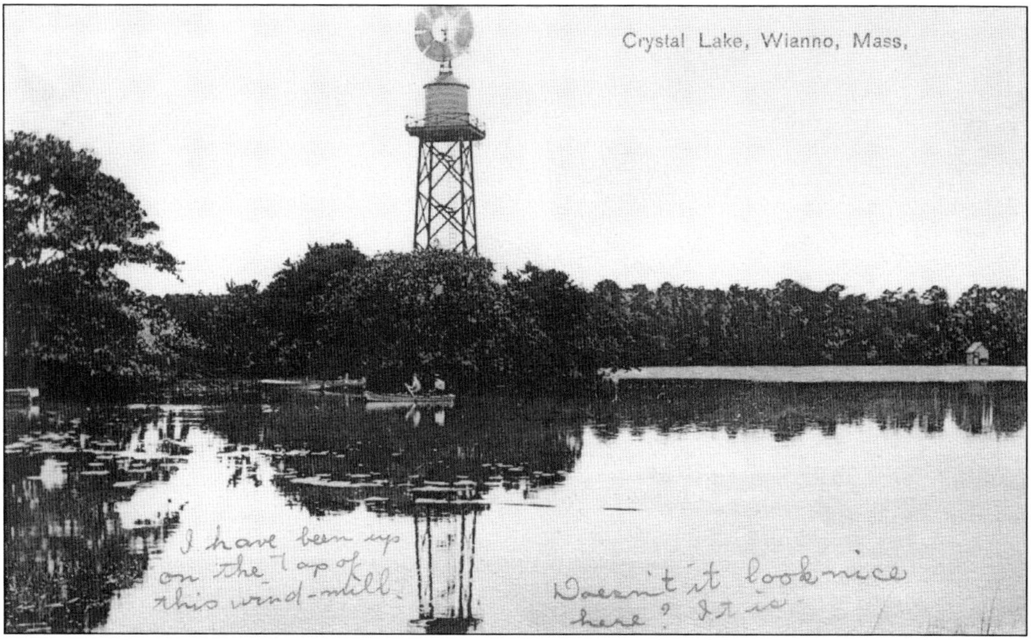

Crystal Lake, a freshwater kettle pond, was another amenity at the Wianno Club. A small beach, along with a dock for small rowboats, offered yet another recreational activity for summer guests. Today, Crystal Lake is the location of the Wianno Club's Junior Activities summer program for children.

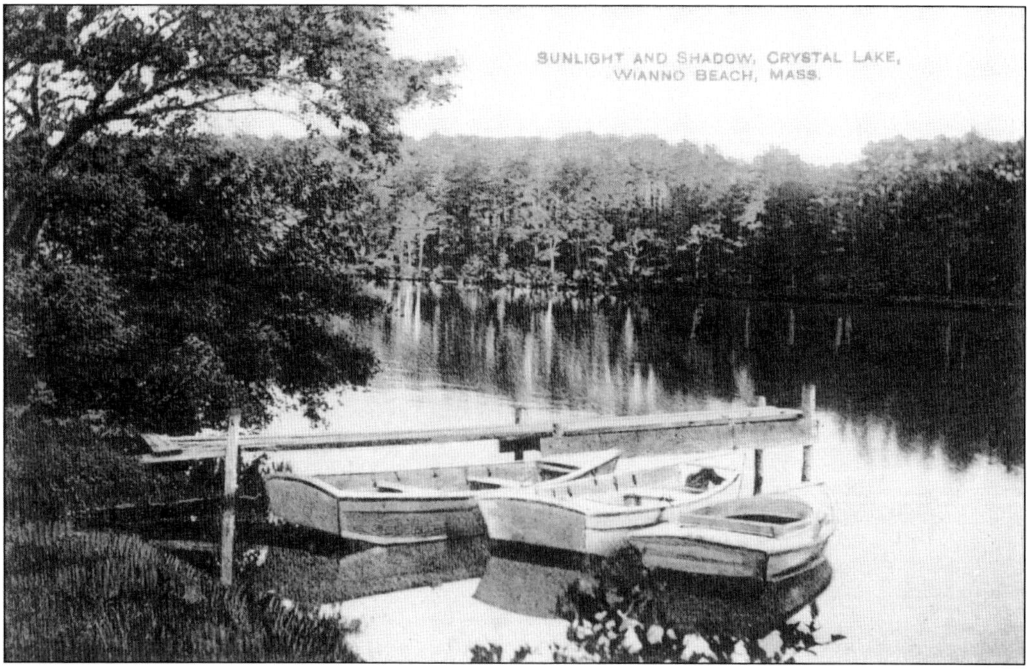

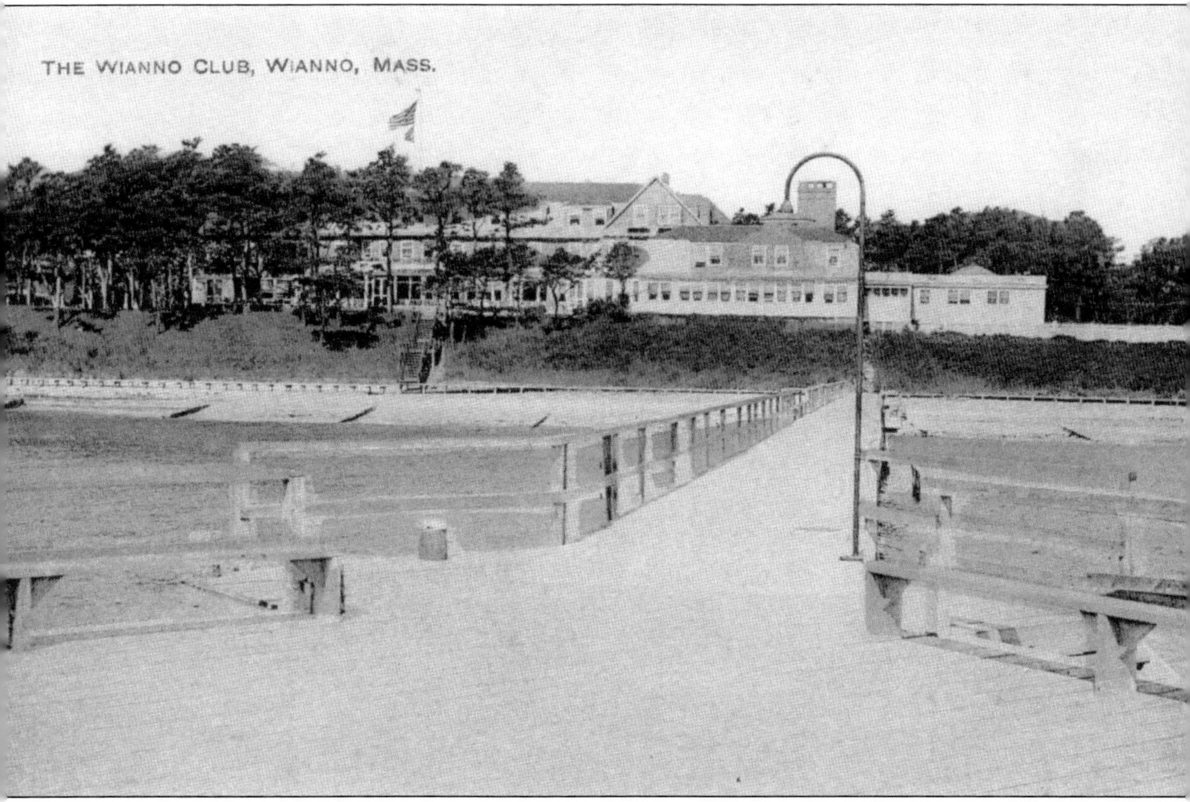

Here is another look back at the Wianno Club from the long-gone Wianno Pier. During certain astronomically low tides, one can still see remnants of the pilings in the ocean. In 1919, renowned golf architect Donald Ross was hired to redesign the original nine-hole golf course and to add an additional nine holes. The Wianno Club today encompasses over 156 acres and includes an 18-hole golf course, a golf clubhouse, 9 tennis courts, 45 rooms (only some of which are located in the 50,634-square-foot main clubhouse building), 2 paddle courts, 2 beaches, Crystal Lake, and a children's Junior Activities program.

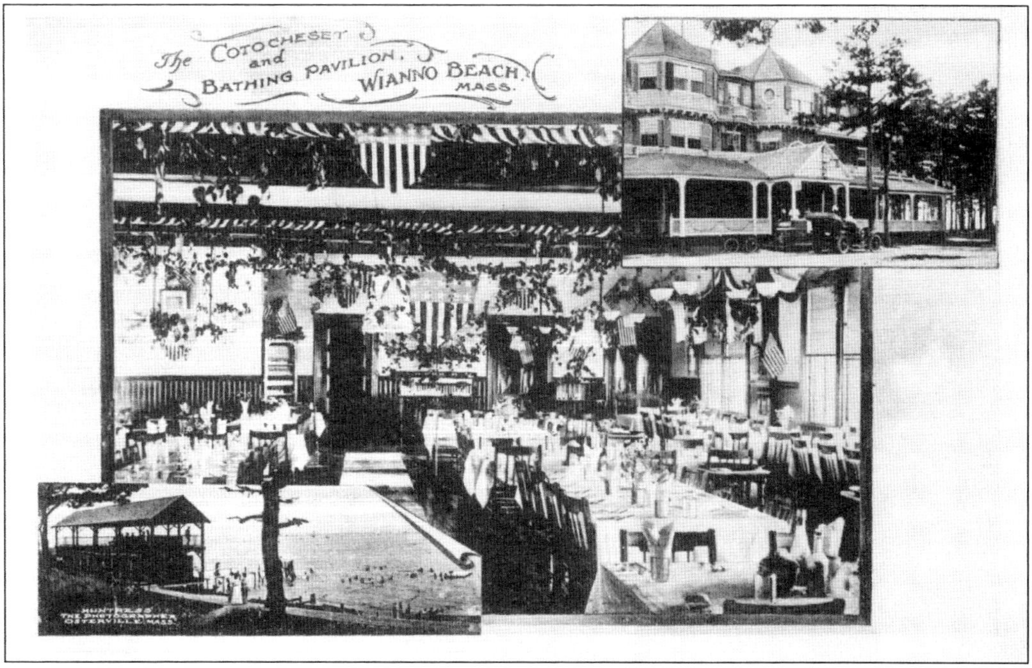

From the images on these two postcards, it is easy to see the draw of the Cotocheset Hotel. The bathing beaches below the bluff, the fine dining in the main dining room, and the magnificent views of the Crosby boats sailing in Nantucket Sound were quite enticing.

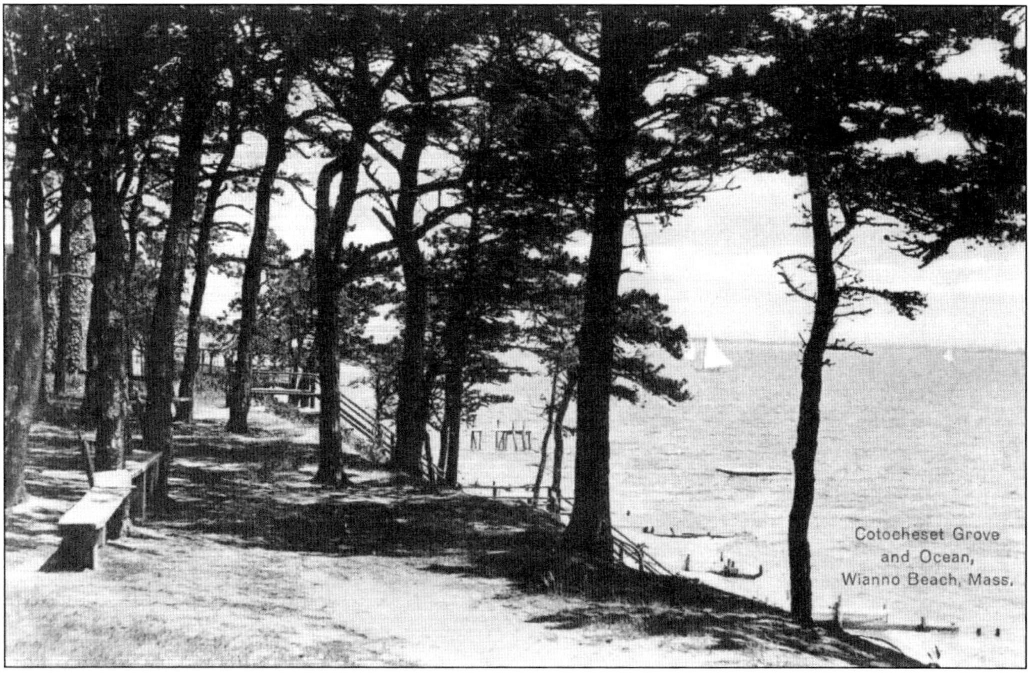

Eight

The Oyster Harbors Club and the Seaput Club

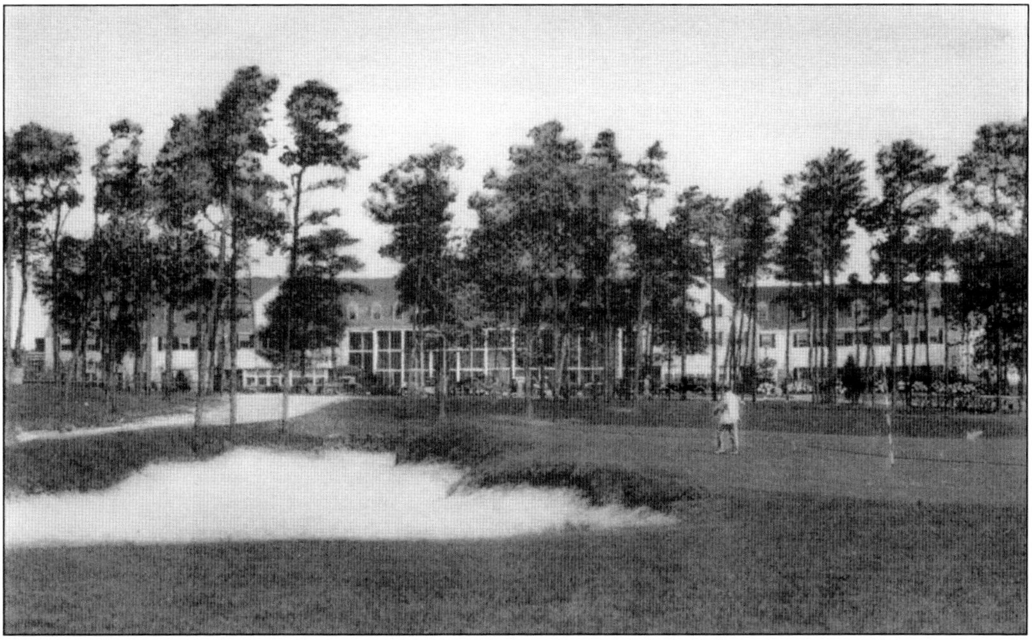

This postcard shows an overview of the Oyster Harbors clubhouse with the golf course and greens in view. Oyster Harbors is another private club with sweeping ocean vistas and a golf course, designed by Donald Ross. A developer named Norris purchased it in 1925. Construction of the clubhouse was complete in 1929 and cost approximately $300,000. The 18-hole golf course was completed at a cost of $250,000. Olmsted Brothers, landscape architects, developed the plans for Oyster Harbors. By the time the entire 300-acre island was developed with roads, a causeway, stables, bridal paths, tennis courts, the golf course, bathing beaches, piers, a water system, and the main clubhouse, expenses totaled almost $2 million.

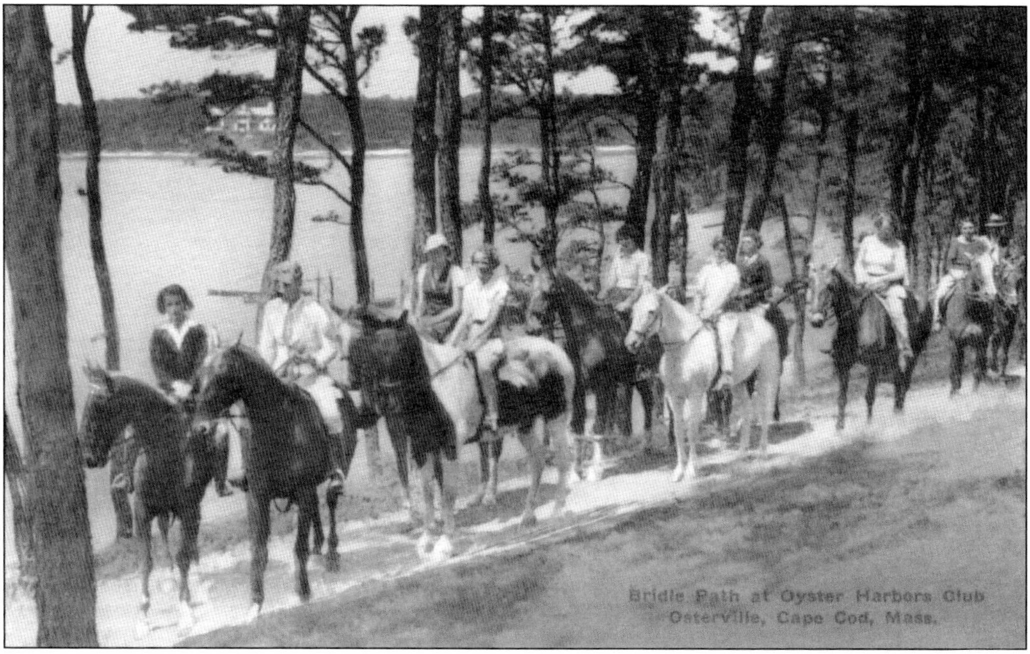

These cards show the bridle path at Oyster Harbors and people "returning from the hunt." Note windmill below at left. The windmill served as the gatehouse for this private community. Foxhunts were frequent events, and the club had its own stables and a popular annual horse charity show. In the 1930s, the admission to see the horse show was 25¢. The postcard below was sent on September 17, 1940, to a Sue Staples at the Viking in Newport, Rhode Island. The message read, "Hi Toots! Having a swell time. Dad."

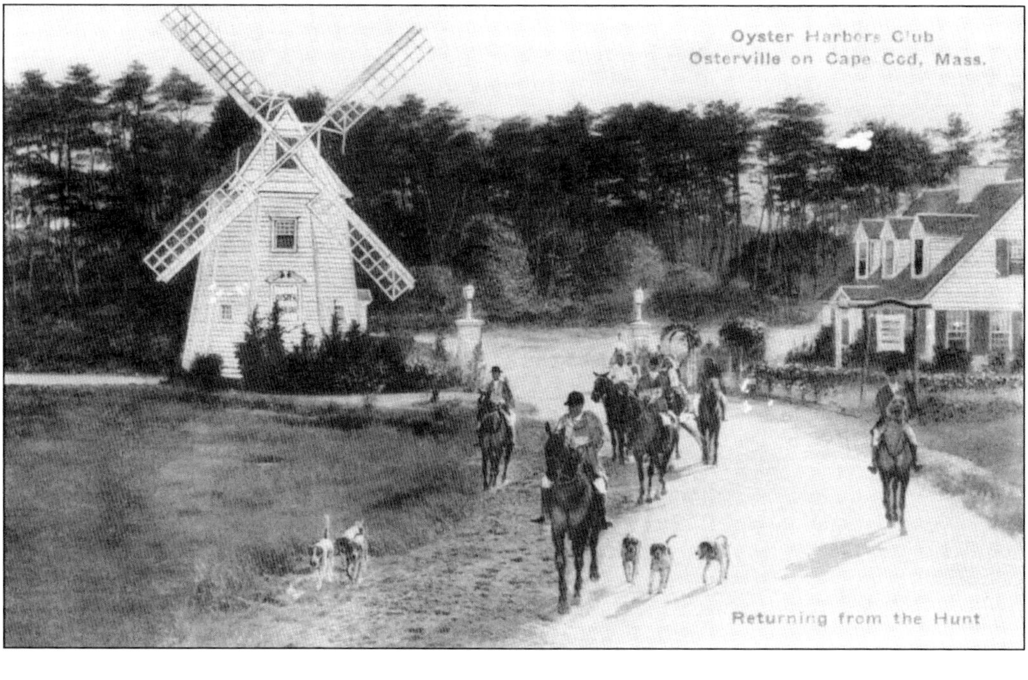

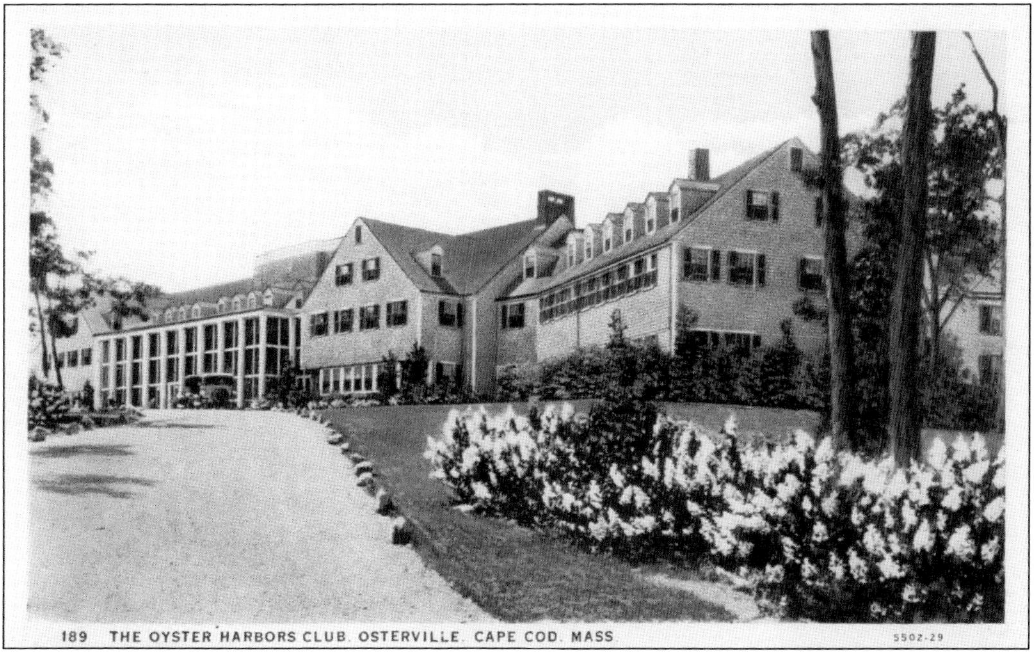

These two images show the driveway to the main clubhouse and the rear of the building with arbors and landscaped grounds and the umbrella tables and chairs set out in the middle of a manicured lawn. From 1925 until 1967, Oyster Harbors was owned by a number of stockholders and investors. The Mellons and DuPonts were among them. The presence of these magnets of industry led to Osterville being the first on Cape Cod to have direct dial long-distance telephone service. In the 1960s, Paul Mellon was credited with saving this private residential island community from commercial development by Howard Johnson and others. The reverse on this card, postmarked in July 1946, states, "The weather has been delightful here on the Cape since we arrived."

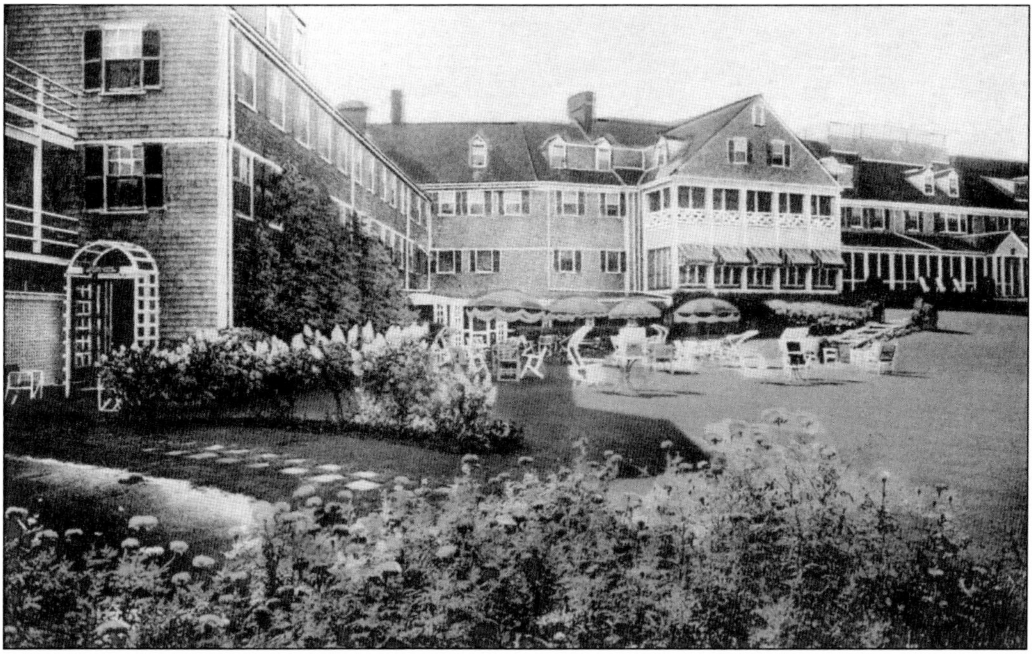

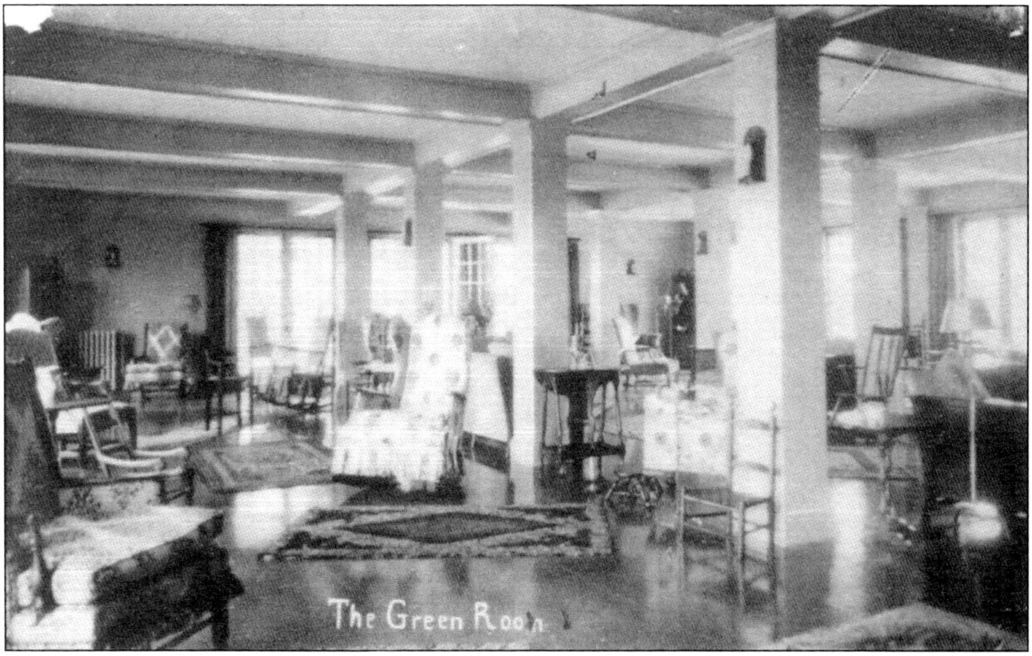

Pictured above is the Green Room interior with upholstered furniture and Oriental rugs on the floor. Seen below is the main dining room with white linen tablecloths and china. The island on which Oyster Harbors is located is sometimes called Oyster Island, Grand Island, or Schreecher Island. Legend has it that the famous pirate Captain Kidd buried his treasure on the island to be protected by Hannah Schreecham.

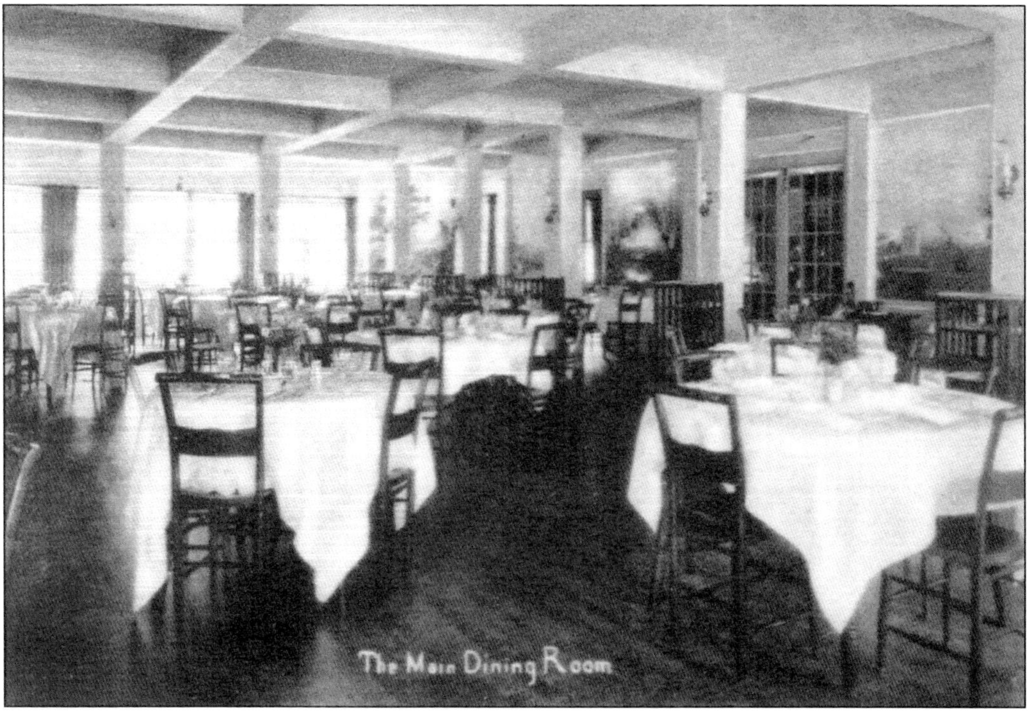

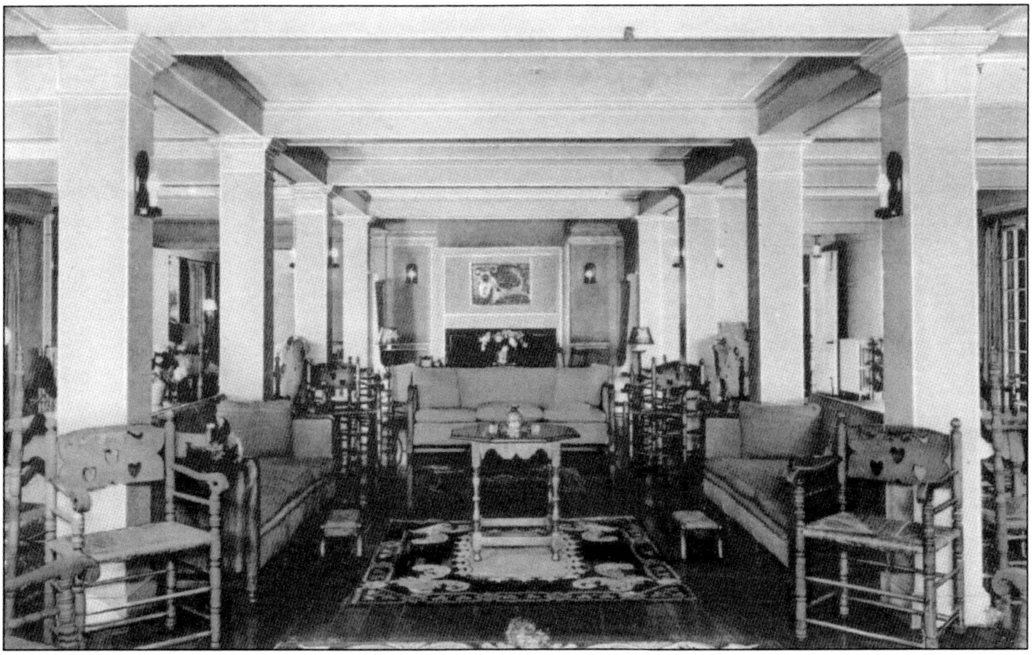

Two additional interior scenes show upholstered furniture with Oriental rugs covering the floor in a parlor. A map of Cape Cod hangs above the mantel. In the postcard below, the front lobby is shown with the front desk visible on the right edge. The boxes on the counter would be used to sort messages and correspondence for guests. The postcard below was sent to Cambridge, Massachusetts, on July 21, 1936, and the message reads, "Am here for the night and tomorrow. Am not sure when I shall arrive home."

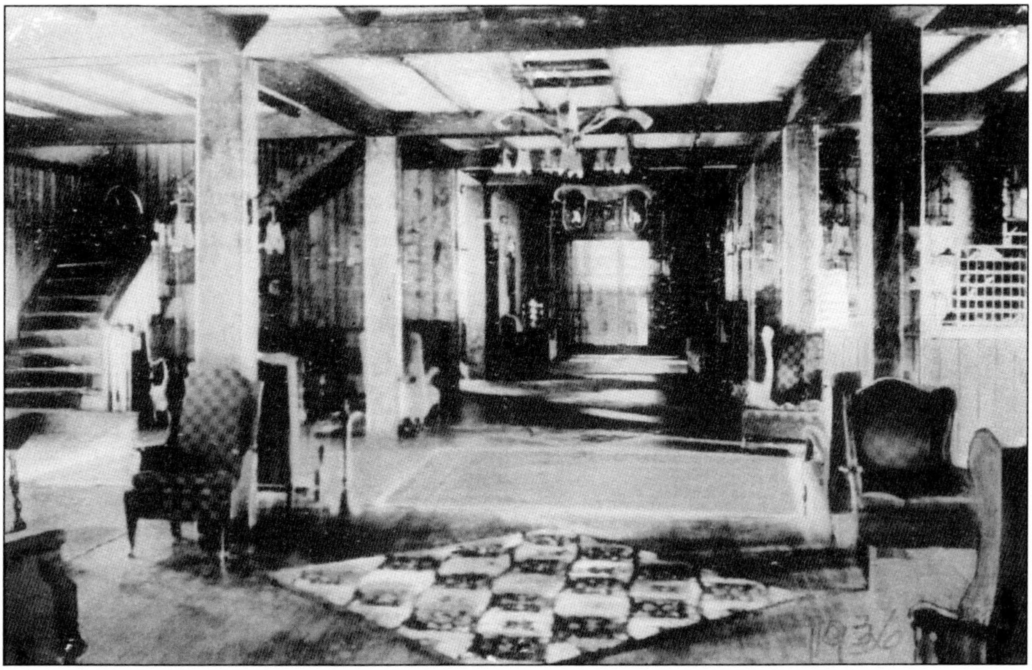

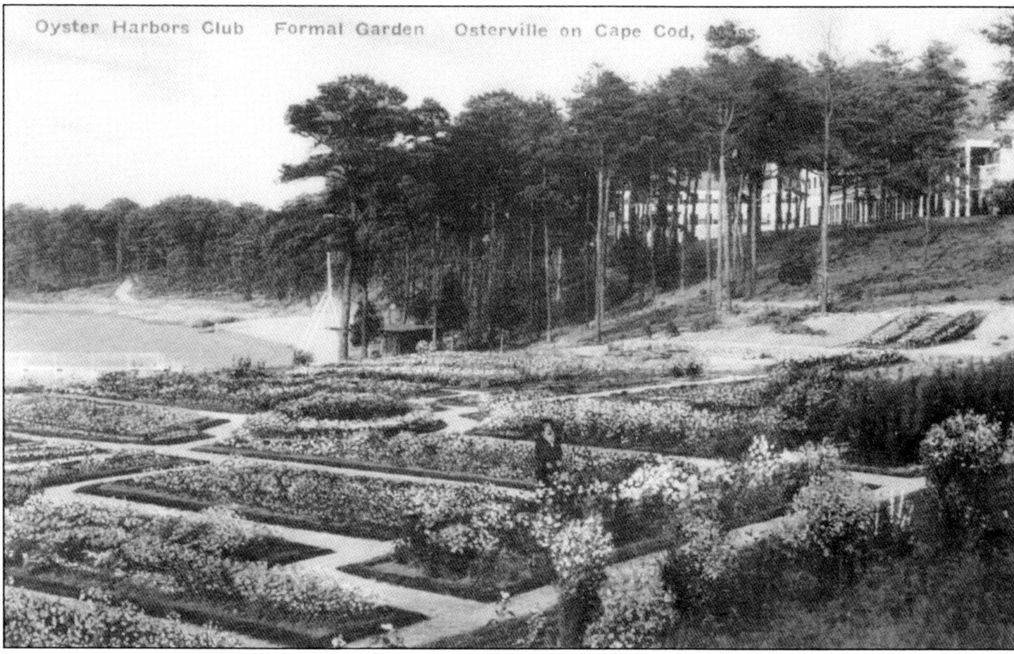

These two postcards illustrate the beautiful formal gardens at the Oyster Harbors Club. They led right down to the water. In the postcard below, one can clearly see one of the other amenities—tennis. Two courts are visible with games in progress. To the right, one can also see the wharf leading into the water and a dock.

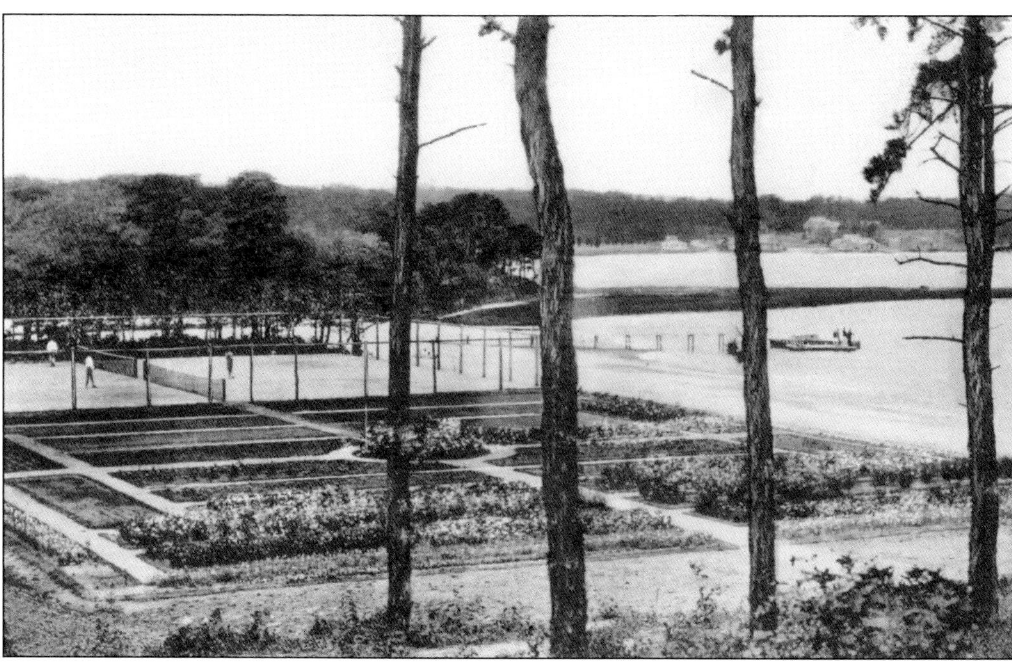

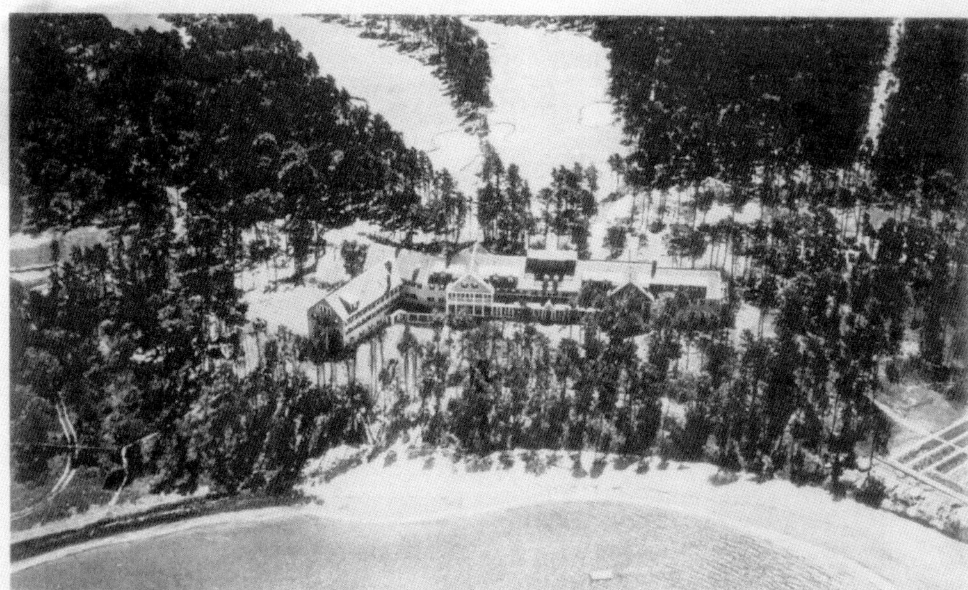
A view of the Oyster Harbors Clubhouse taken from above the waters of Cotuit Bay

Here is an aerial view of Oyster Harbors from above the waters of Cotuit Bay. The card below shows boats moored in the water near the pier as well as folks sitting on the bluff above the beach. One can also see the path and stairs leading down to the beach on the right. This card was sent on July 27, 1950. It reads, "Dear Helen, The old head is doing much better, Chuck is really getting relaxed and both of our noses are burned to a crisp. Hate the war news. Hope Tom's eyes are better—Helen."

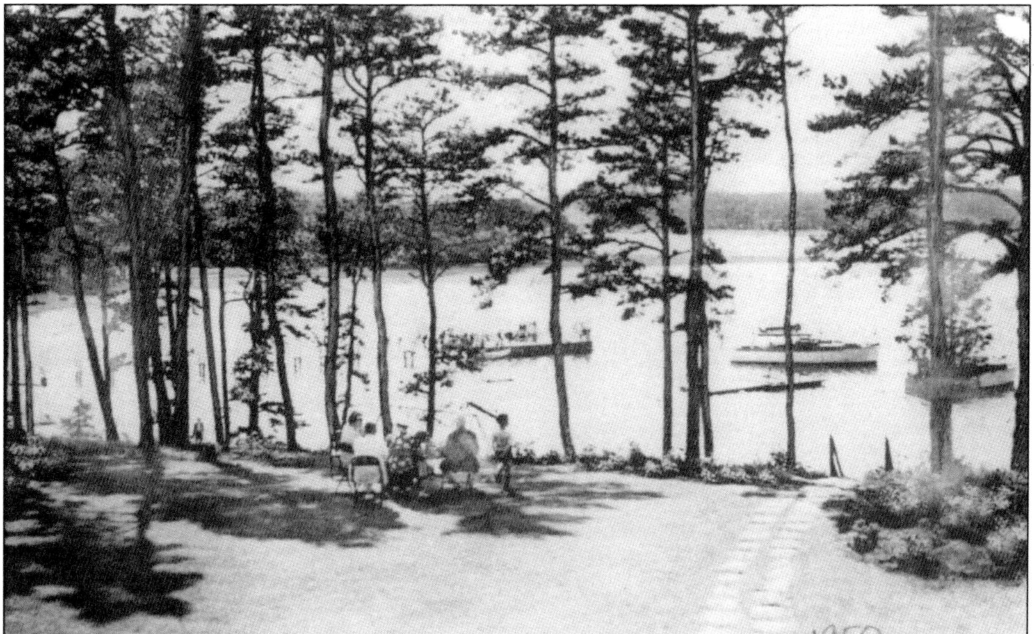

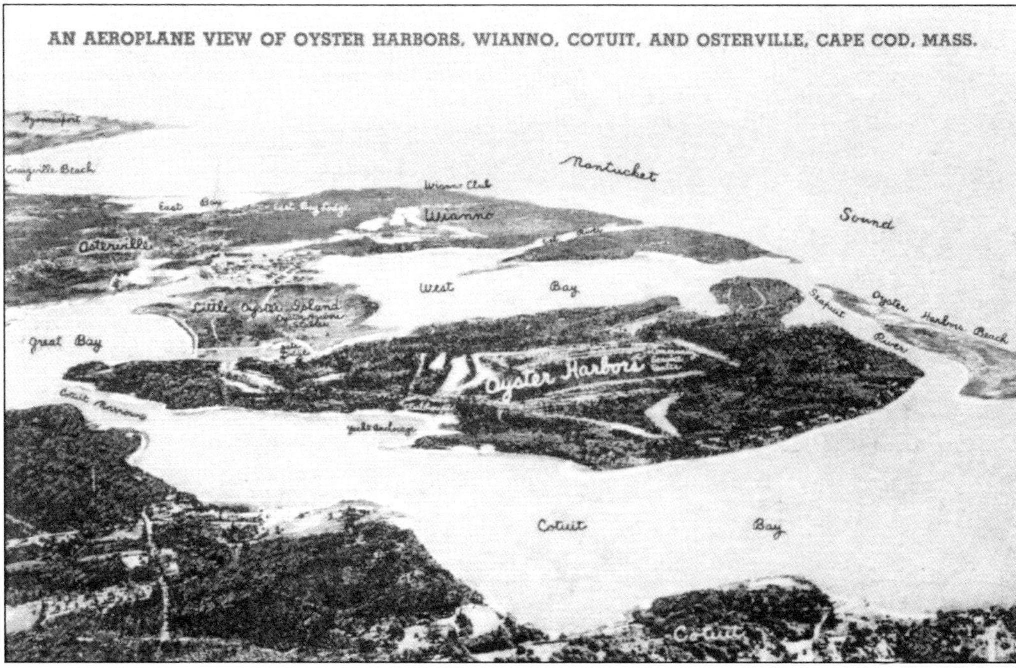

"An Aeroplane View of Oyster Harbors, Wianno, Cotuit, and Osterville, Cape Cod, Mass." is the title of this postcard. It illustrates the series of bays that encircle Osterville. The c. 1915 card below shows the Grand Island Bridge. The drawbridge is raised to allow boat traffic through. A Wianno Senior with full sails can be seen going through on the left. Horace Manley Crosby designed the Wianno Seniors, which first sailed in the summer of 1914.

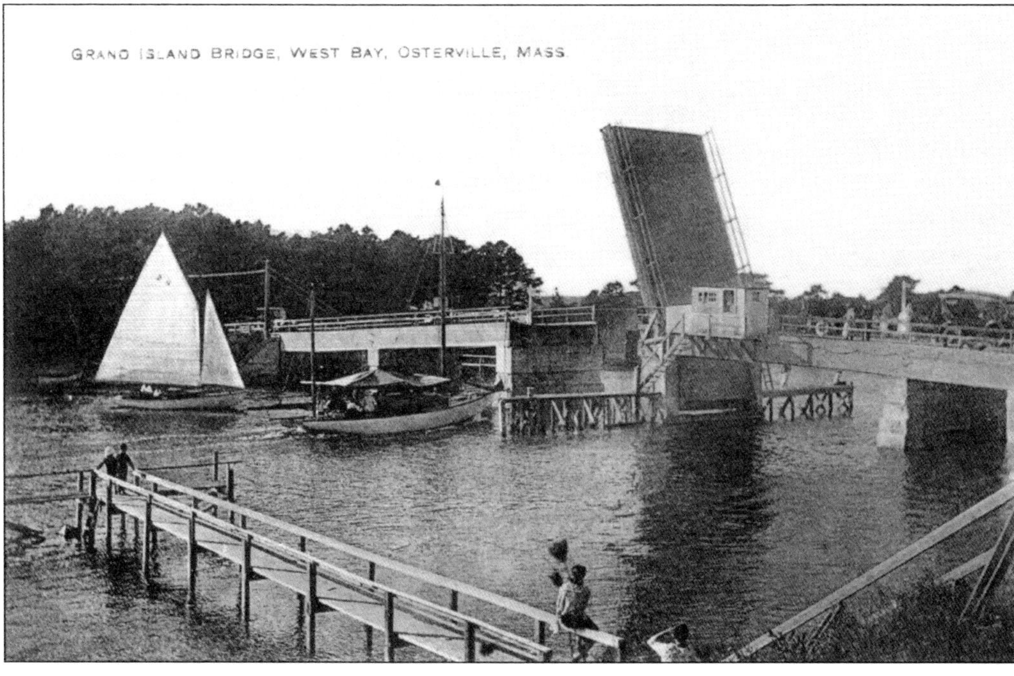

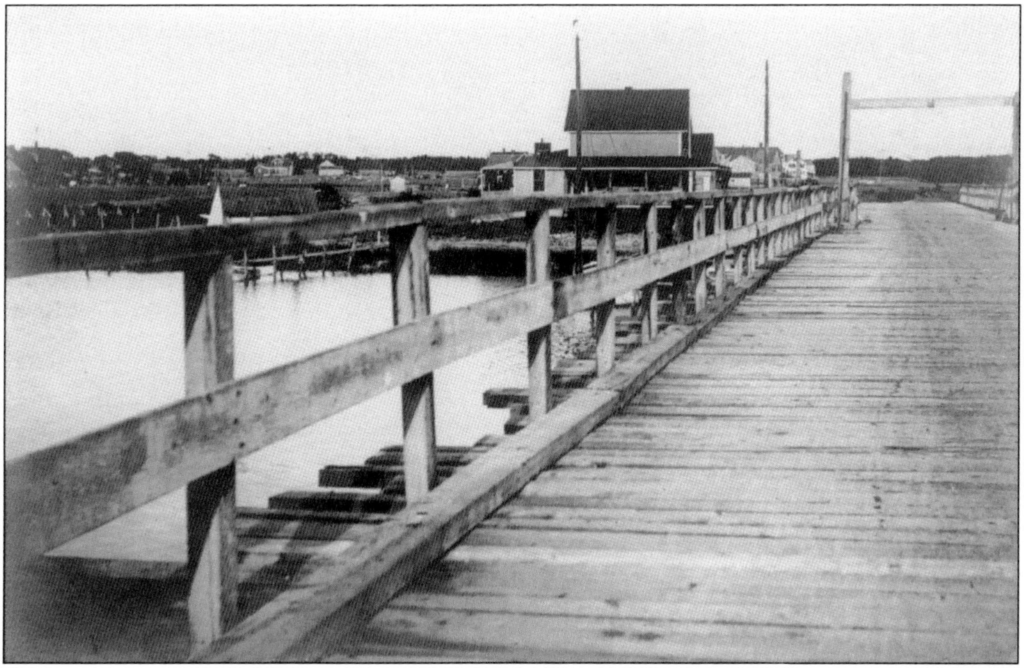

Here are two more views of the wooden bridge connecting Little Island to Grand Island. The postcard below was sent on July 12, 1906. "Imagine my going under this bridge," writes the sender. The Lincoln Club with its distinctive roofline can be seen on the right. The building to the left is the Cornelius Driscoll house. C.R. Williams, the owner of the ice cream parlor next to the Star Theatre, photographed the scene found on the postcard.

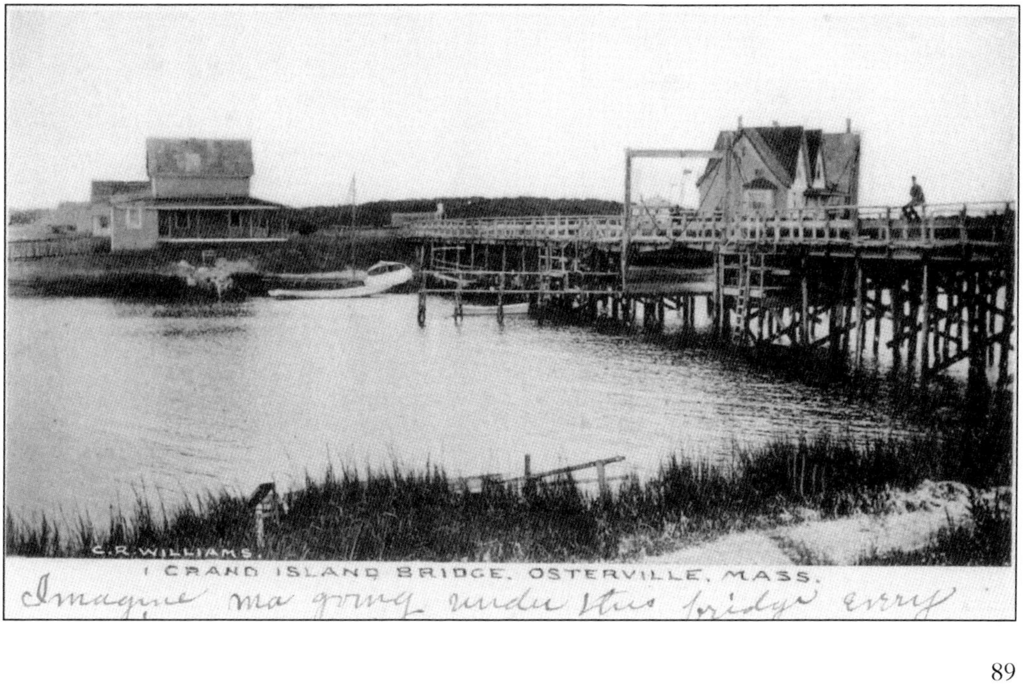

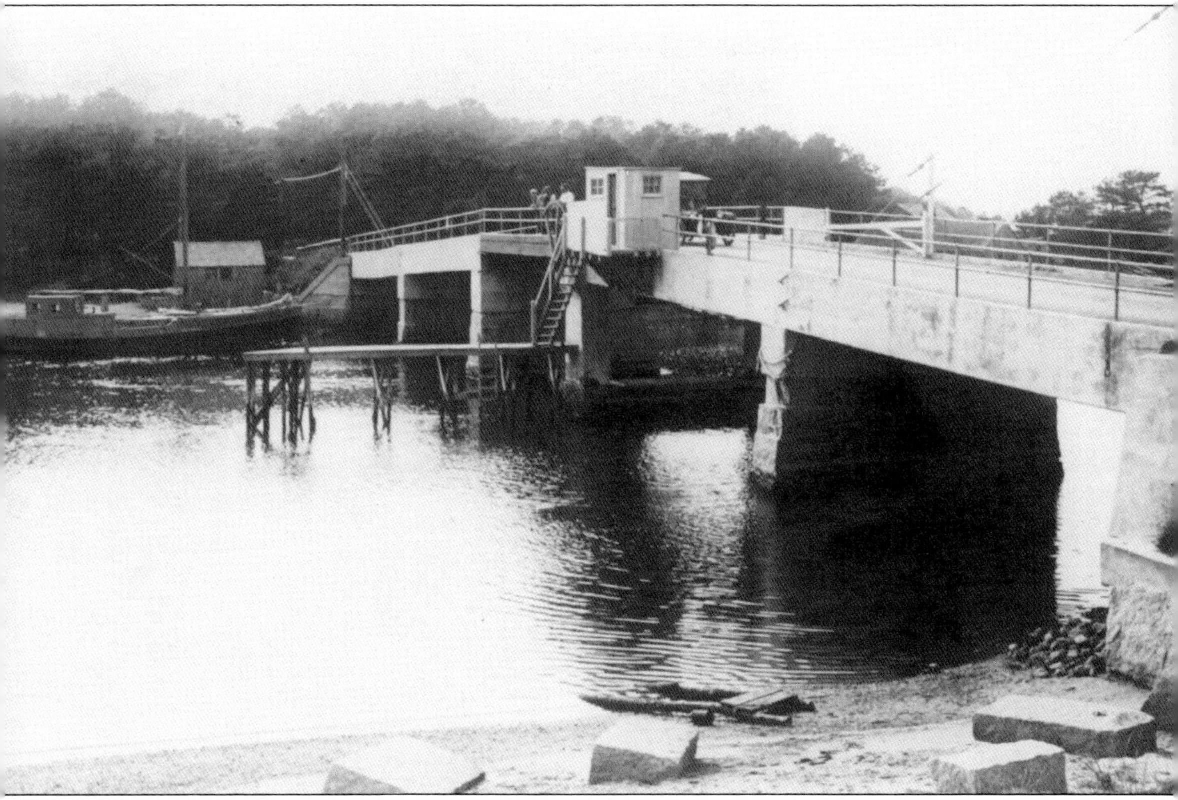

This view of the bridge highlights the difference in construction through the years. Instead of the old timber construction with wood pilings and a primitive double-draw bridge design, a modern bridge appears. In this image, the concrete blocks and a more formal guard shack can be seen. The cement bridge was built in 1911, and major improvements occurred in 1946 and 2012.

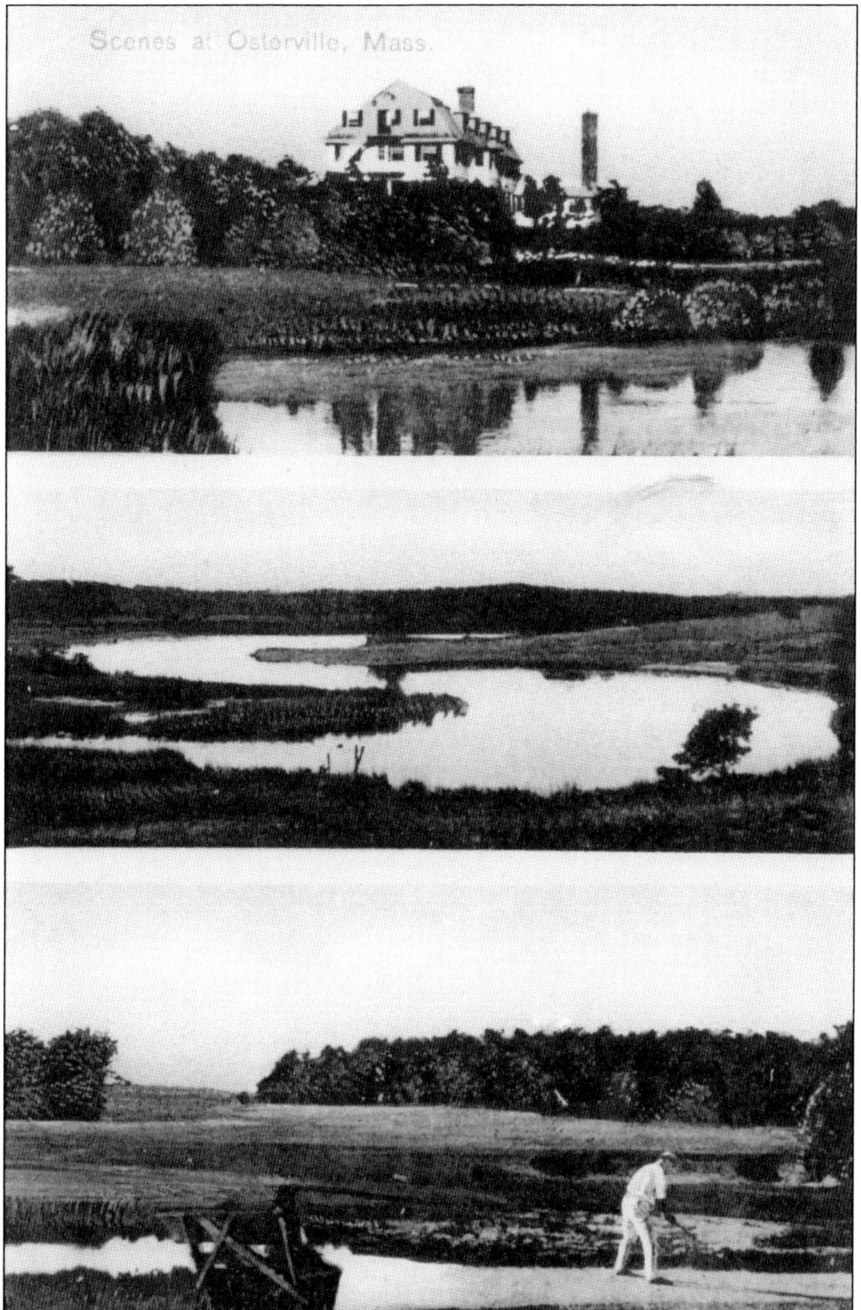

This postcard illustrates the beautiful vistas from the golf course at the Seapuit Club. The Seapuit Club and golf course stretched over 1,000 acres in Osterville and Marstons Mills. Designed by a Scottish architect, the nine-hole golf course is believed to be the second oldest in the United States, having opened in 1898 and closed in 1942. It changed owners several times but was originally owned by Francis Parsons, who named the inn after a local Native American chief. In 1926, the golf pro was James Shepherd Jr., and the rate for the season for an individual was $35. The daily greens fee was $1.50 for a weekday and $2.50 for the weekend.

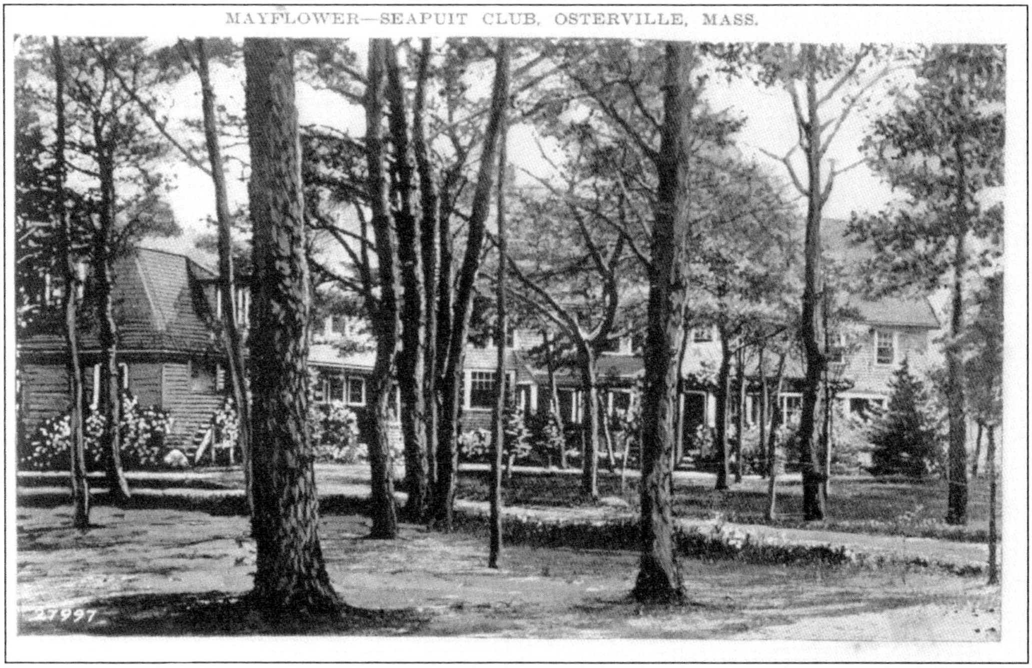

Seen here are two images of the Mayflower at the Seapuit Club. The one below was taken from the water. In the 1970s, the Davis family, who had owned it since 1930, began a master plan for the site. Eventually, it was carefully divided into more than 50 house lots and conservation land.

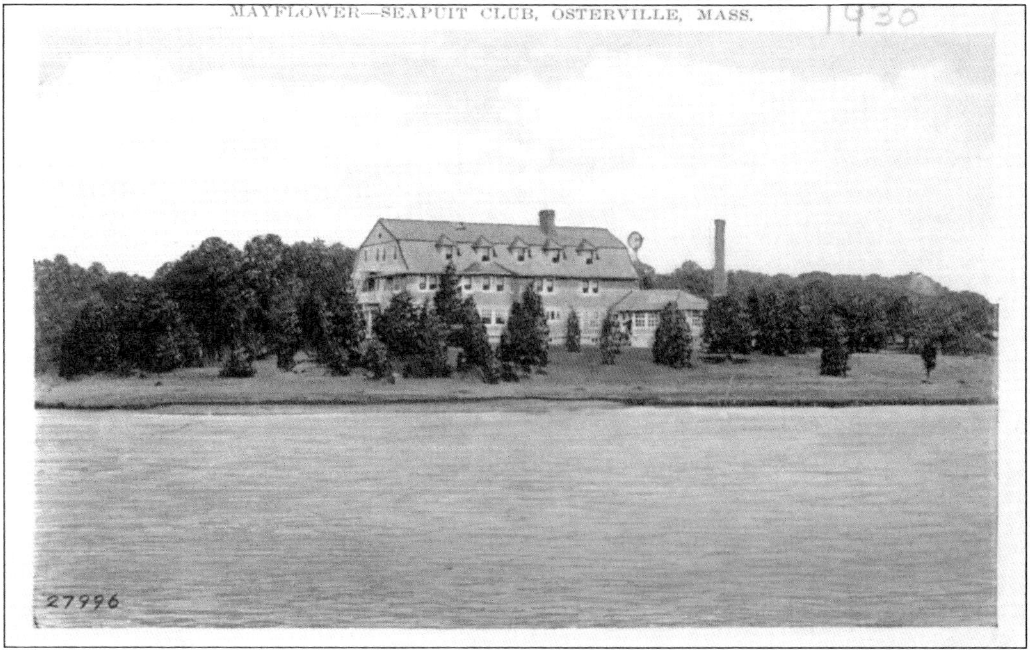

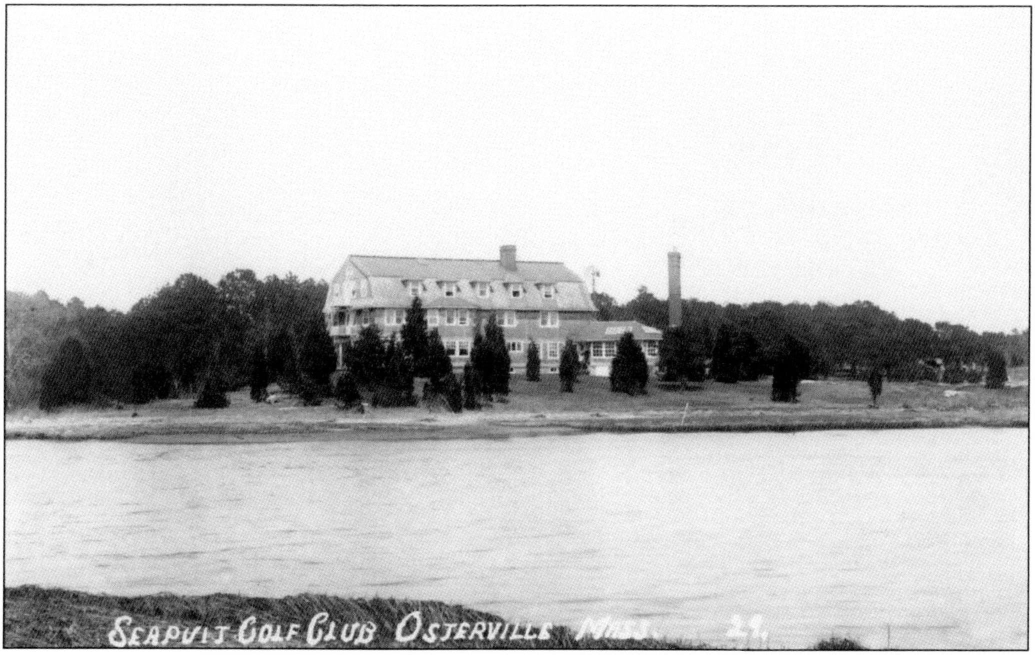

Shown is the main club. On the postcard below, one can see the boardwalk stretching across the marshland. The Mayflower appears as if in a storybook setting with vegetation obscuring the view. The inn had over 50 rooms. Although the golf course was still used for several more years, the inn was torn down in 1932 at a cost of $400.

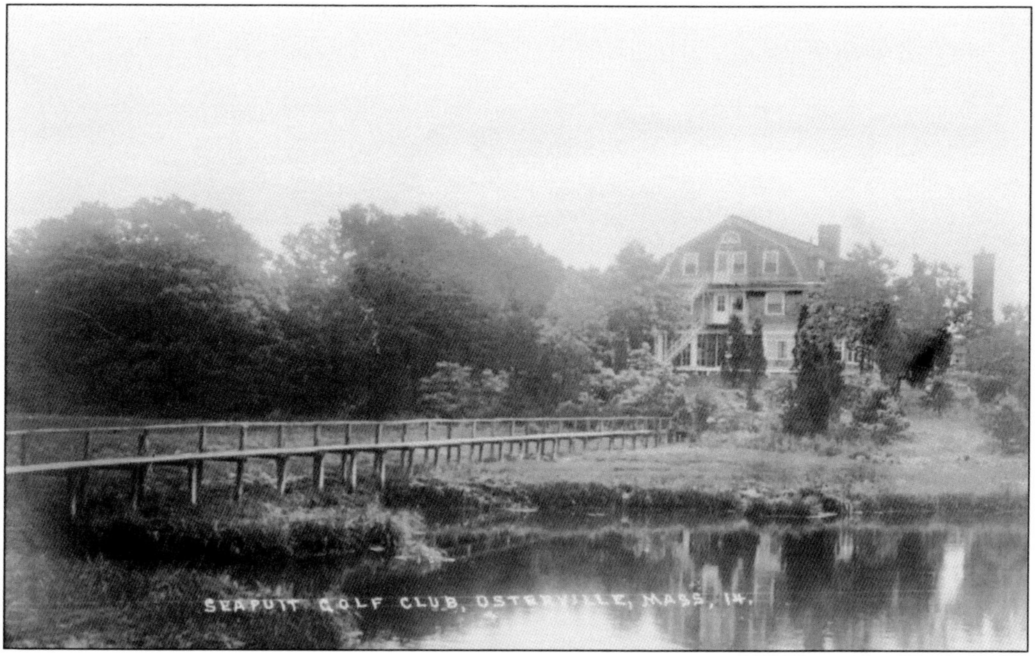

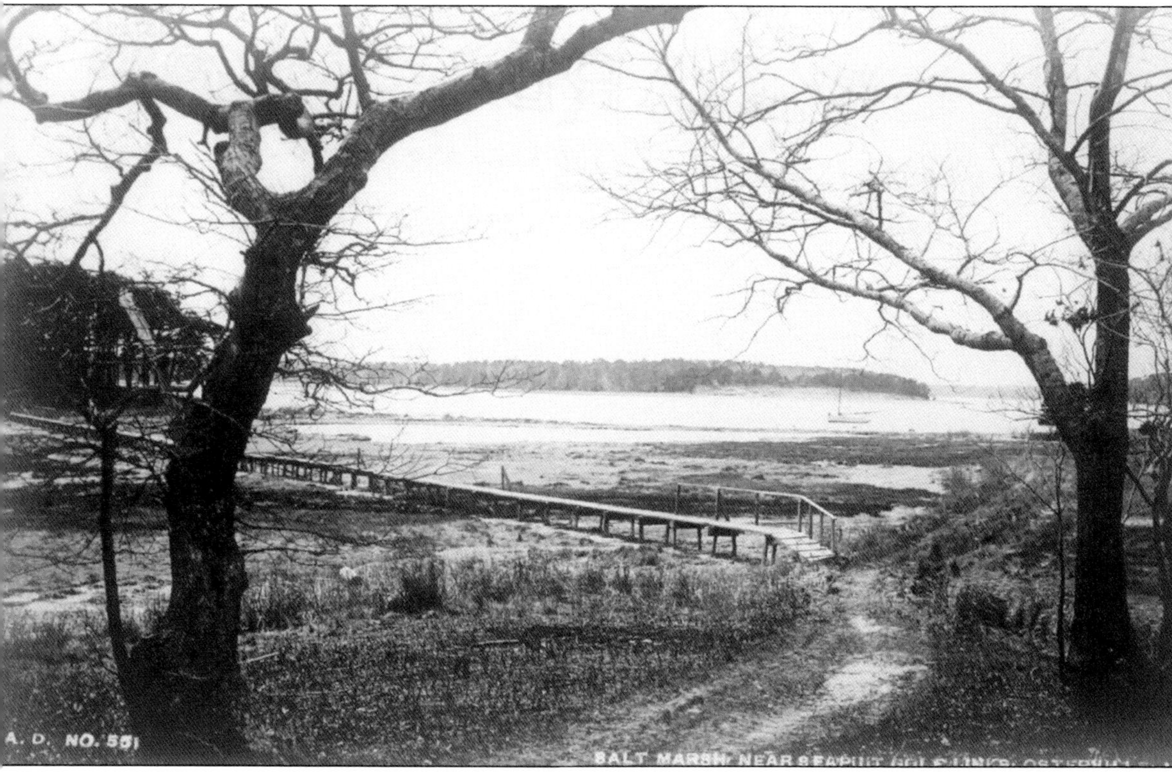

This is a beautiful view of the boardwalk crossing over the salt marshes at Seapuit. On the ninth green was the "Head House," where golfers could sit on the porch to watch the final play and register their scores. There were also locker rooms for both men and women. The course went through several cranberry bogs, and the property also contained a working farm that had horses and chickens.

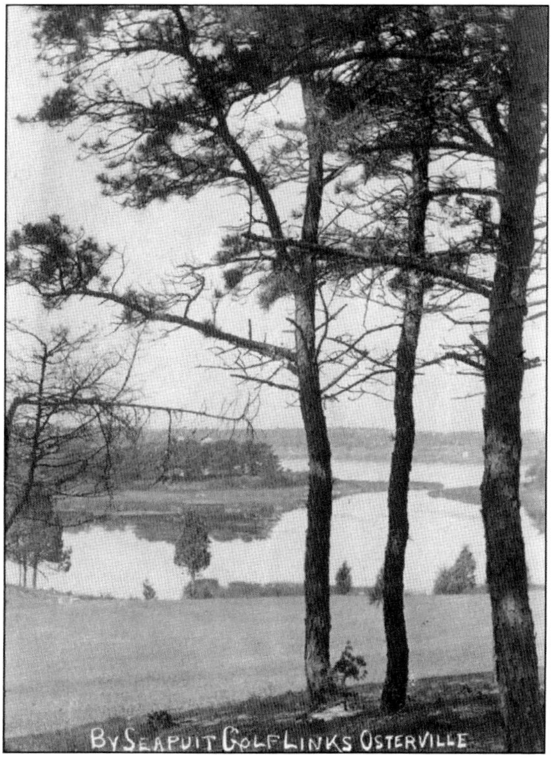

Here is another spectacular view of the golf links at Seapuit. The postcard below was mailed on October 20, 1906, from Osterville, and the sender states, "It was near here we made our best haul quahoging. Cedar tree near golf links. Love, Matthew." On the turn at the end of the third hole, golfers could have a raw oyster or two courtesy of the Hinckley oyster shanty.

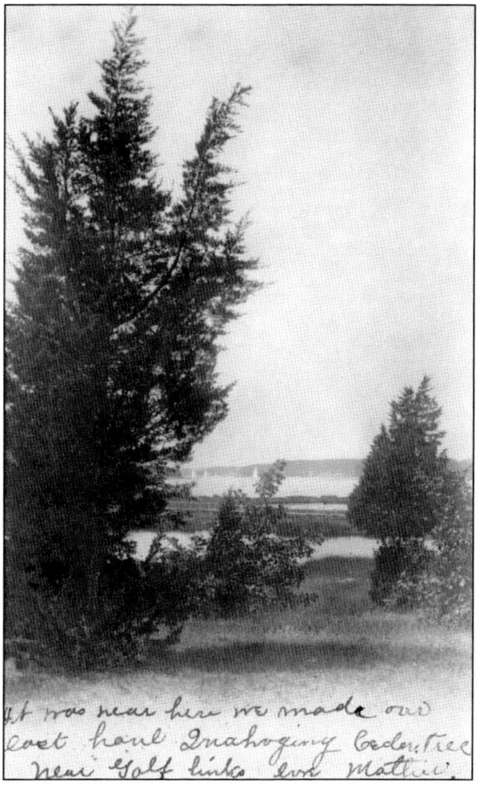

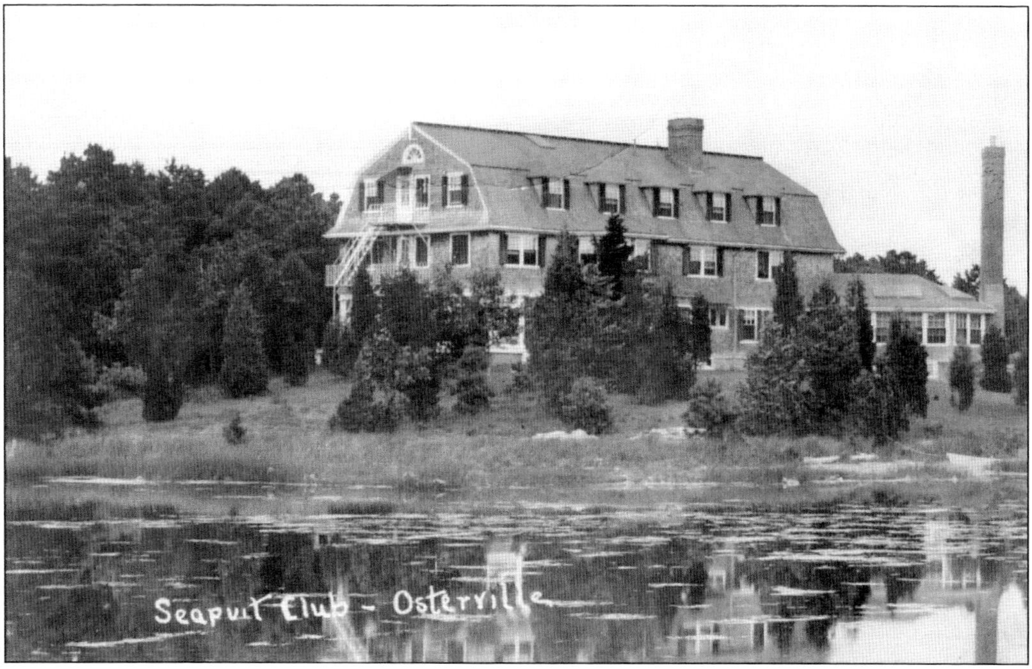

"The golf here is pretty grand for a winter course," declared the sender of the card above in 1913. The postcard below, sent in August 1910 to a Crow Point resident in Hingham, Massachusetts, reads: "Dear Pat, Deep class here. The water is darn warm. I had a puncture last night and I was alone. Will be home Friday. Paul."

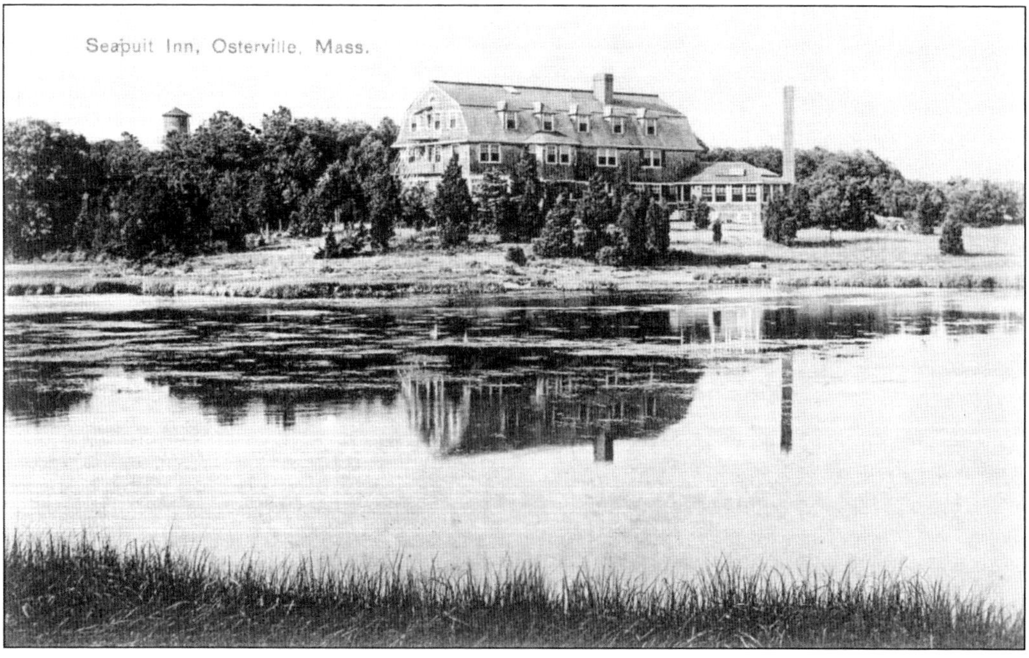

Nine

The Crosby Boatyards and Boats by the Sea

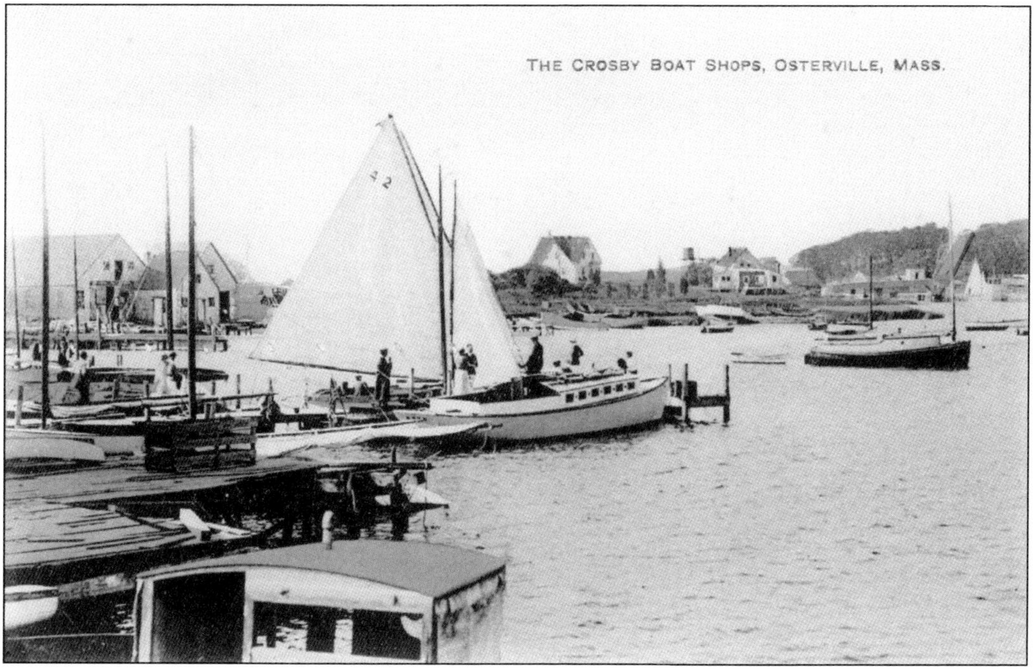

Here is a view of the Crosby boat shops looking southwest toward the entrance to West Bay. Who would have imaged the Crosby legacy of boatbuilding when in 1798 the first two Crosby brothers leased land on North Bay? Their craft was passed down from uncle to nephew and grandfather to grandson. There was an oral tradition of art and skill handed down through the generations by family members who knew these Cape Cod waters and were a part of the fabric of the village. Today, in Osterville, eighth-generation Crosby boatbuilders are actively practicing their craft. The Crosbys remain America's oldest currently active wooden boatbuilding family.

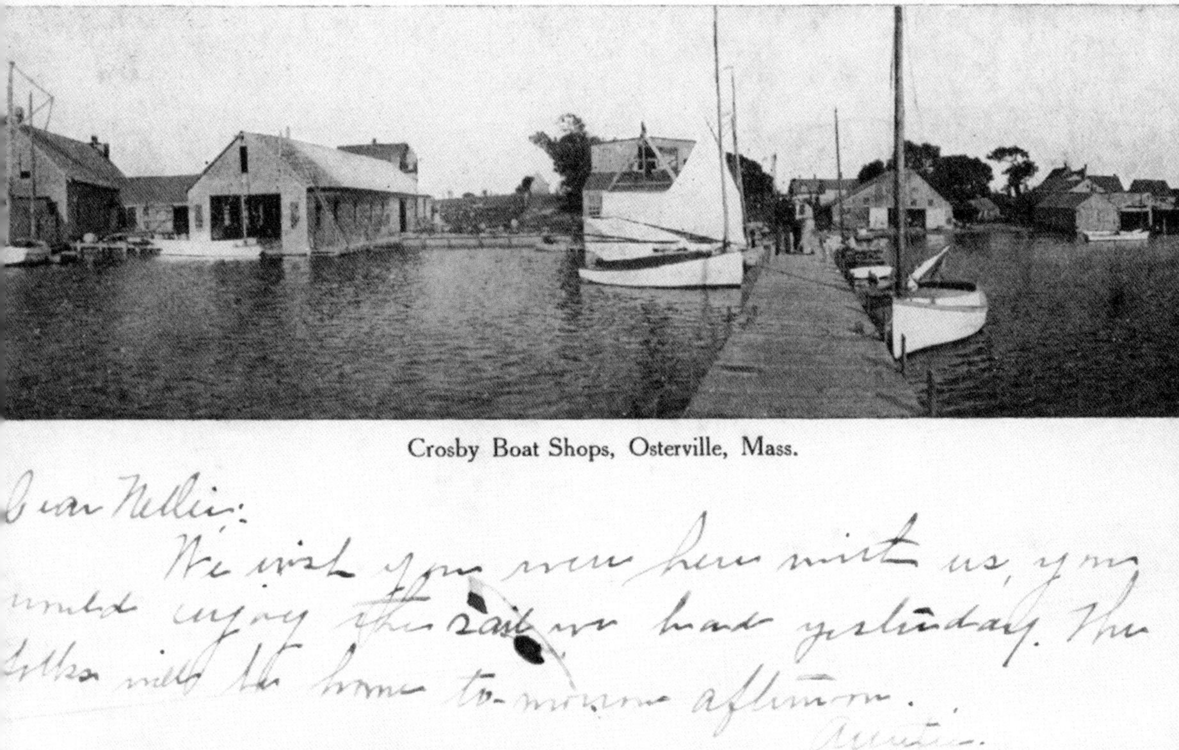

A view from the end of a dock looks back toward land and the Crosby boat shops. The dock is lined with catboats, including one on the left with its sail raised. The smallest of the catboats—the beetle cat—is still used today at the Wianno Yacht Club to teach kids to sail in its junior sailing program.

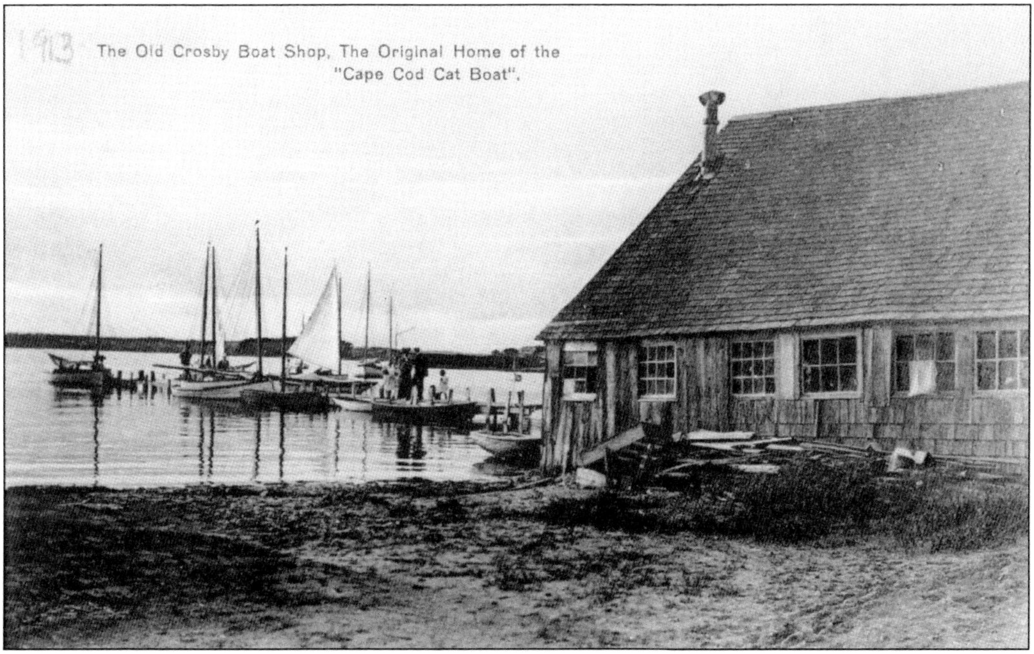

"The Original Home of the Cape Cod Catboat" (above) and "Launching a Power Boat" (below) proclaim these postcards regarding the Crosby boat shops. The card below was postmarked August 1, 1909. The three pictures show a newly constructed boat emerging from the boat shop, sliding down the ramp, and entering the water. Finally, it is shown at the dock where the final part of the building and outfitting process will take place. In the early 1900s, power motors began to be added to some boats.

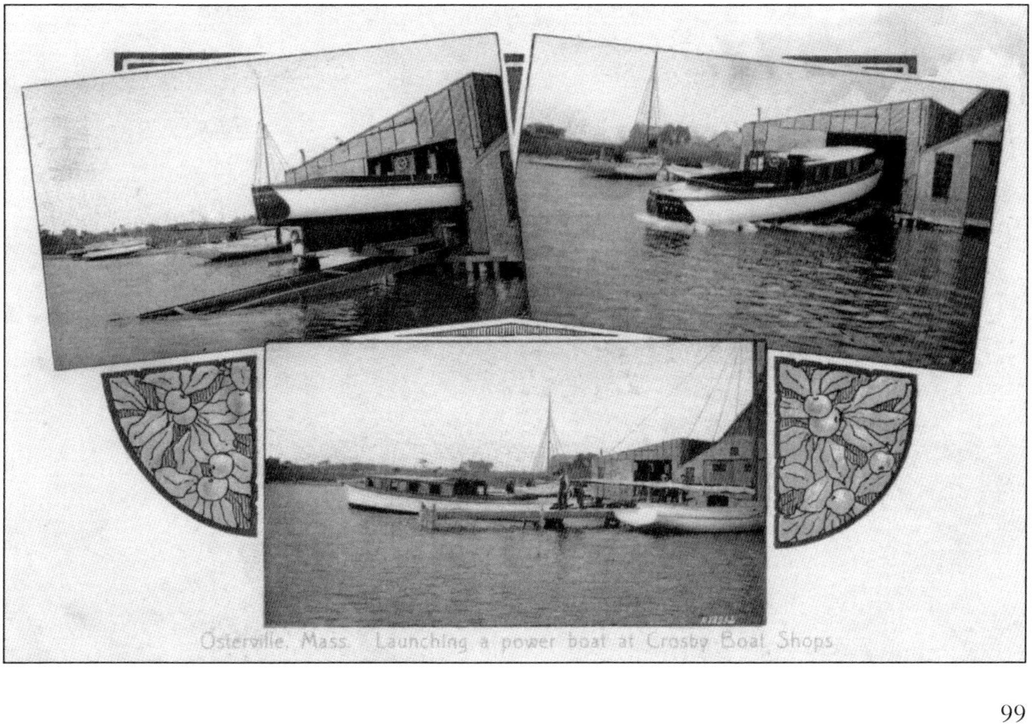

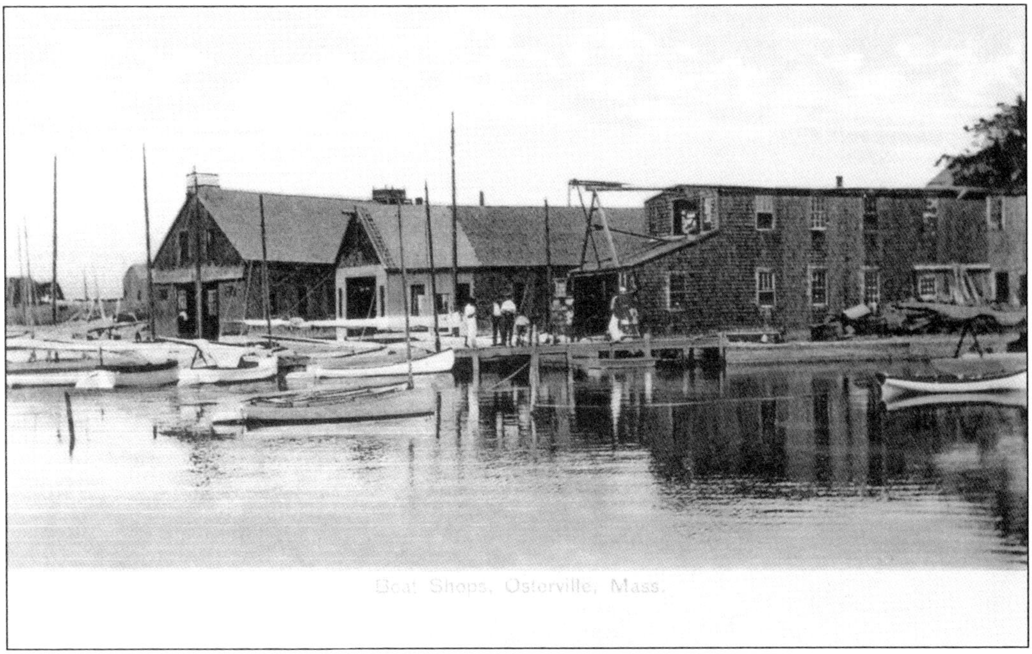

In July 1907, the sender of the postcard above wrote, "Forget all your trouble. I forget mine for two weeks. Am having a good time but I sleep too late in the morning." The postcard below, sent to Mansfiled, Massachusetts, on July 27, 1908, reads, "Dear Mildred, This is where Grace and I are boarding this summer. Having a lovely time. I thank you very much for your invitation which I cannot accept. When we come home we will see you and tell you about our summer here. Fine bathing here, but it is very countrified here. Will write soon and tell you all about it. Lots of love from East Bay Lodge, Osterville."

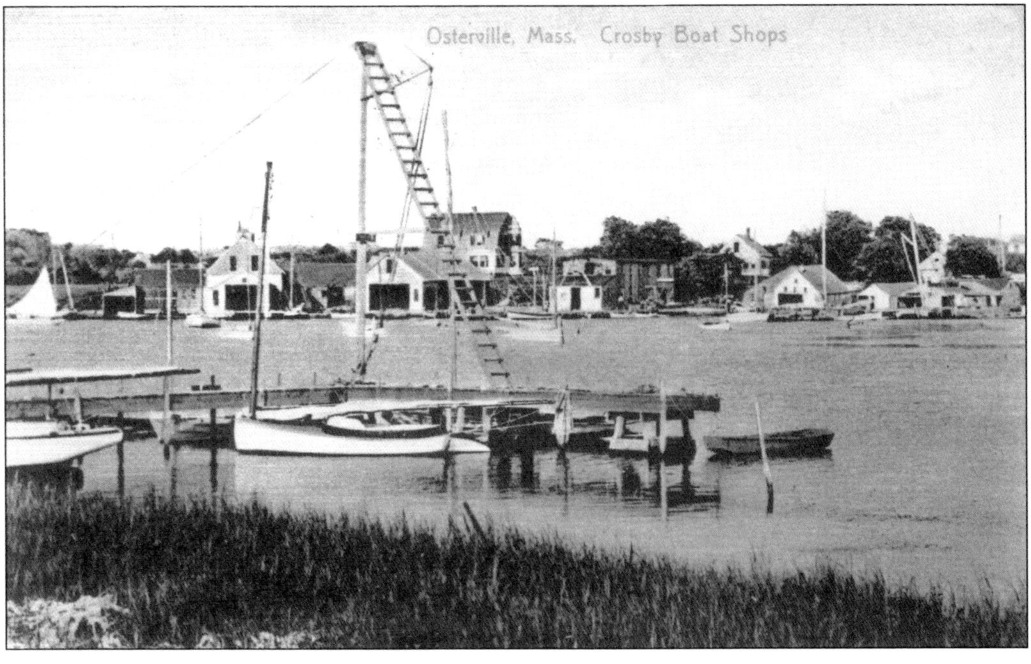

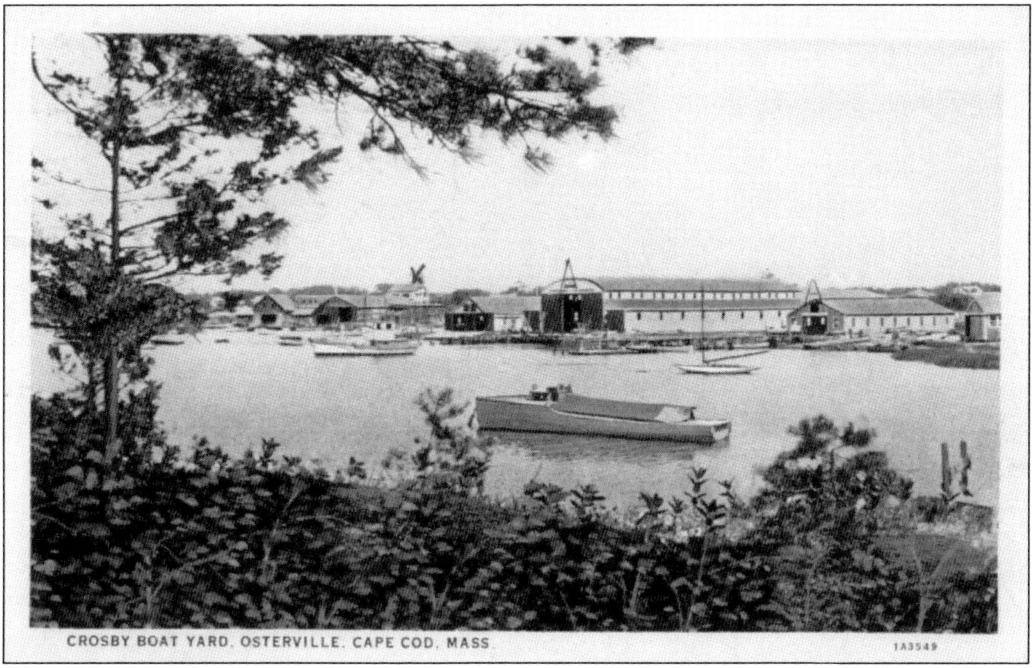

Looking northeast from the entrance to West Bay, the Crosby boat shops line the eastern shore. As time has passed, the boat shops have become more numerous and grown significantly in size. The port side of a boat is visible in the postcard above, reflecting the impact of the tide on a boat sitting at its mooring, and the stern of a boat is visible in the foreground of the postcard below. The largest boat shed, in the center, belonged to Crosby Yacht Yard. This storage shed burned in a December 2003 fire that destroyed 113 wooden boats, 21 of them Wianno Seniors. No lives were lost in the inferno, and the wooden shed was rebuilt and replaced by sheet metal.

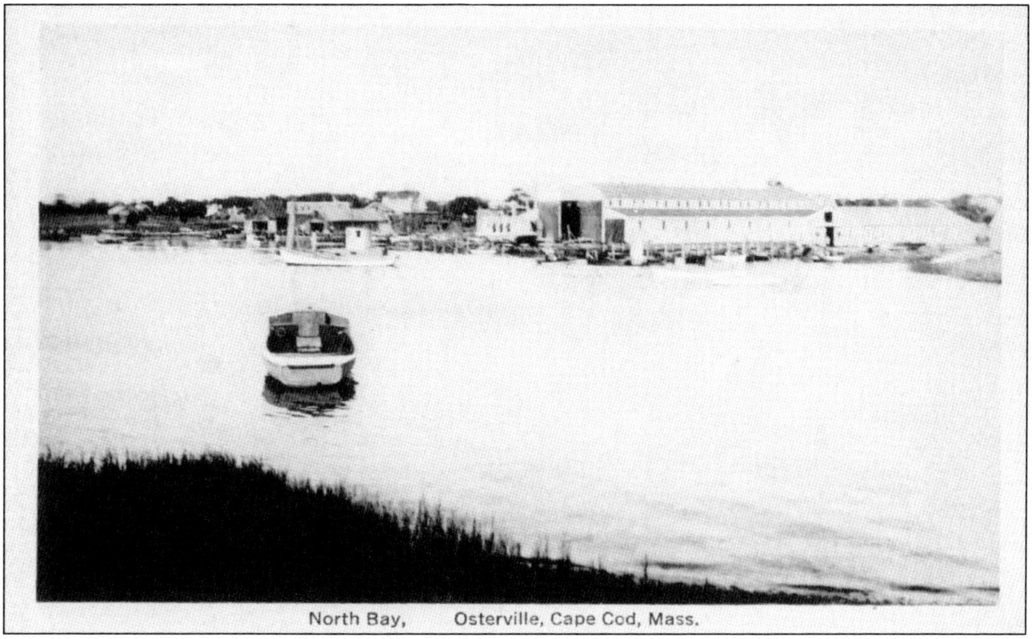

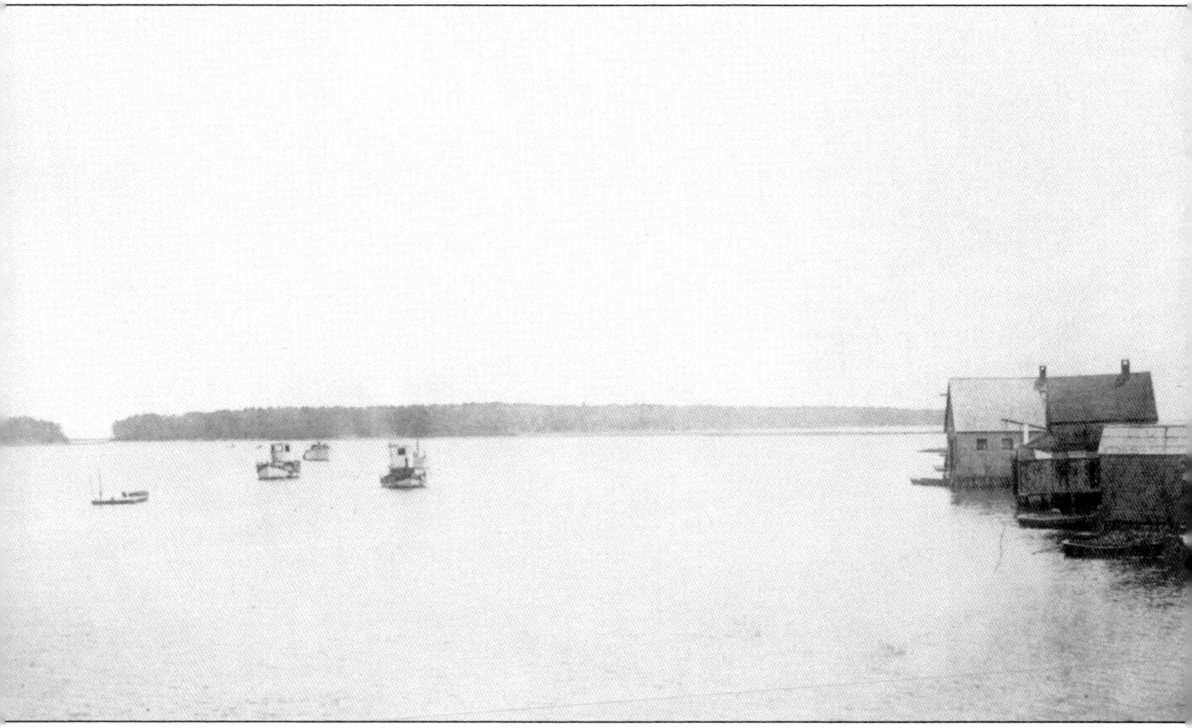

The tranquil waters of West Bay are home to several boats in this card postmarked September 6, 1919. A row of oyster shanties can be seen on the right, while Eel River can be seen in the distance on the left. The sender of this postcard headed to New Bedford, Massachusetts, laments, "They say, 'Silence is golden.' I guess you believe that."

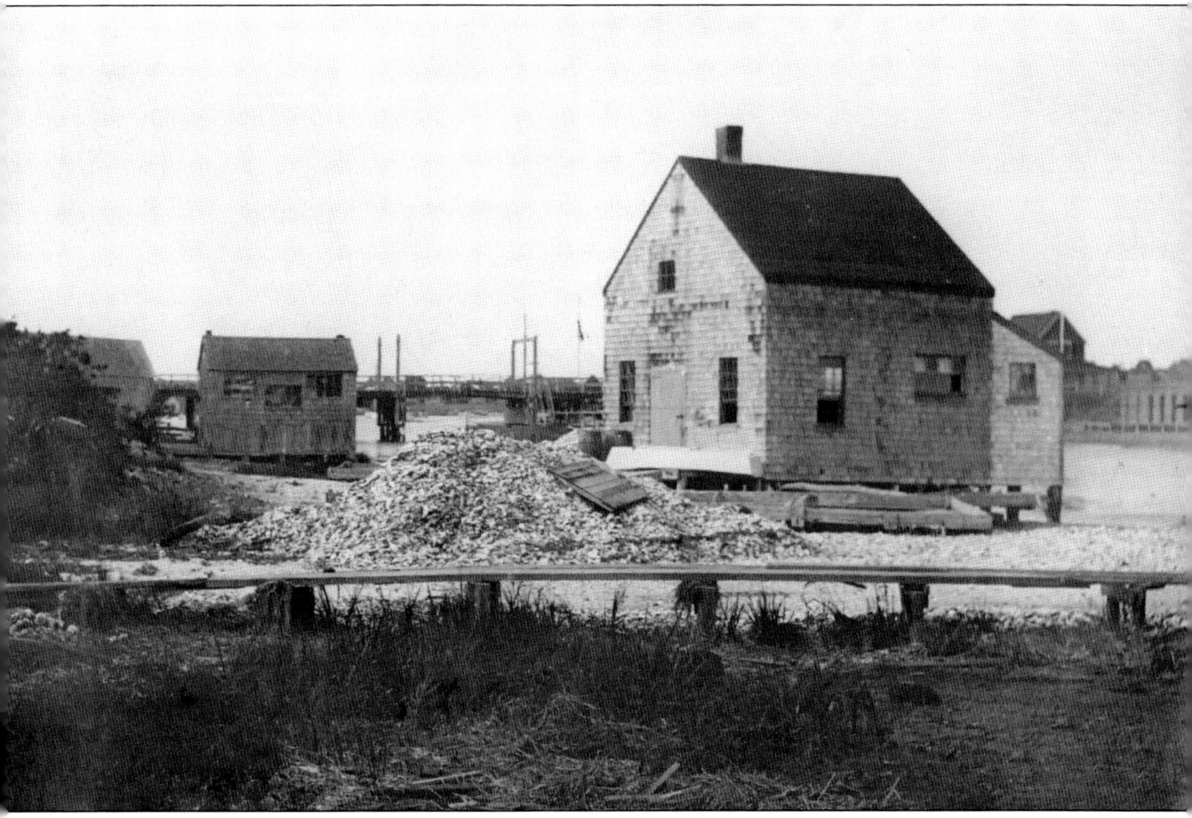

Joseph C. Crosby's oyster shanty is shown with thousands of shells amassed on the shore. Oyster shanties belonging to members of the Lewis, Tallman, and Hinckley families, among others, dotted the bays around Osterville. The famous Cotuit oysters were packed in barrels and sold at market. Crosby was also owner of a boat named *Hooker*, which brought guests from the West Bay Inn dock to the bathing beaches.

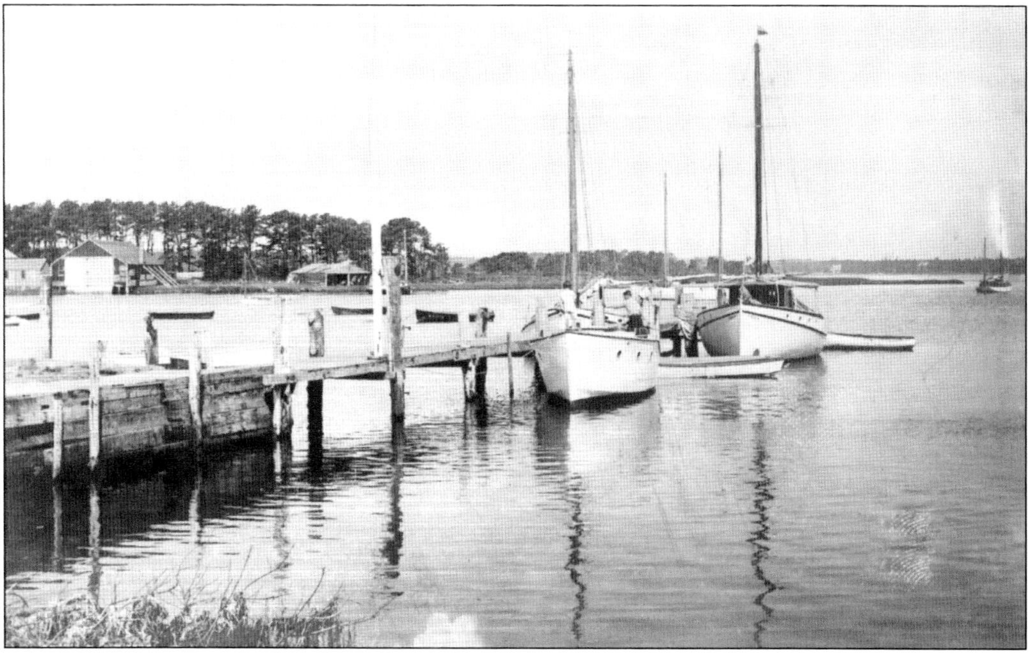

This is a view up North Bay from Crosbytown. The storage sheds on Little Island have been replaced. Until the advent of the West Bay Cut, boats had to take a longer path around Cotuit Bay to enter West Bay. A number of boats would dock in East Bay for ease of access.

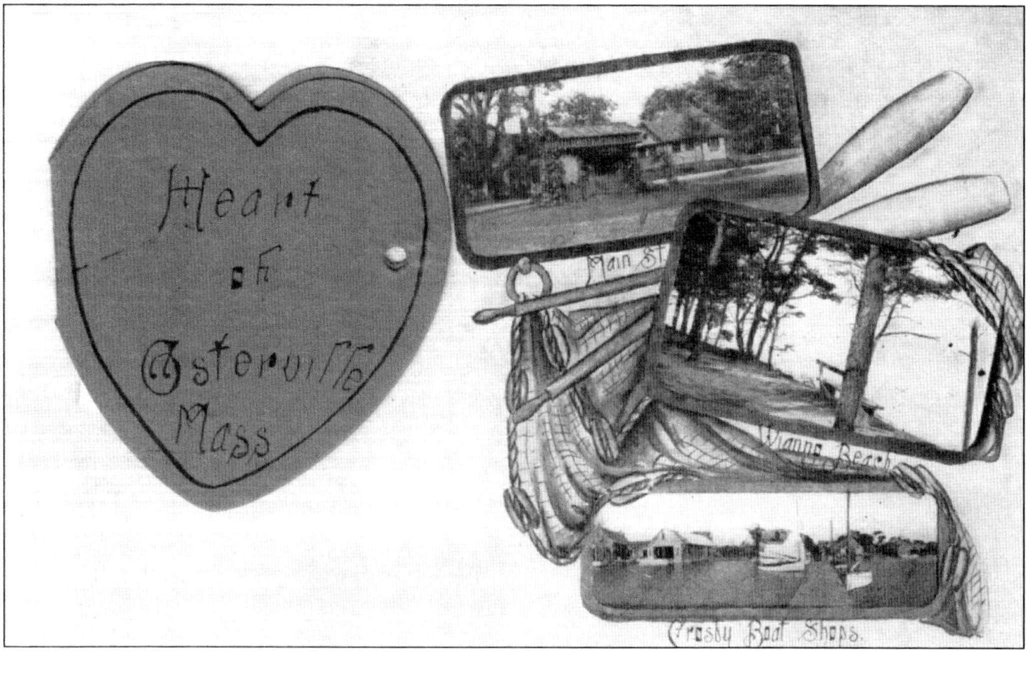

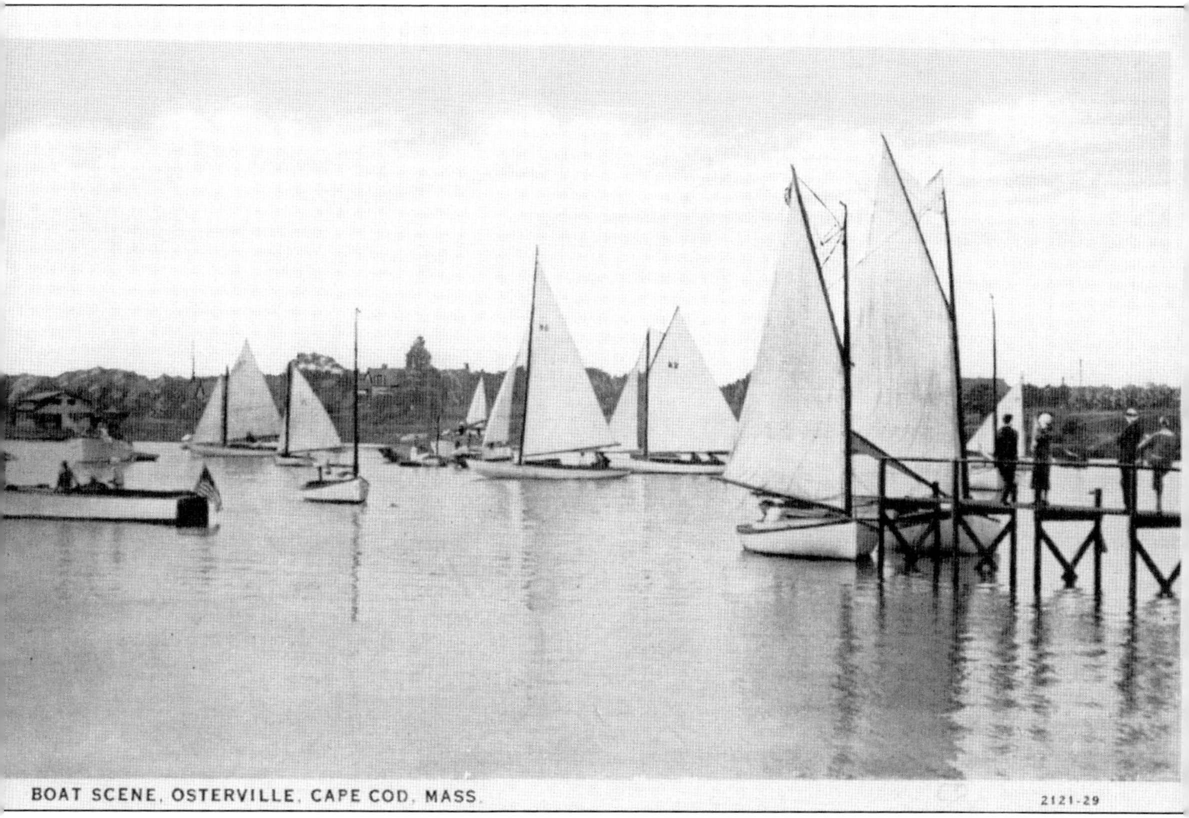

This card depicts catboats at the East Bay dock and at sail. The catboats can be identified by their single sail and mast placed near the boat's bow. At center, in the distance, is a Wianno Senior at sail, easily identified by the sleek design of its hull and its jib sail in front of the mast. Horace Manley Crosby designed the Wianno Seniors, which first set sail in 1914. The gaff-rigged sloop is 25 feet long. They were the first one-design class of racing boats and can still be seen sailing the waters around Osterville and worldwide. The year 2014 marks the centennial celebration of the Wianno Seniors.

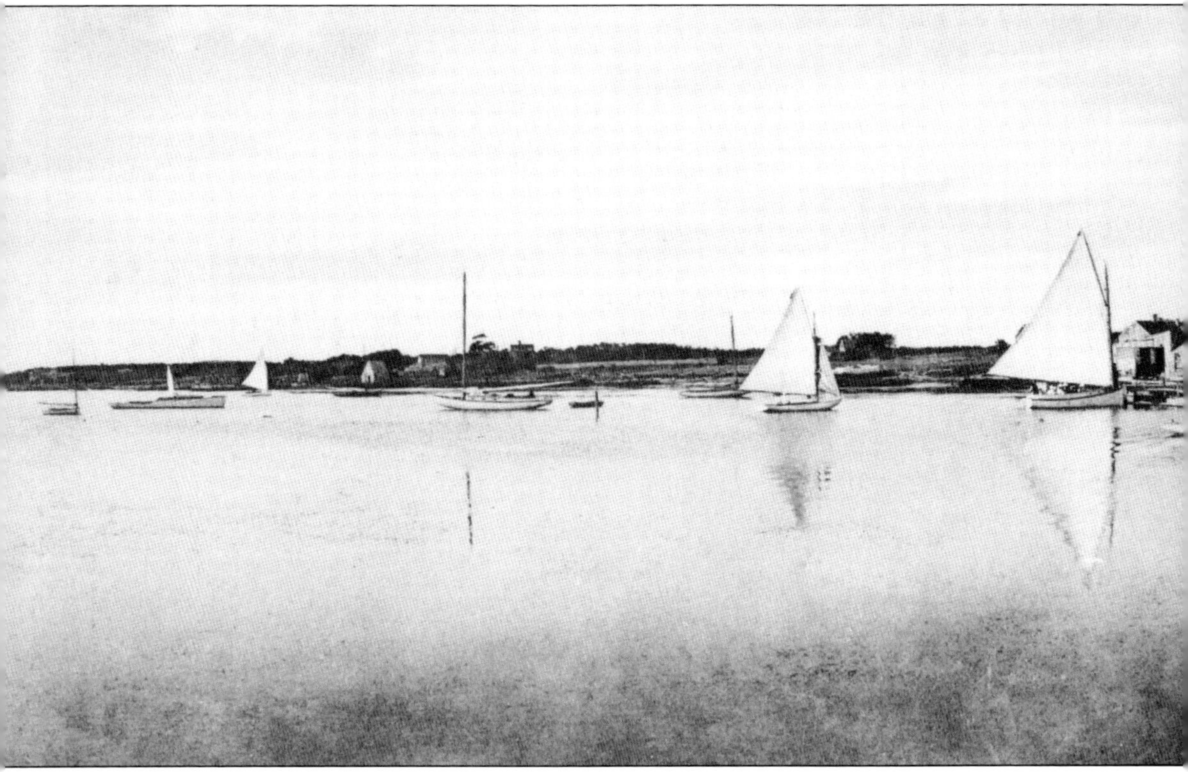

Here is a c. 1908 view of the Crosby boat shops, seen on the right in inner West Bay, with boats sailing the calm waters. One of those shops is the Herbert F. Crosby boat shop. In the July 1928 issue of *Motor Boating: The Yachtsman's Magazine*, Herbert F. Crosby, the oldest Crosby builder at the time, was interviewed in his boat shop. The following was taken from the interview: "'That's my little cruiser,' he says pointing at a small motor boat at the pier between a big white and mahogany cat of 1927 and a small gray cat of 1897. 'Every year, I have been taking

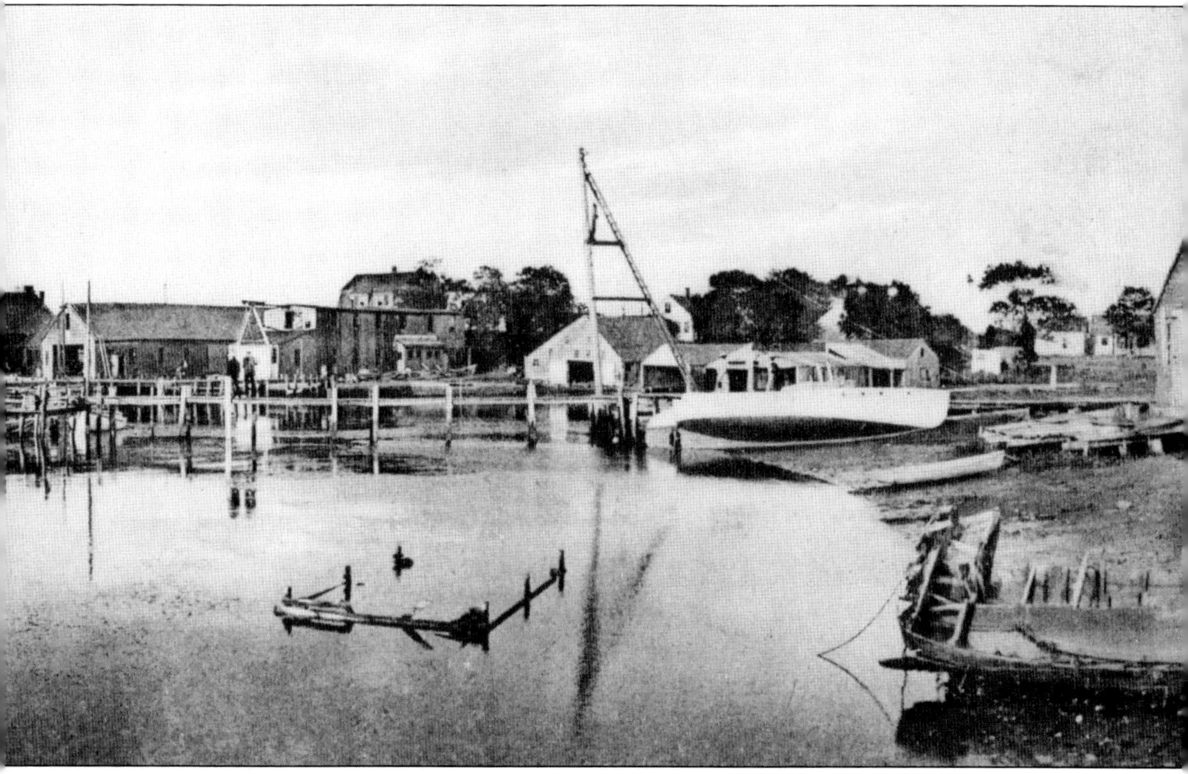

the last two weeks in August for a little cruise just over to the Vineyard.'" At one point, his grandchildren interrupt the interview by bringing in a pail of freshly harvested oysters for "Grandpa Crosby." In 1983, the Herbert F. Crosby boat shop, complete with original tools, rocking chair, and wood stove, was generously donated by Bill Koch (of America's Cup fame) and was moved to the grounds of the Osterville Historical Museum. Koch's Nauticus Marina is now in its original location.

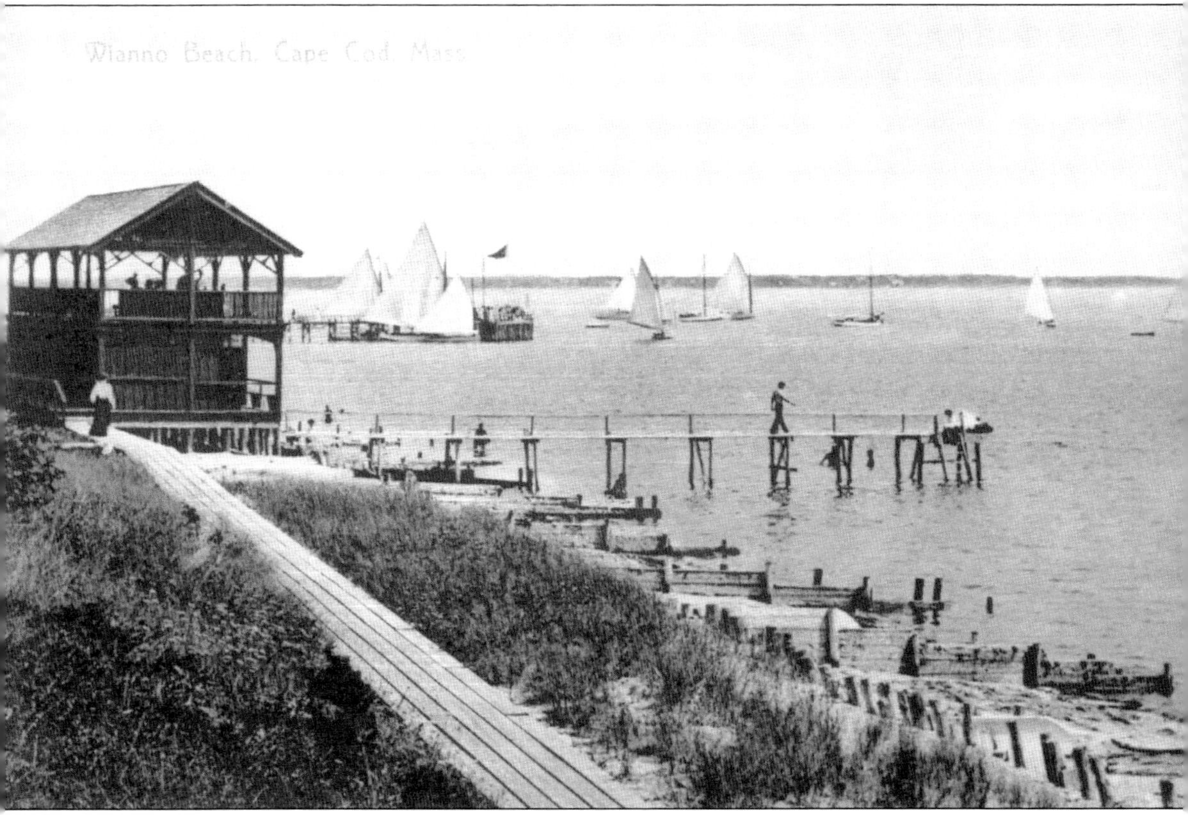

Seniors are seen at sail along Nantucket Sound with the bathing beach pavilion in the foreground. In total, over 200 Wianno Seniors have been built. The Wianno Seniors with hull numbers up to 173 were wooden. Later numbers indicate fiberglass, or "glass," boats. The first 14 boats to sail that first season in the summer of 1914 were, in order, *Fiddler, Wendy, Telemark, A.P.H., Commy, Snookums, Patsy, Sea Dog, Marie, Qui Vive, Fantasy, Whistle Wing, Maxixe*, and *Ethyl*.

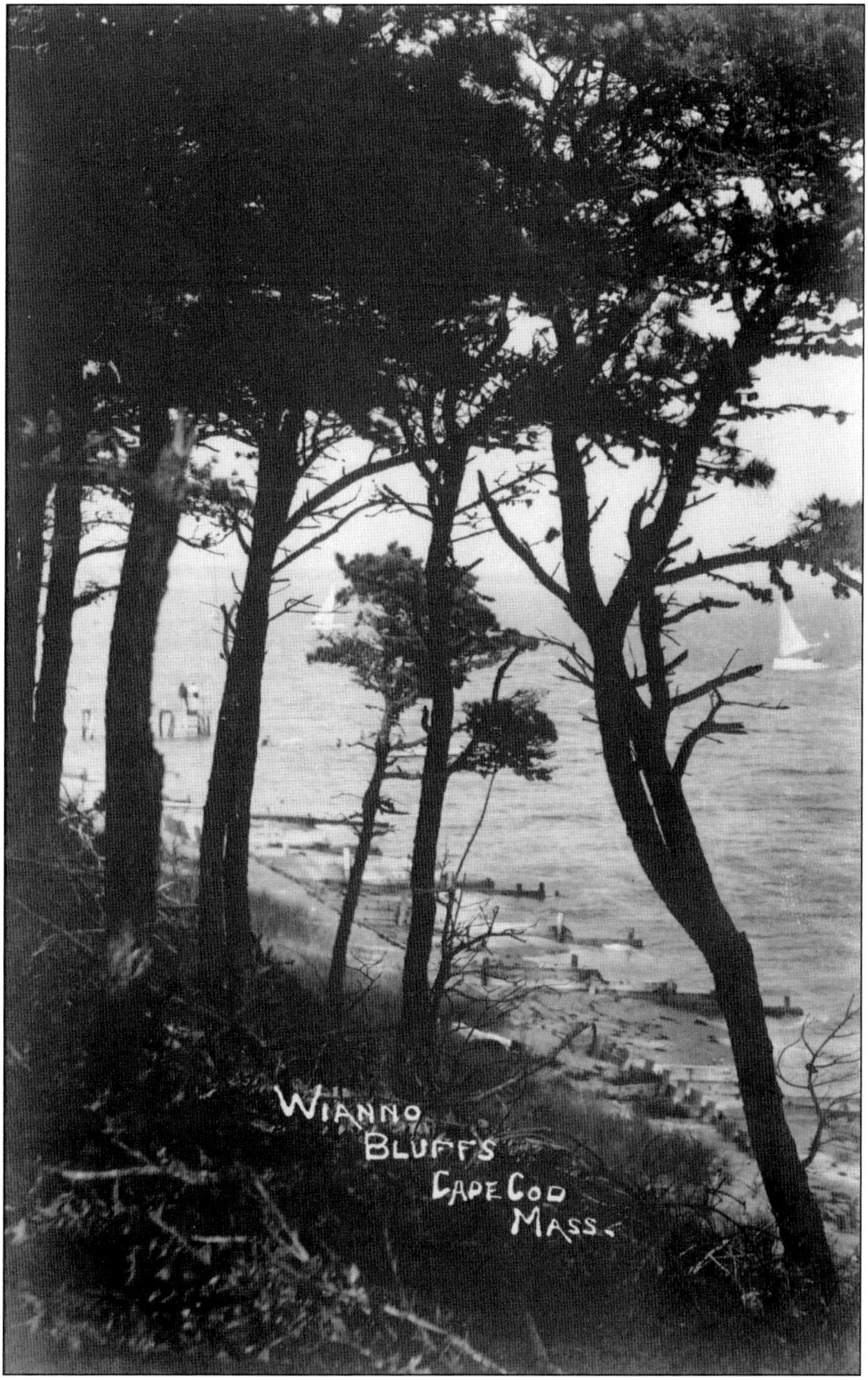

Peering through the trees at the grove on the Wianno Bluffs, a single catboat sails through the sound. In 1852, the first Crosby catboat, built by brothers C. Worthington and Hoarace S. Crosby, was the *Little Eva*, named after a character in *Uncle Tom's Cabin*, published in 1852, and holding true to form, Crosby catboats remain about half as wide as they are long. This makes them very stable at sea.

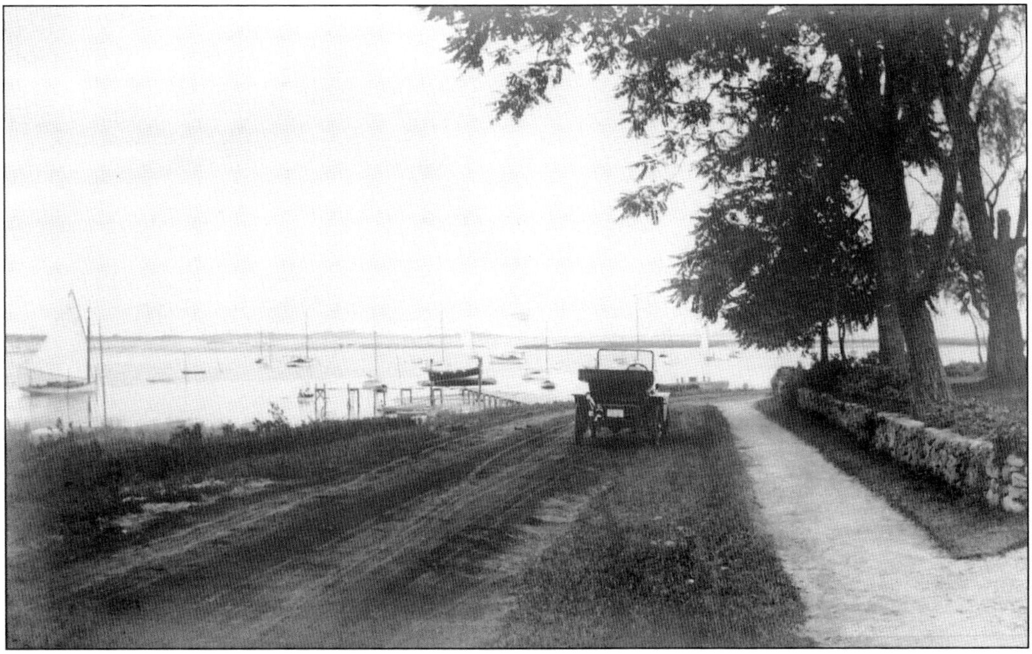

The car, pictured above, is heading southeast on East Bay Road with East Bay just beyond. Hyannis Port is visible on the left. In the distance, on the right, is what would later become Dowses Beach, one of the town of Barnstable's public beaches. Below, in the distance, are the mansions lining Main Street as it heads towards Centerville.

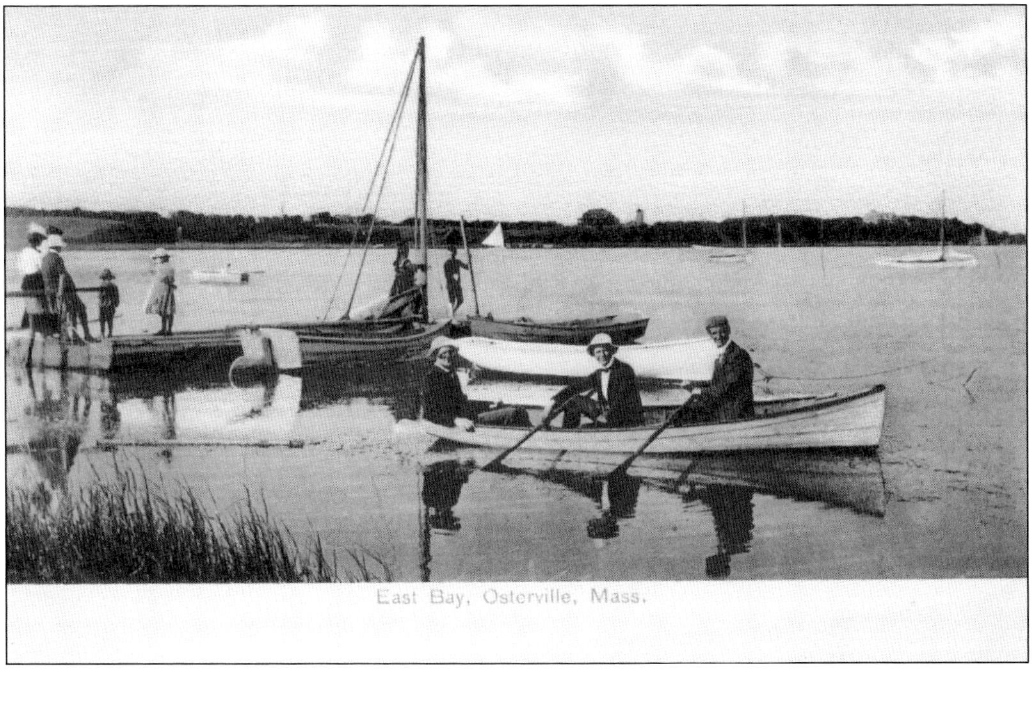

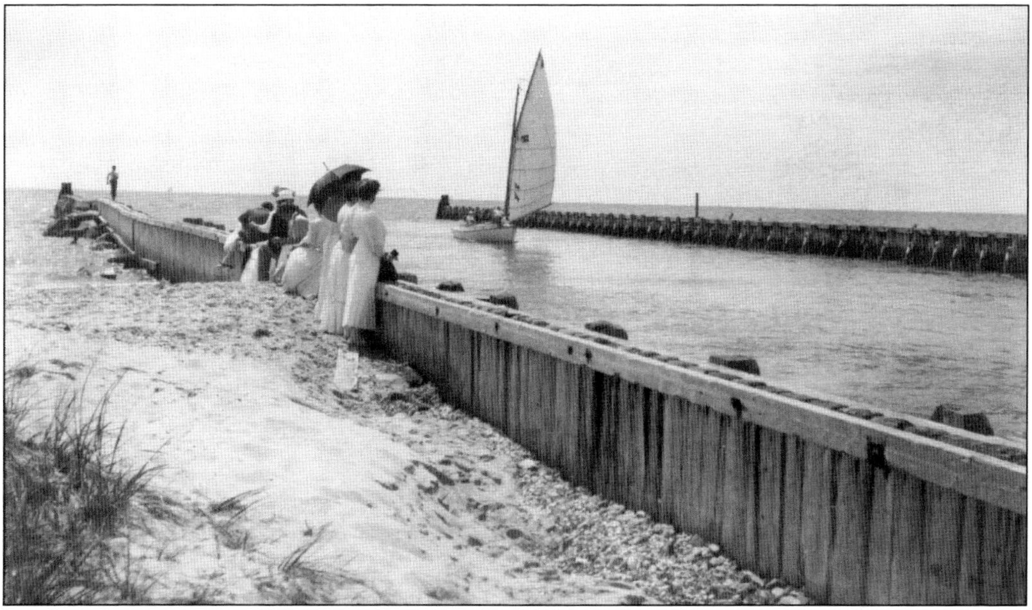

Pictured above is the cut, which was constructed to provide access to Nantucket Sound from West Bay. This is the view from the western end of Seaview Avenue looking south toward Nantucket Sound. Sampson's Island is on the far side of the cut. There are long jetties of rocks extending out into Nantucket Sound to prevent the ocean and its storms from refilling the cut with sand. In the postcard below is the view from the southwestern side of Oyster Harbors looking out at Cotuit Bay with Sampson's Island/Dead Neck in background.

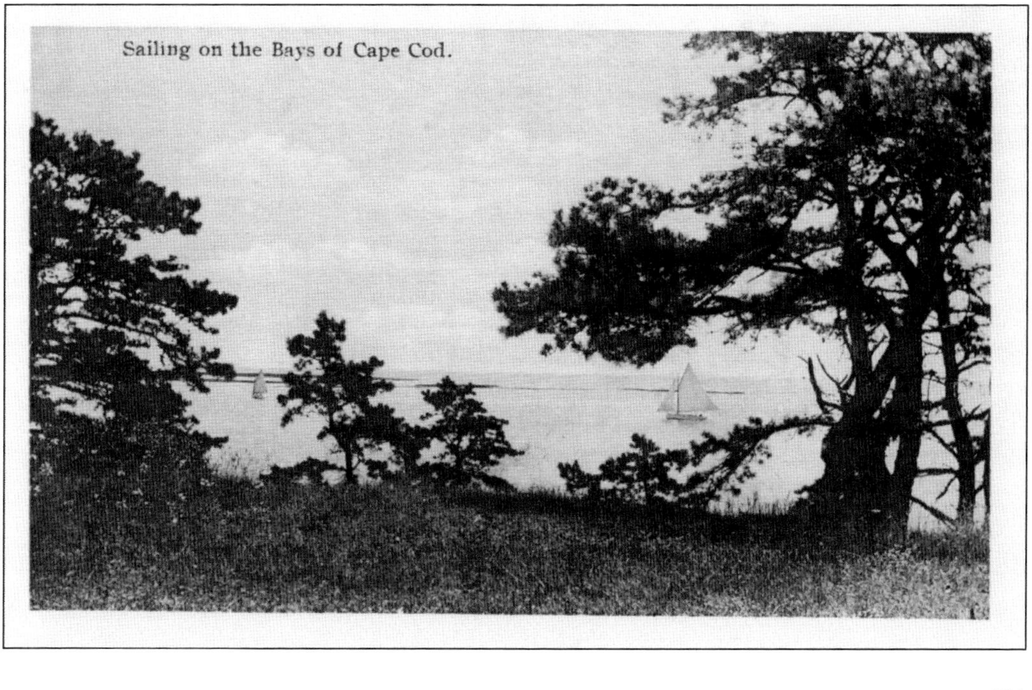

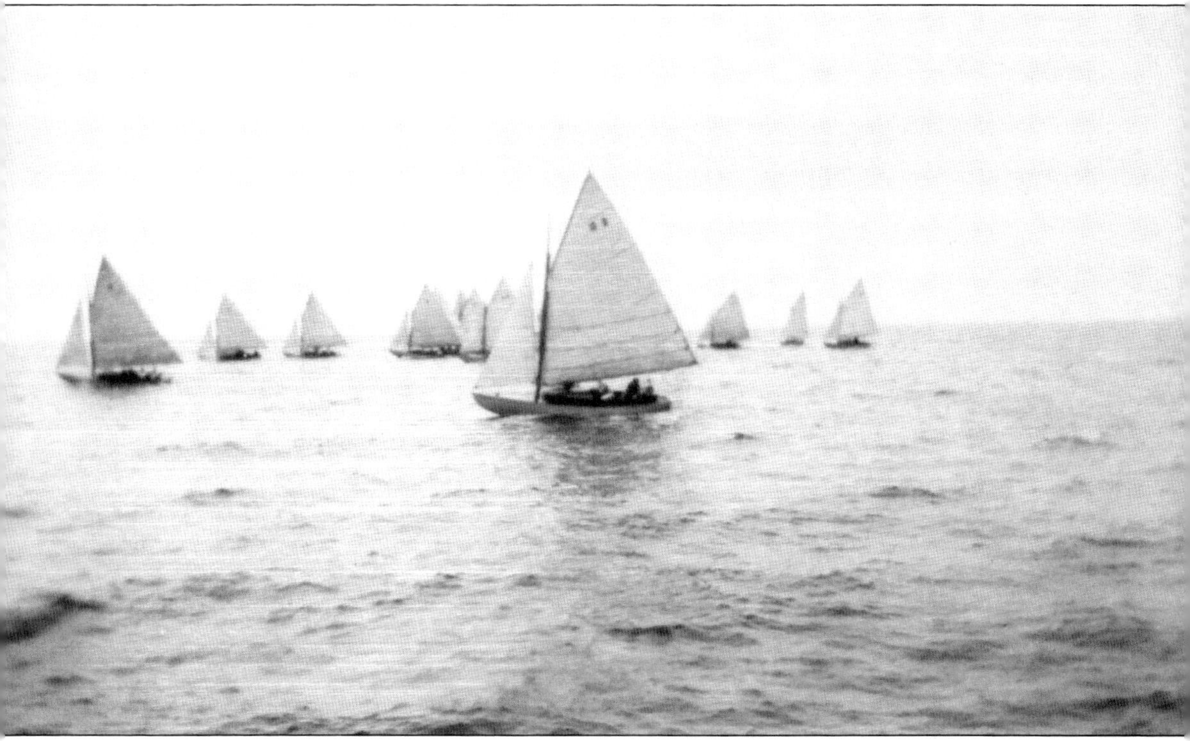

This image shows a fleet of Wianno Seniors racing on Nantucket Sound. H. Manley Crosby's one-design racing class of boats enabled sailors to have evenly matched competitions. The Wianno Seniors, with 600-pound cast-iron keels and 366 square feet of sail area, were built to deal with the choppy waters of Nantucket Sound and the 25-knot southwest winds. The last of the wooden Wianno Seniors was launched in 1976.

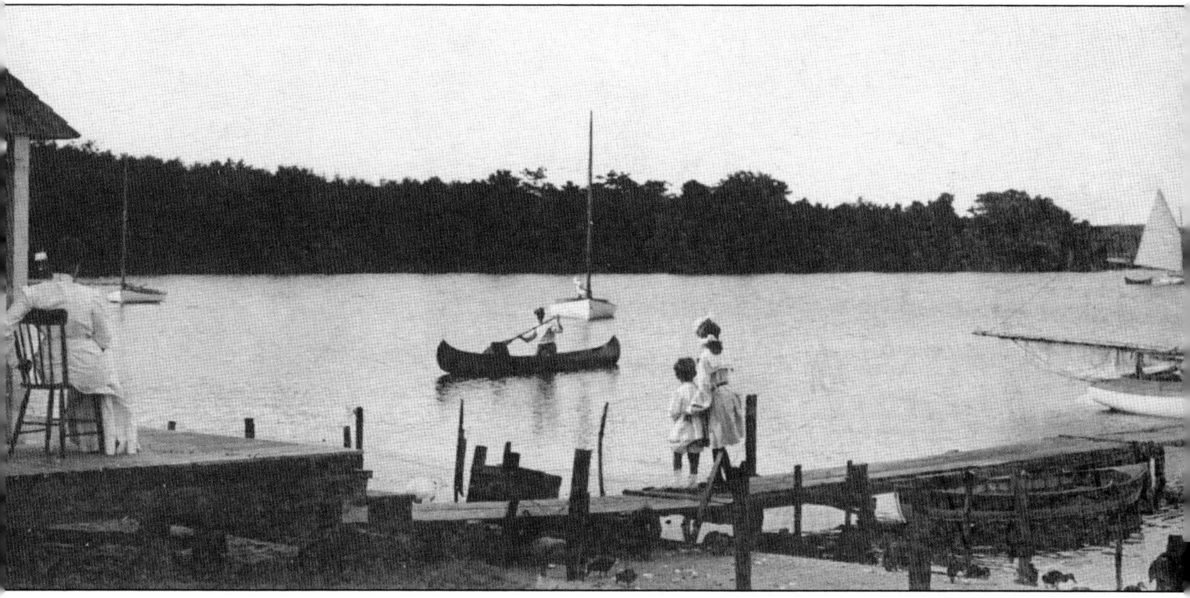

This is the view from the Oyster Harbors Beach, just below the Oyster Harbors Club, on the western side of Grand Island/Oyster Harbors. The sailboat leaving the cove will enter Cotuit Bay, which separates Oyster Harbors from Cotuit.

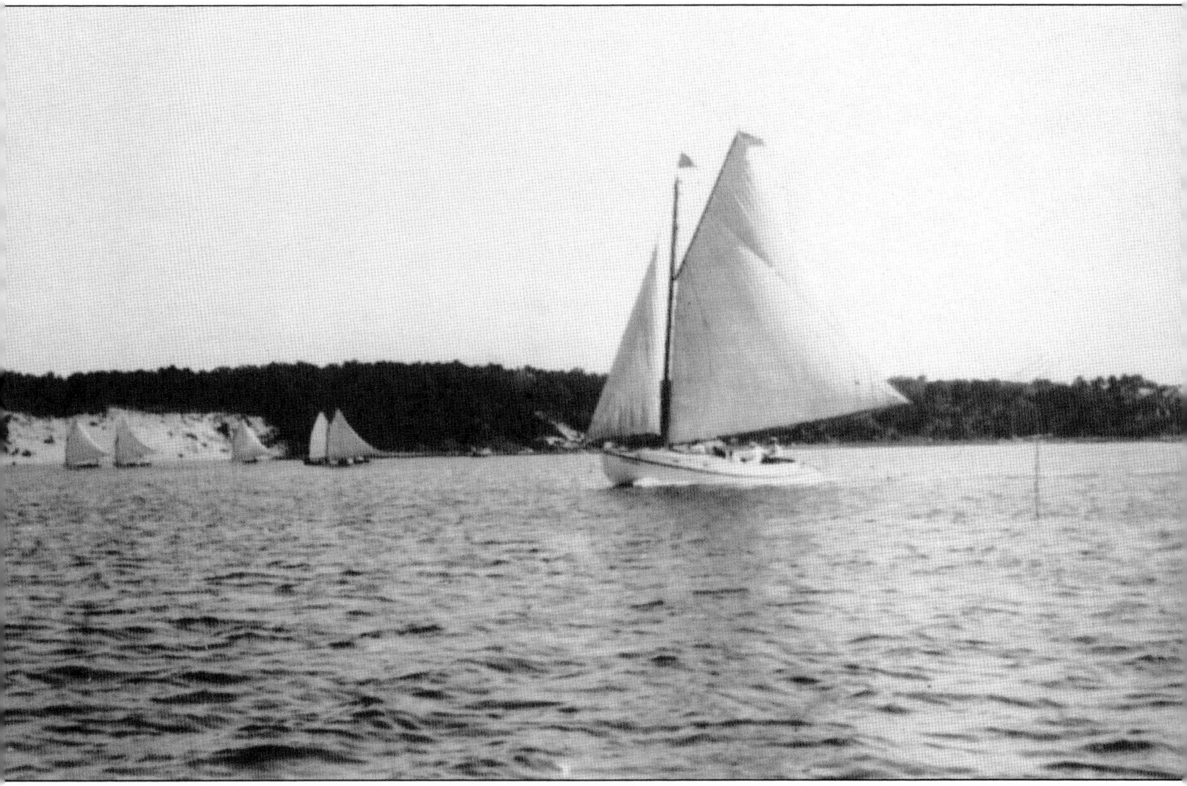

A gaff-rigged sailboat is seen sailing on North Bay. A gaff-rigging means that a boat has a four-cornered sail that is controlled at its peak and usually headed by a pole called a spar.

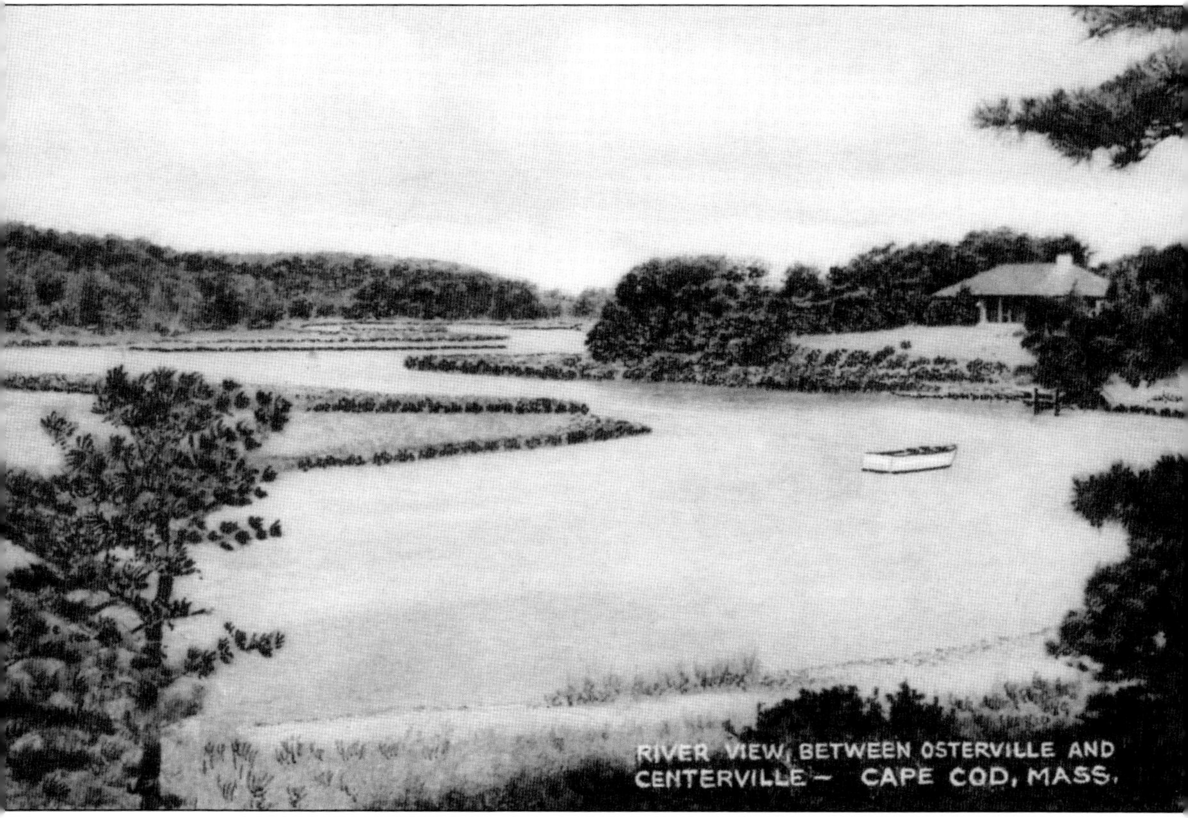

This is another view looking north of the Bumps River, which is an inlet rather than an actual river. Bumps River separates Osterville on the west and Centerville on the east. The house visible on the right is located on Cove Road in Centerville.

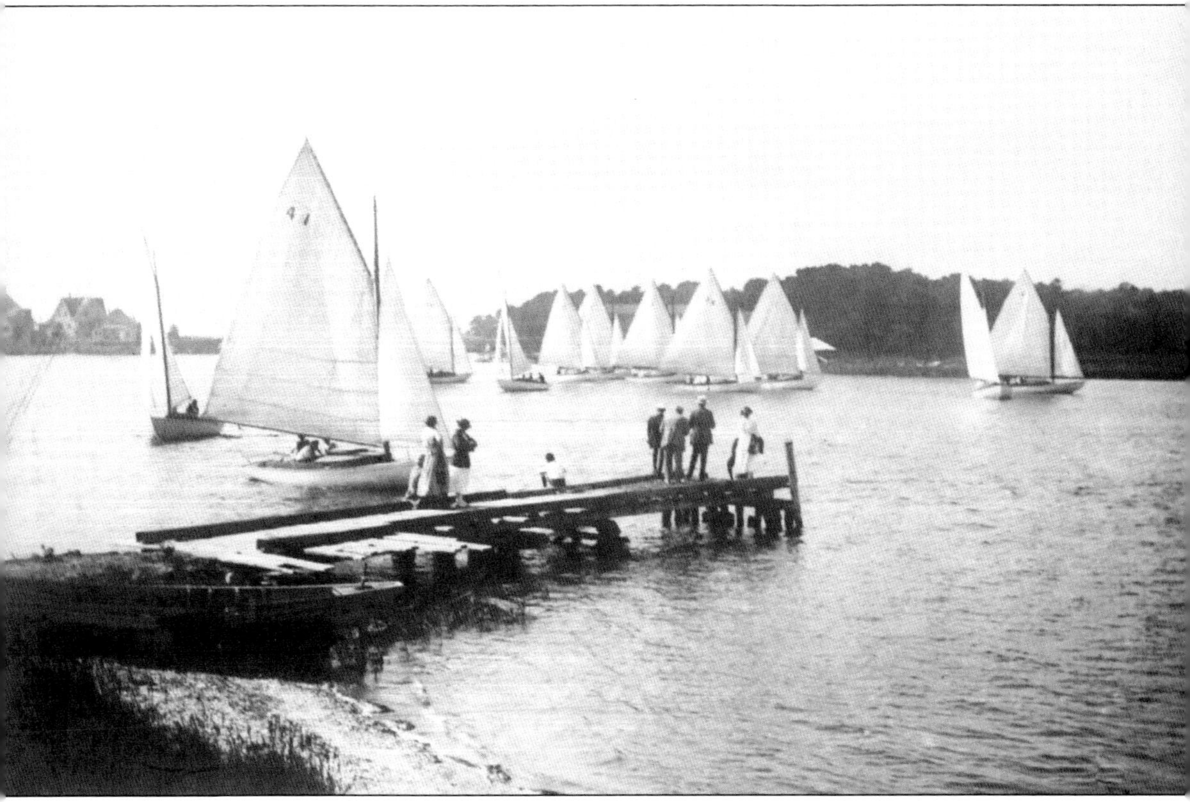

In this scene at the coal dock, patrons watch the Wianno Seniors racing in the afternoon on inner West Bay. The Crosbys are also known for building another boat called the Wianno Junior. It was not until the advent of the Wianno Junior that racing opened up to children. Prior to that time, it had been reserved for adults only. Other boats made famous by the Crosbys include the Crosby Striper and the Oyster Harbors Catboat. In 2013, Crosby Yacht Yard reintroduced the Oyster Harbors Catboat from their original design of 1937. It is billed as follows: "A Crosby catboat is an investment in the future that honors the past."

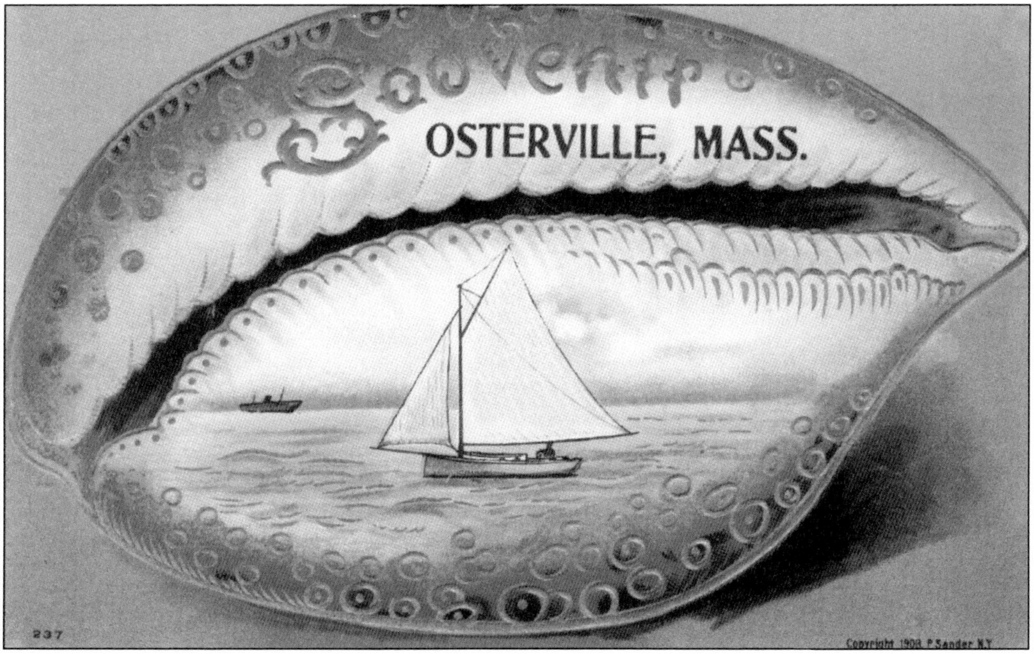

Shown above is a souvenir postcard with an artist's rendition of a sailboat drawn in a seashell. The souvenir postcard below says, "It iss Awf'ly Lone-some 'round Osterville While You Are Avay."

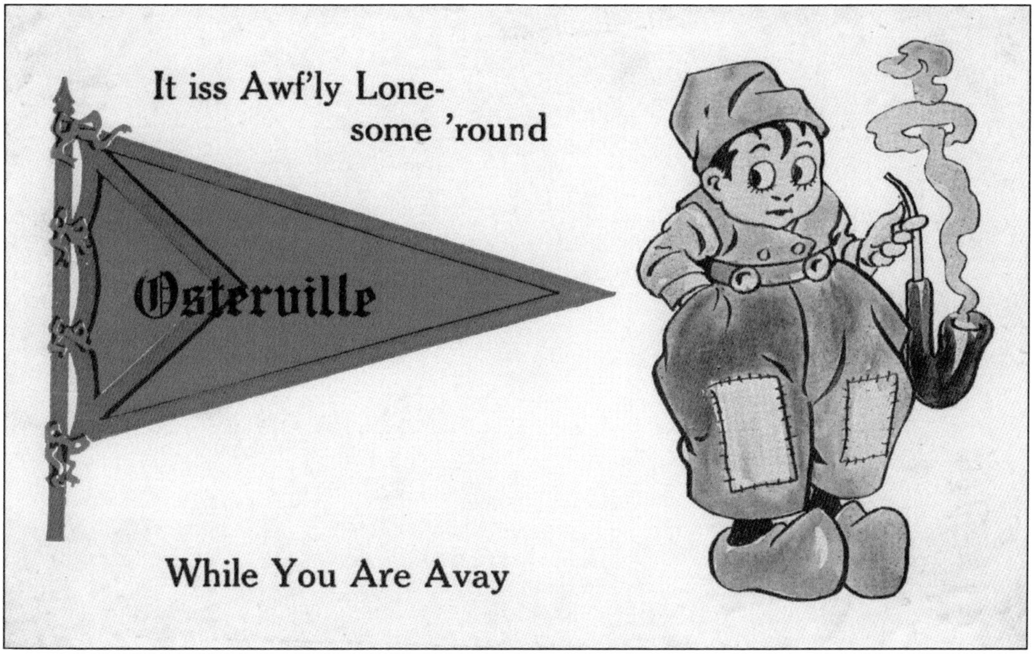

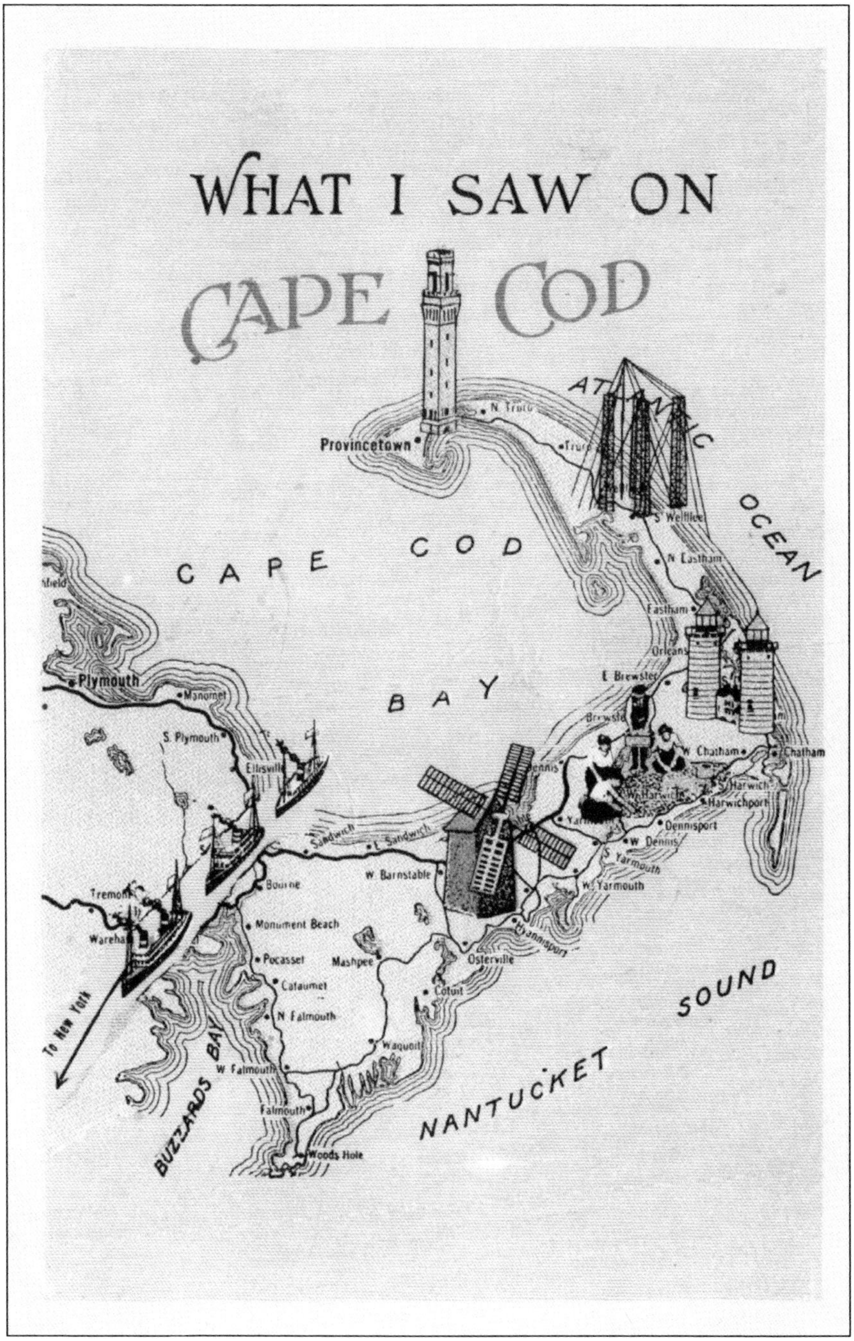

"What I Saw on Cape Cod" is another example of a souvenir postcard but points to the nautical heritage of this coastal community. In 1914, the Cape Cod Canal was made. Two automobile bridges—the Bourne Bridge and the Sagamore Bridge—connect Cape Cod to the mainland. The bridges opened in 1935. The Cape Cod Railroad bridge replaced an earlier railroad bridge and opened at the end of 1935. All three bridges were built as part of the Public Works Administration (PWA) by the US Army Corps of Engineers. (Note that those three bridges are not seen on this pre-1935 postcard.)

Ten

Homes Around Osterville

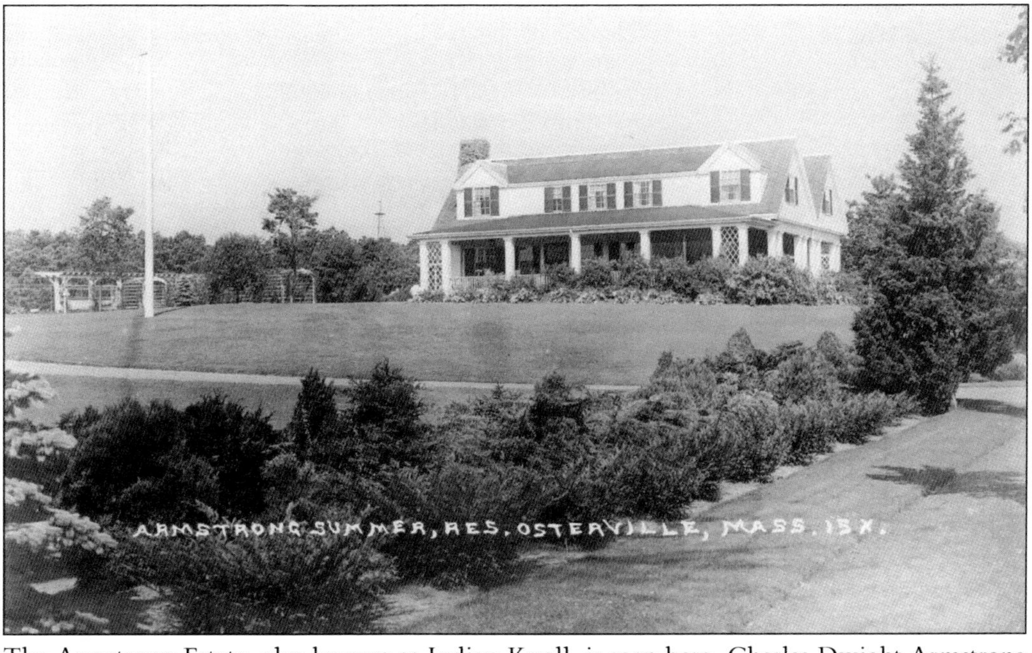

The Armstrong Estate, also known as Indian Knoll, is seen here. Charles Dwight Armstrong was president of the Armstrong Cork Company in Pittsburgh. In 1930, Armstrong donated over eight acres to establish what is now Armstrong-Kelley Park. The park was owned and operated by the members of the Cape Cod Horticultural Society, which began in 1928. To this day, Armstrong-Kelley is Cape Cod's oldest and largest privately owned park. It features 30 rare and unusual trees and over 250 rhododendrons.

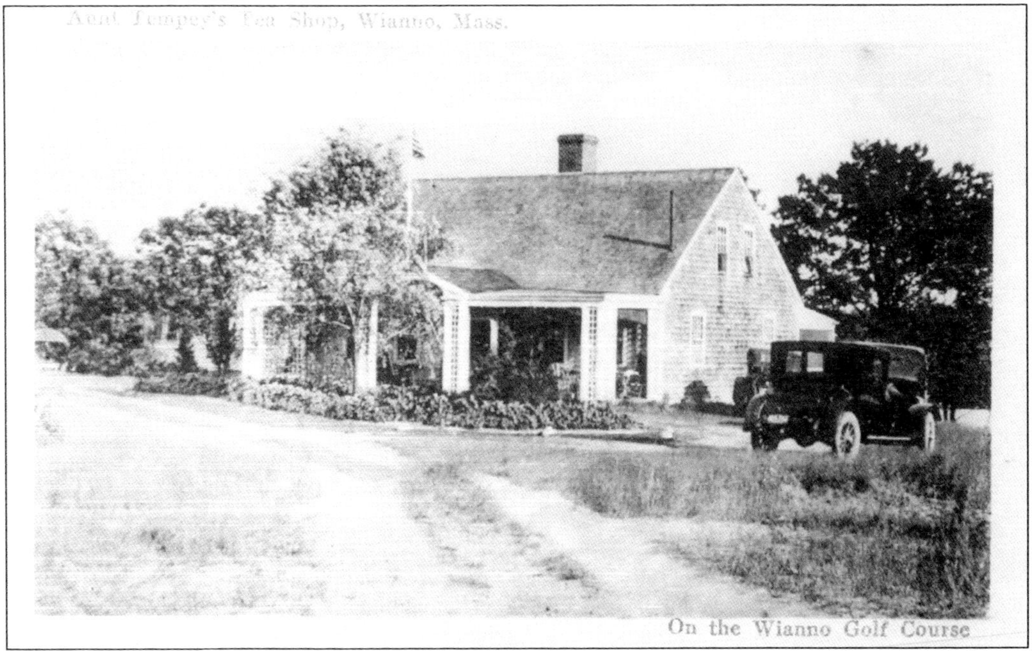

These postcards show the well-known Aunt Tempy's Teahouse. The original Aunt Tempy's was located on the eighth green of the Wianno golf course (above). Later, the restaurant and small inn (below) was located on Parker Road. It was named after Temperance Crocker Parker. The restaurant and small inn was located on Parker Road, just down the road from the 1820s Capt. Jonathan Parker House. Parker was a coastal schooner captain and lived at the corner of Parker Road and West Bay Road. The house eventually belonged to Gladys Brooks Thayer, one of the original stockholders in Oyster Harbors. In 1961, Thayer donated the building along with two acres of land to the Osterville Historical Society, and it is now the home of the Osterville Historical Museum.

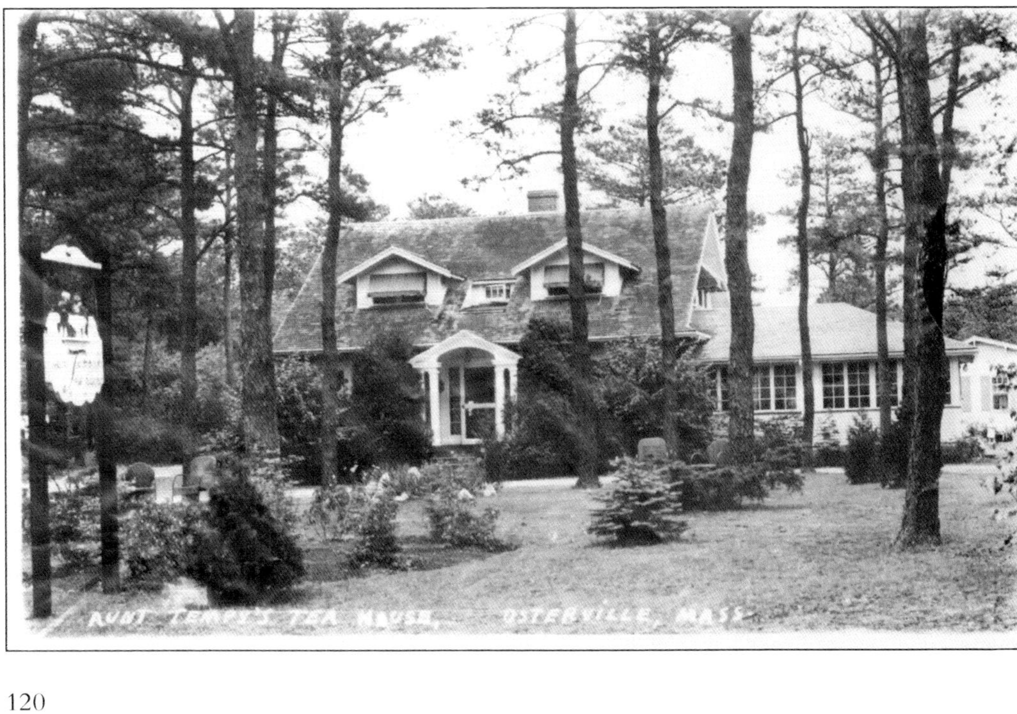

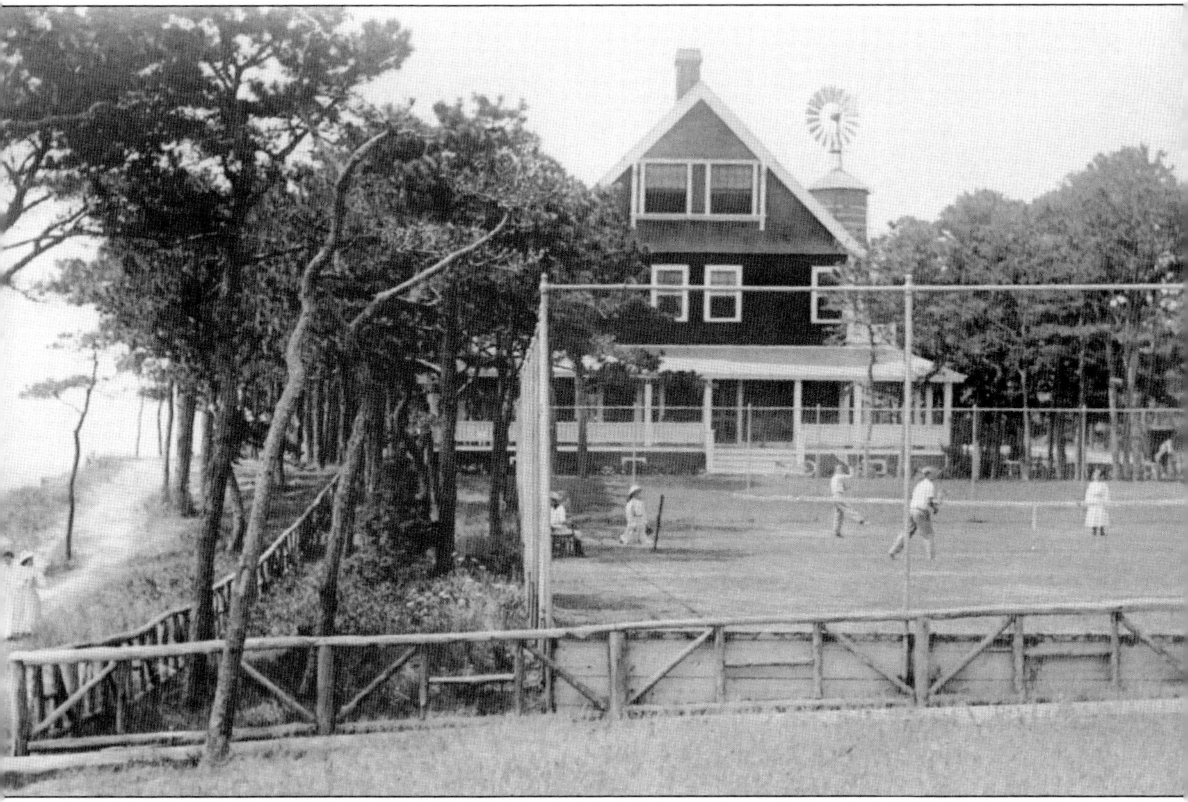

The Blodgett House is at the corner of Wianno and Sea View Avenues. This house is typical of the family homes built facing Nantucket Sound.

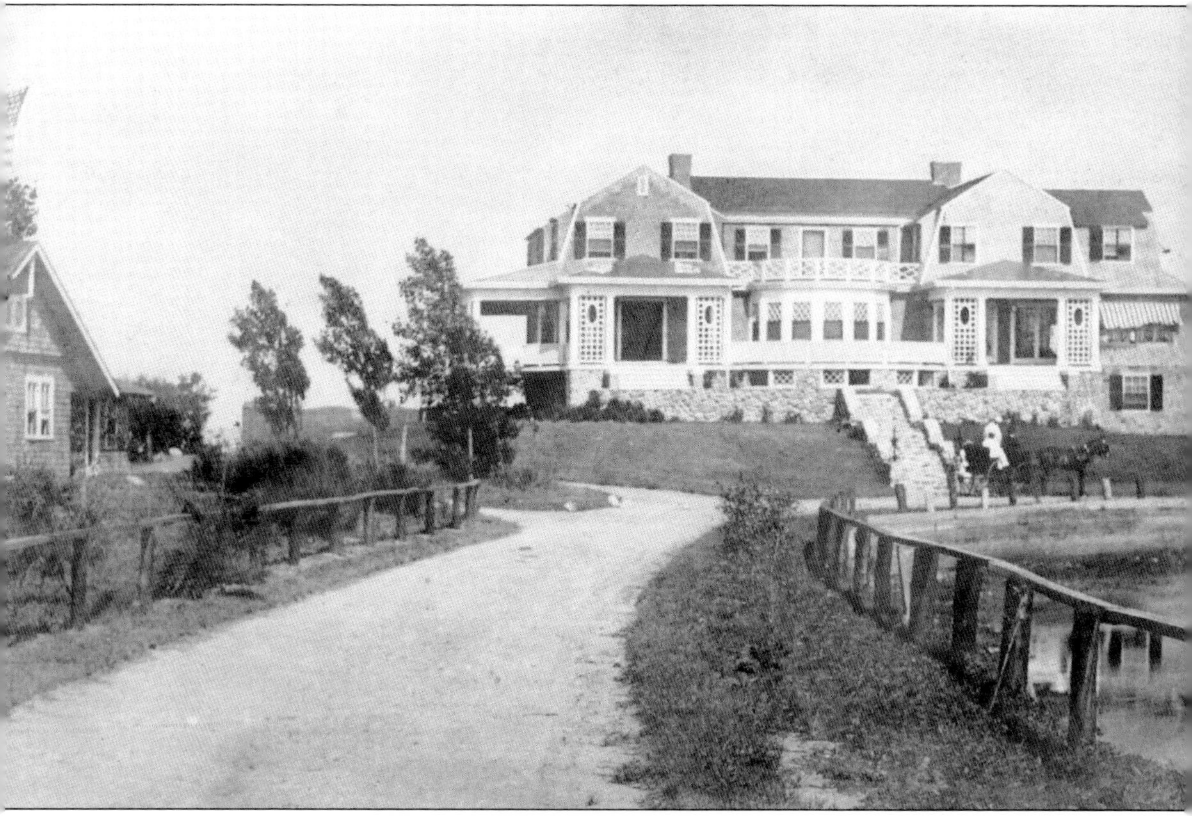

This postcard features a close-up of the Dowse family mansion at Dowses Point, overlooking Nantucket Sound with East Bay to the left. This house was destroyed in the hurricane of 1944. All that was left was the foundation. Today, the bathhouse for Dowses Beach sits atop the old foundation.

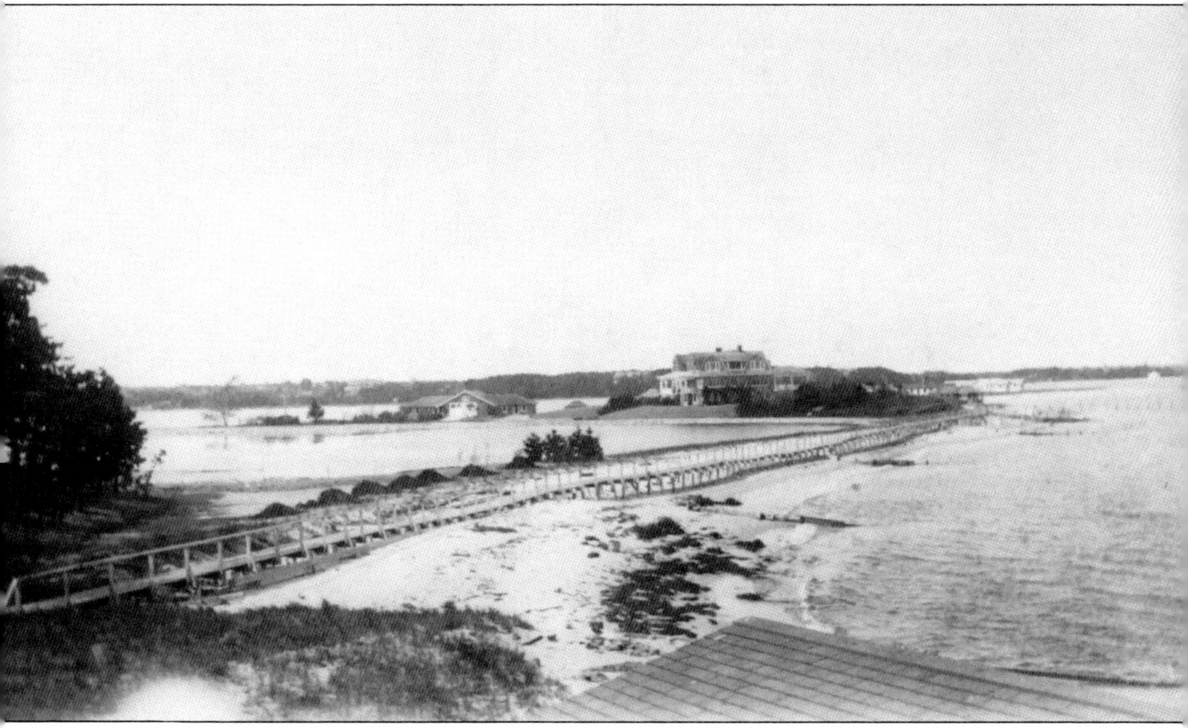

This is another view of the peninsula on which the Dowse family resided. After the home was destroyed by the storm in 1944, the family donated the property to the Town of Barnstable so that residents could have access to a beach within Osterville. Today, Dowses Beach remains popular with all ages and still offers sweeping views of Nantucket Sound and East Bay. Scallop shells still wash up upon the shoreline after a storm.

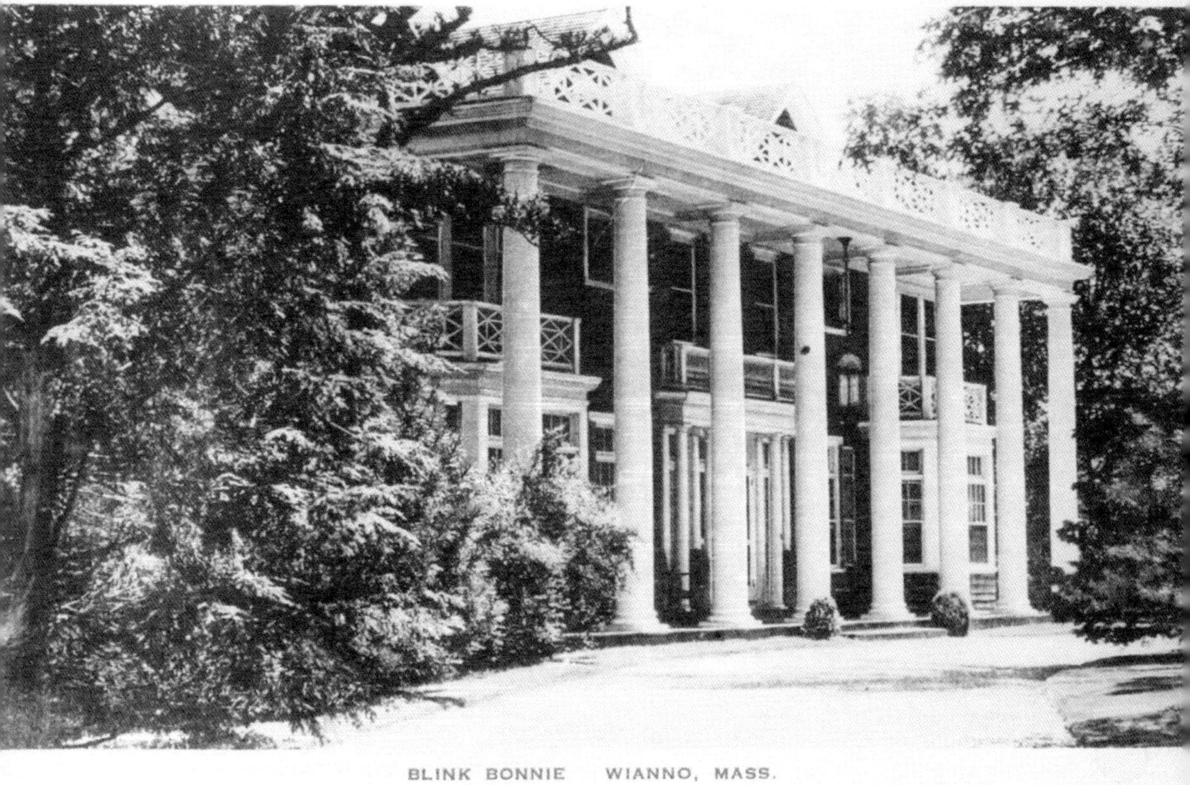

This house on Wianno Avenue, located a short distance from Sea View Avenue, was known as Blink Bonnie. Originally, it belonged to the Underwood family. Born in 1857, John Thomas Underwood was an inventor who founded the Underwood Typewriter Company.

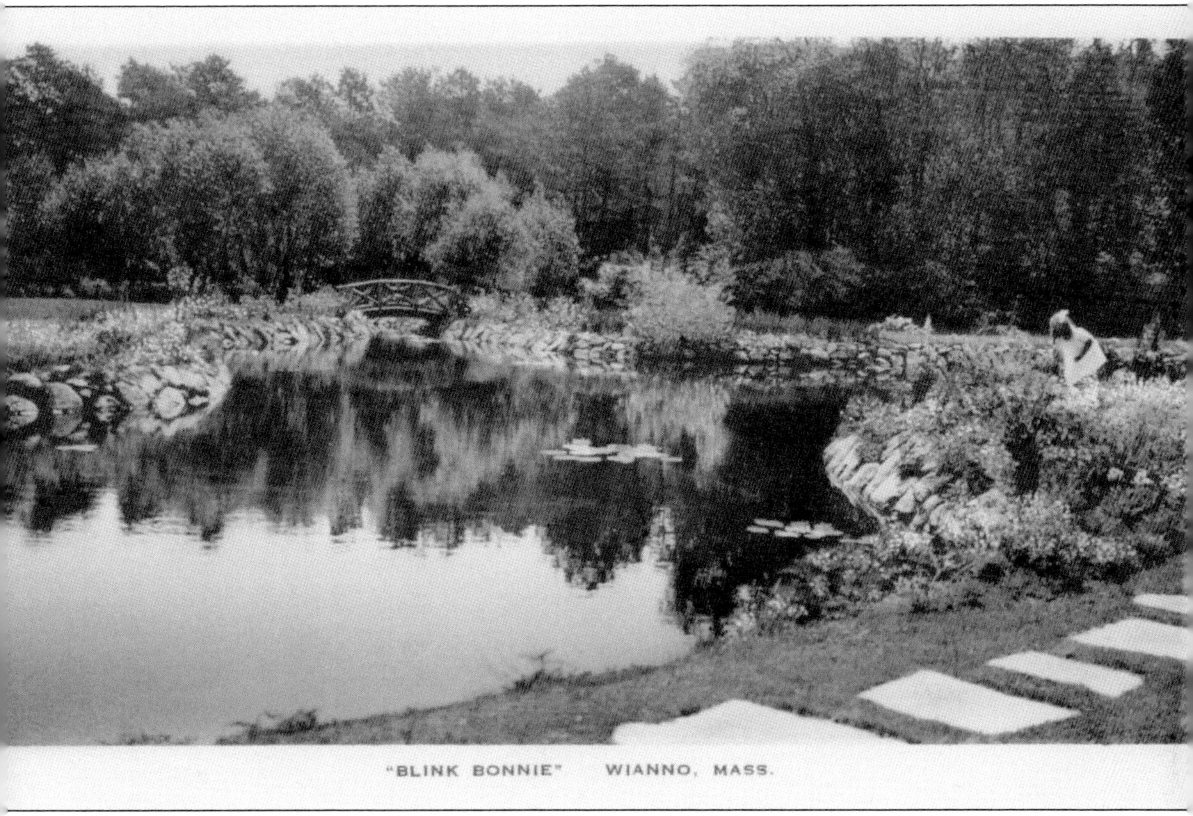

The glorious gardens that were hidden behind Blink Bonnie are shown in this image. The manmade stone walls and bridge are paired with a freshwater pond. The glass-like water reflects the thick cedars and pine trees that buffer the ocean in the distance.

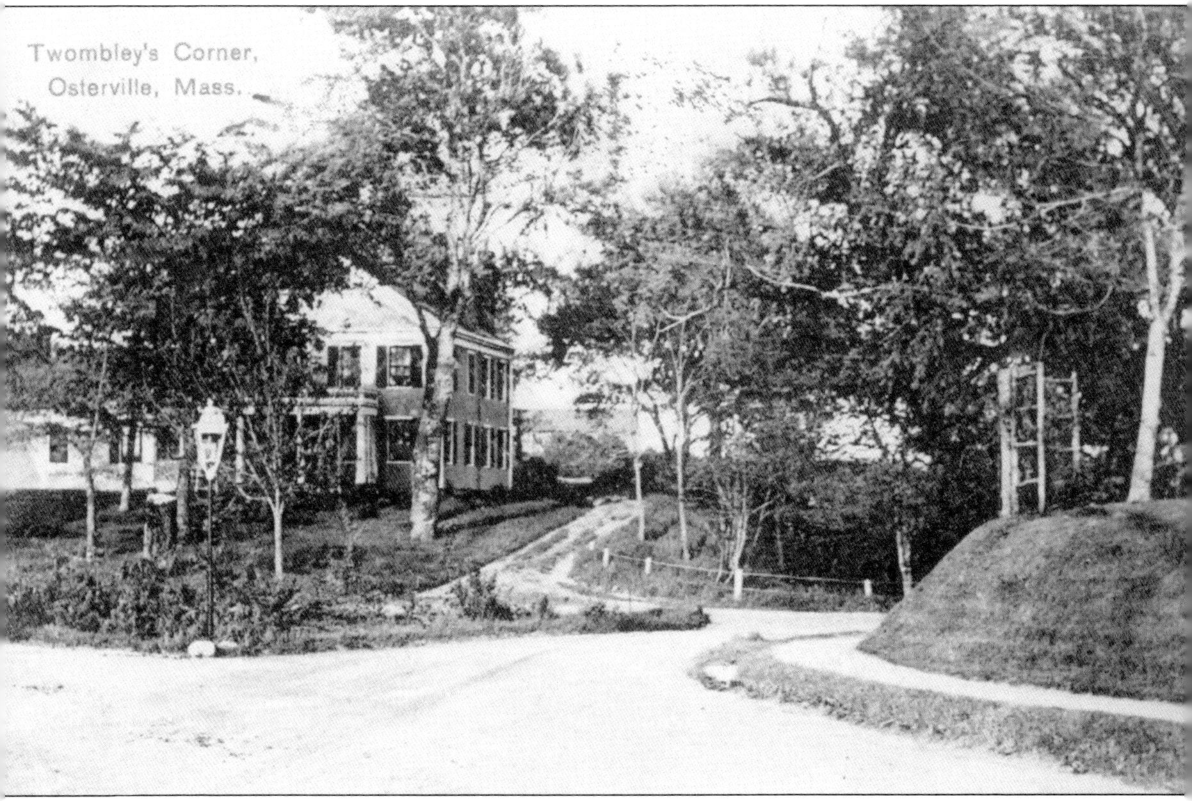

The image in this postcard shows Main Street heading out of town toward Centerville. East Bay Road is on the right. The house straight ahead belongs to one of Osterville's founding families, the Lovells. George Lovell and his second wife, Adeline de La Mott Hallett Lovell, lived in this house on the hill. Lovell, a War of 1812 veteran, was instrumental in the establishment of the Osterville Baptist Church. He also was the first director of the Barnstable Bank and established the first packet line between Boston, New York, and Albany. Adeline Lovell was one of the 12 daughters of Capt. Benjamin Hallett, a soldier during the Revolutionary War.

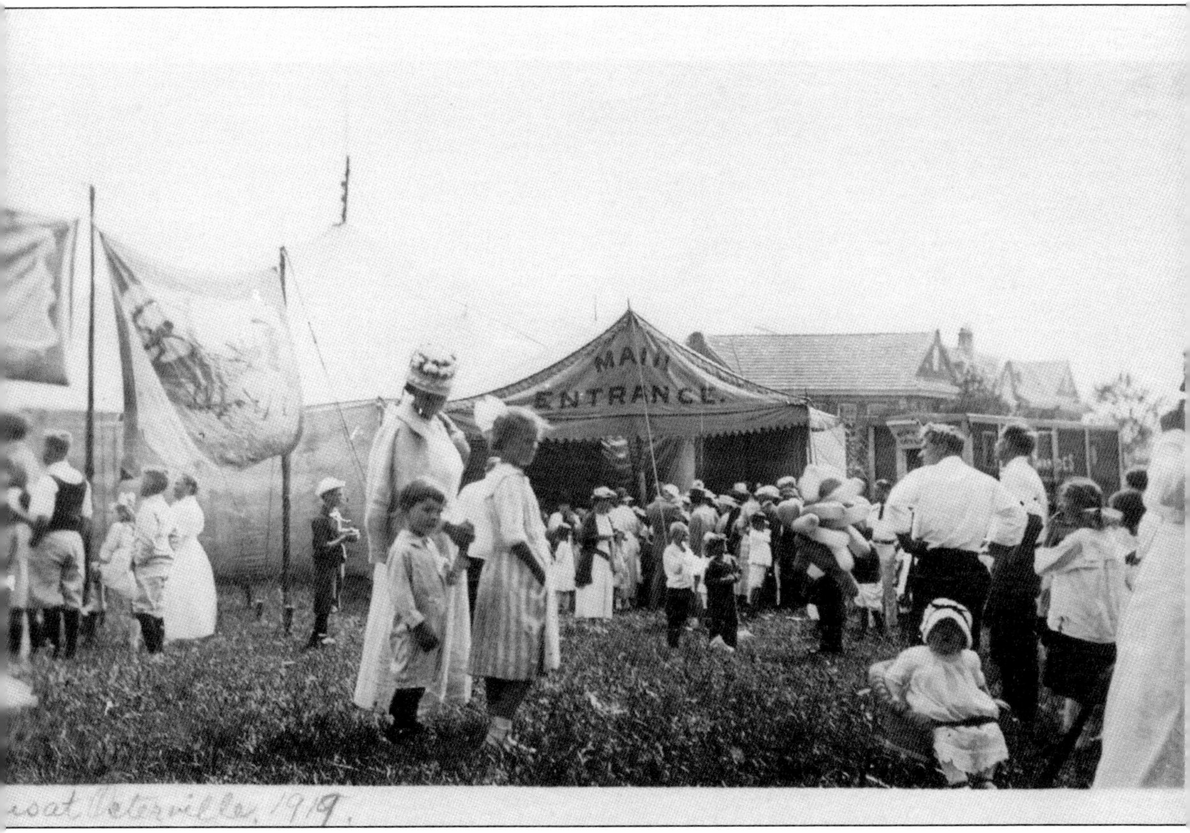

In the 1920s, the circus came to town in Osterville, drawing a large crowd, as seen in this postcard. The tents were placed in the fields on West Bay Road, next to the Bay School. The Bay School, built in 1915, can be seen behind the tents to the right. The building cost just over $13,000 to complete, and the school operated until 1961, when the Osterville Elementary School opened on Bumps River Road. The structure served many purposes over the next decades, including town school administration offices, a special sixth-grade annex, and the first home of Cape Cod Academy. When it closed in 2008, it was the oldest school still in use on Cape Cod.

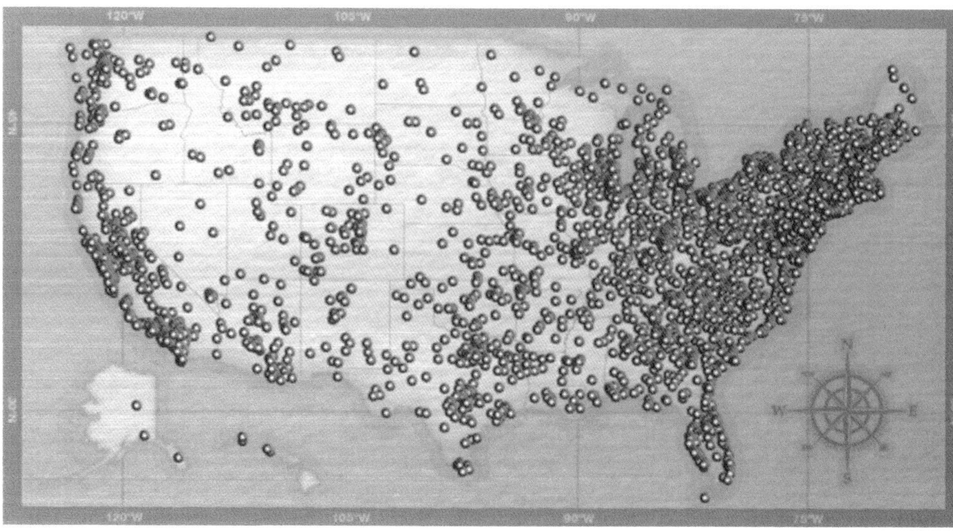